The Small Rural Primary School
A Matter of Quality

For Kathleen and Marilyn

The Small Rural Primary School

A Matter of Quality

Adrian Bell
and
Alan Sigsworth

 The Falmer Press

(A member of the Taylor & Francis Group)
London, New York and Philadelphia

UK The Falmer Press, Falmer House, Barcombe, Lewes, East Sussex, BN8 5DL

USA The Falmer Press, Taylor & Francis Inc., 242 Cherry Street, Philadelphia, PA 19106-1906

© A. Bell and A. Sigsworth 1987

First published 1987

Library of Congress Cataloging in Publication Data

Bell, Adrian (Adrian B.)
 The small rural primary school.

 1. Education, Rural—Great Britain. 2. Rural schools
—Great Britain. I. Sigsworth, Alan. II. Title.
LC5148.G7B45 1987 370.19′346′0941 86-32777
ISBN 1-85000-155-3
ISBN 1-85000-156-1 (pbk.)

Jacket design by Caroline Archer

Typeset in 11/13 Bembo by
Imago Publishing Ltd, Thame, Oxon

Printed in Great Britain by Taylor & Francis (Printers) Ltd, Basingstoke

Contents

120749

Contents

List of Figures and Tables

Figures

Tables

Acknowledgements

We have received much help from many people whilst writing this book. Teachers have given generously of their own time to talk with us, as have members of rural communities who have welcomed us into their homes and shared their views of small school education and also their sense of what it is like to experience school closure. To them we express our gratitude.

Advisers and administrators too have found space in their busy schedules to talk to us, to take us on to 'their patch' and to read and advise us on parts of this book. Particularly, we would like to thank Mike Slipper and John Bradford, Senior Primary School Adviser and Principal Assistant Education Officer respectively in Norfolk for their willingness to read and comment upon particular draft chapters. Our thanks go also to Denis Jones, Senior Primary School Adviser for Gwynedd, for a day freely given to accompanying us on visits to several small rural schools and to discussing their work with us. It was then that we knew we would write this book.

Molly Stiles we must thank for her sustained interest in the progress of our work and her donation of much precious archive material on school closures. We also wish to express our gratitude to Rex Gibson of the Cambridge Insititute of Education for his ready help both in discussing our work with us and also reading and commenting on one of our chapters. In a similar way we must also thank Bev Labbett and Malcolm Moseley; our colleagues, and also Sally Paramour, for their readiness to read material at short notice and to offer their advice and criticism. We also received valuable help from Ian Gilder of St Edmundsbury Borough Council, Tony Mackay an economist from Invernesshire, and Debbie Finch, an urban student who 'discovered' rural schools.

Finally, we wish to salve our consciences by acknowledging the way in which our wives have put up with those times in which we have been lost to the world and for reading and correcting our typescripts.

Adrian Bell
Alan Sigsworth
University of East Anglea
December 1986

A Preface of Quotations

I watched the swallows, so soon to go, swoop screaming over the garden, and wondered if Mr Hope, that unhappy poet-schoolmaster, who had lived here once, had sat here, as I was doing now, looking back. He, and, for that matter, all my predecessors, whom I knew so well from the ancient log-books, although I had never seen their faces, must have joined in the hotchpotch of fetes, sales, outings, festivals, quarrels, and friendships that make the stuff of life in a village.

The click of the gate roused me. There, entering, were Mrs Coggs and her two daughters. They gazed about them with apprehension, with monkey eyes as dark and mournful as their brothers'.

I put the past from me and hurried down the path to meet my future pupils.

'Miss Read' (1955) *Village School*, Penguin

Children's Song

We live in our own world
A world that is too small
For you to stoop and enter
Even on hands and knees,
The adult subterfuge.
And though you probe and pry
With analytic eye,
And eavesdrop all our talk
With an amused look,
You cannot find the centre

Where we dance, where we play,
Where life is still asleep
Under the closed flower,
Under the smooth shell
Of eggs in the cupped nest
That mock the faded blue
Of your remoter heaven.

R.S. Thomas

... in order to secure the necessary range and mix of teacher experience and expertise, particularly for older primary pupils, it is desirable that 5–11 schools should have at least one form of entry.

... the number of pupils in a primary school should not in general fall below the level at which a complement of three teachers is justified, since it is inherently difficult for a very small school to be educationally satisfactory.

But geographical and social factors need to be given their full weight. In isolated communities it is often right, given appropriate augmentation of its resources, to retain a small village school.

HMSO (1985) *Better Schools*

A school should be sufficiently small that all of its students are needed for its enterprises. A school should be small enough that students are not redundant.

Roger Barker

Introduction

In the late 1960s, the college of education in which we worked, set as it was on the edge of Norwich and within one of the largest agricultural areas in England, had a policy whereby its first-year student teachers were placed mainly in small rural schools for their first teaching practice. Thereafter, their remaining practice placements were in larger urban schools. The college policy was based upon a commonsense view, born of experience, that small rural schools were good places for beginning students to take their first steps as practitioners. As tutors, it was our privilege to visit many small rural schools and, sometimes, to participate in their activities.

What was inescapably evident from our experience was that, whether vividly exciting, or just plain dull, small rural schools were markedly different from the larger schools to be found in towns and cities in the ways they worked, the social relationships within and around them, and in their community contexts. Reduction of student teacher numbers and an adverse economic climate in the early 1970s largely ended the mutually beneficial contact between student teachers and the small schools. We, however, remained intrigued by the way in which many of the small schools we had come to know seemed capable of providing a stimulating, if sometimes idiosyncratic, education for their children, the warm social climates they often contained and the many different ways in which they and their local communities interrelated. Since that time, we have been able to visit small and large schools in other parts of the United Kingdom and also in the Republic of Ireland, Norway, Sweden, Finland and the United States of America. What that experience has seemed to tell us is that the ethos and style of small schools in rural communities are more similar across societies than they are to larger urban schools within their own societies. In short, we have come to regard the small rural school as something worthy of study in its own right.

Over the period that our interest has developed, the future of the small rural school has become increasingly uncertain. Since the late 1960s, a substantial opinion has grown among the politicians and administrators in many shire counties that, by virtue of their size, small rural schools are inherently disadvantaging, both educationally and socially, and should, wherever possible, be closed and their pupils educated in larger schools. That substantial opinion, structured into a policy of small school closure (and more recently given greater impetus by central government views on the minimum size of primary schools) has, over the seventies and early eighties, encountered increasingly determined opposition from normally quiescent rural communities. Although never directly involved in the conflicts sparked by school closure proposals, we have found them of considerable interest, for it is in the intense arenas of argument which they have created that policy-makers and rural inhabitants alike have been driven, necessarily, to articulate the qualities which they prize in primary schooling.

The intersection of those two elements, the educative experience which a small school can provide within a small rural community, and the conflict over what size and kind of school is necessary to provide a worthwhile education and how the school should relate to its community, has increasingly sharpened the focus of our professional interest and indeed, has provided the motivation to write this book.

Two things are very soon apparent about the contemporary rural education scene. First, whilst the conflicts provoked by school closure proposals allow a sight of what people do or do not value about the education which small schools can offer, the assertions that are made, on either side of the argument, are grounded in very little substantive evidence. They consist of hot rhetoric rather than cool information. The second point follows from the first. Relative to the research effort which has gone into urban concerns in the post-war years, that directed to rural affairs has been miniscule. Little exists upon library shelves. Beyond what it is possible to glean from such limited research as can be found upon rural education, both here and abroad, we have therefore had to draw upon our own enquiries and from the work of teachers with whom we are associated both in their schools and through in-service education programmes. Additionally, we have made use of reports of local initiatives aimed at supporting small schools in their work, and from our own activities in this field. To the extent that gathering information upon rural education rests very much upon word of mouth and the chances yielded by informal networks, we apologize in advance to those rural educators whom we may appear to have overlooked.

The organization of the book virtually suggested itself. The first section seeks to portray the differing views which people have possessed and possess about small rural schools and the sets of ideas which those views contain. Chapter 1 presents two case studies of the conflicts which developed around school closure proposals and from them two perspectives of the small rural school are derived. In the second chapter, the history of the small rural school is explored in order to see ways in which perceptions of it have changed over time in relation to wider educational developments. Against that background, chapter 3 traces the growth of advocacies for the retention or the closure of small schools and considers the ideological nature of the conflict which they engender.

Section II is given over to a discussion of three features of the rural school which, its critics allege, makes it educationally disadvantaging. Chapter 4 considers the first of these criticisms, namely that by virtue of its small size, the rural school cannot provide adequately sized peer groups for its children who consequently suffer educationally and socially. A second charge, that the location of small rural primary schools and the limited size of their staffs create a condition of teacher isolation, is addressed in chapter 5. In chapter 6, the third principal criticism, that small rural schools cannot provide a curriculum of adequate breadth and balance, is considered. This is set against current national views as to what should be the structure and scope of the curriculum and recent moves by central government to create a national curriculum framework.

A major local authority concern, though rarely given great prominence in individual school closure debates, is the financial cost of maintaining educational provision in a dispersed network of small schools. This is the focus of section III; chapter 7 examines the direct economic costs and benefits, whilst chapter 8 considers the nature of the indirect costs and benefits which, though they rarely figure in the formal equation, nonetheless exist.

The theme of section IV is future directed inasmuch as it is concerned with ways in which the small rural primary school can be enhanced. Chapter 9 examines ways in which relationships within, and between, clusters of schools can be fostered to provide a form of professional support and in-service education appropriate to their settings. Chapter 10 looks at small rural schools in their settings. It speculates upon how schools can harness the knowledge both of adults and children to improve the quality of life and learning in the community and in its school.

Section I
The Closure Debate

Chapter 1

Two Battles and Two Perspectives

The recent history of rural primary schooling has been one informed by the efforts of politicians and educational planners to achieve economic and educational rationalizations in the school system they seek to provide. The consequence for many village communities has been to find themselves confronting the possibility that their school may close and their children be sent elsewhere for their schooling. Commonly, communities have resisted attempts to remove their schools and, when set against the tacit acceptance which they have accorded to the removal of other institutions — the pub, the policeman, the post office — the fierceness of rural opposition to school closure is remarkable. Faced with threats to an institution which is obviously cherished above others, rural inhabitants have been forced into action in its defence. In the mounting of such defence, rural communities necessarily have reflected upon the qualities which they prize in the small school in their midst. The crisis, as it were, has caused them to disinter taken for granted assumptions about why they value the school and its relationship to community and to articulate them. Equally, as opposition to rural school closure has stiffened, politicians and planners have been required to marshall their arguments more ·cogently. It is upon the battlegrounds created by proposals to close village schools that the two opposed perspectives are engaged.

Our purpose in this chapter is to render an account of the conflicts which ensued when proposals for closure were made against two village schools. From them, we will be able to see what characterizes community action and official action and what components constitute each of the opposing perspectives.

The Battle for Aldcaster School

Aldcaster is an unexceptional English village. It possesses a cobbled square in which one finds the village inn and shop set amongst houses of grey stone. It has an air of permanence. If one leaves the small square from its northern corner, the road crosses an old pack bridge and climbs towards semi-moorland. Two hundred yards up the hill, a lane takes off to the right and here, beyond the corrugated-iron chapel and close by the ancient church, is the village school, now almost 120 years old. Built in the years just before the 1870 Education Act, it is typical of schools of that time — a schoolroom with a headteacher's house attached. A more recent annexe, built in the thirties, affords an extra classroom and, in common with many similar schools, the headteacher's house has been converted to educational use.

Although the village contains a commuter element, it possesses a fairly balanced population of incomers and natives who seem to mix rather than to separate. On the southern side of the village square, another road leads out and soon forks. One branch, running to the south-east passes a disused quarry and continues through Lower Aldcaster from which come some of the school's pupils. It is the south-westerly fork which provides the surprise. Rising steeply, it leaves the houses behind, passes the sparse remains of a small Roman fort and, in a little over a mile, crests a rise before intersecting with another road. Here, to the west, one is confronted unexpectedly with the outer suburbs of a town possessing a population of 73,000. Within this suburban area, recent building activity is evident, the house prices pitched attractively within range of young families. A little to the south of the Lordseat suburban development is a former railway stockyard, now converted to a permanent travellers' site whose present users seem principally to be involved in the horse trade. Within the suburban development, school enrolments are healthy. By constrast, a major problem for Aldcaster village primary school at the time which we are to recount, was the decline in its school roll — this in a period when the stringency axe was finely honed.

Intimations of Closure

The beginnings of the move to close Aldcaster School followed a familiar pattern. By December 1981 decline in the birthrate had reduced enrolment so that numbers were hovering close to thirty. In that month, the long-serving headteacher announced his intention to retire at the end of the school year. Parental anxiety over the future of the school, as a consequence of the confluence of these two features, was allayed, however, at a meeting of the Parent-Teacher Association, when the Chairman of the school governors informed them that, in a consultation with the Chief Education Officer and the Area Education Officer, he had been assured that the school would remain open.

Anxiety returned to the village when, in April 1982, the Area Advisory Sub-Committee decided not to proceed with the appointment of a new headteacher and instead, invited the school's governors and the retiring headteacher to discuss the future of the school with them. There can be no doubt that the governors were aware that the possibility of closure was in the wind. As the following note from their record of the May 1982 meeting with the Advisory Sub-Committee indicates, their impression was that a decision to recommend closure had already been framed.

> Although we had been invited to discuss the future development of our school, we felt that we were, in fact, expected to defend our school against, in our opinion, a foregone conclusion.

Driven into an on-the-spot defence of the school the governors had asserted reasons for retaining the school within the village. These included the influence of the school upon community ethos, the secure atmosphere which a small school provides for beginning pupils and for those with special needs, the close contact possible between parents, children and teachers, and the richness of the local setting as a learning resource. It was also pointed out that the school, small as it was, had been commended by a group of educational researchers for its work with the children of travelling folk. Subsequent to the meeting, the governors observed that the assurances given earlier by the Chief Education Officer and the Area Education Officer had not been reiterated. Ten days later, the governors were informed by letter of the Sub-Committee's recommendation that the school should close. On 10 June parents were sent a letter which informed them that 'the Advisory Sub-Committee feel that there would be clear educational advantages in closing the school'. The letter also announced a date and time for a meeting at the school to discuss the proposal. Eight days later, at a meeting organized by the Parent-Teacher Association, a unanimous decision to fight closure was taken and the Save Aldcaster Village Education (SAVE) Group was formed.

A first move of the Group was to seek information from the

Authority on their grounds for the closure recommendation in terms of pupil numbers, financial savings and educational reasons. The CEO in his letter of reply, indicated that with an expectation of no more than five new houses in the area to 1990, the forecast pupil numbers from 1982–86 would be in the range thirty-five to thirty-seven. Against two scenarios of alternative school placements for Aldcaster pupils, financial savings were depicted in the range £25–27,000. He cited two educational advantages for closing Aldcaster School. These were:

1 The size of the peer groups in a school of approximately thirty pupils limits that part of the learning process which arises from stimulation and competition between pupils. The authority believes that peer group interaction is important for the learning process and that children should have a sufficient number of children of similar ability in a year group.
2 Teachers have to teach children spanning several year groups which requires a very high level of teaching skill and effort. The school is dependent upon finding versatile staff who can offer several specialisms and undoubtedly, curricular opportunities are restricted by the limited range of teacher skills and experience.

While noting that no decisions had been taken on alternative recipient schools the CEO observed that. 'As the Bloxton Yard Travellers' site is in Bloxton, it would seem logical that the travellers' children should attend the nearest school in Bloxton (Turley Primary School) should Aldcaster School close.'

The Battle Joined: The Public Meeting

The public meeting took place on 10 July 1984. The meeting was chaired by the Chairman of the Area Advisory Sub-Committee. With him were the Principal Assistant Education Officer and the Area Education Officer. Fifty-eight parents and villagers, including several traveller parents, attended.

Two versions of the meeting exist — the 'official' notes made by the LEA representatives and those made by the Secretary of SAVE and confirmed and amended by other members who were present. What follows is an attempt to portray the main issues thought worthy of record.

The Official Version

The Chairman, after his opening remarks, requested the Principal Assistant Education Officer to outline the factors influential upon the Sub-Committee's decision to recommend closure in terms of the advantages and disadvantages of small schools. Summarized, these were as follows:

Advantages	Disadvantages
1 A family atmosphere providing security especially for younger children.	1 Professional limitations of two full-time teachers catering for the full 5–11 age group.
2 Close individual attention.	
3 The development of close home-school liaison.	2 The small size of peer group within a year group and the need children have for interaction with children of the same age, sex and ability.
4 The availability of a community facility.	
	3 The professional isolation of teachers accruing from difficulties of attending in-service training and the absence of inter-staff discussion to be found in larger schools.
	4 The disproportionately higher unit costs of small schools.

The Chairman also remarked that larger schools too could create a family atmosphere and provide individual attention in a context of a larger staff deploying a greater range of skills to classes of children of the same age. After observing that, as yet no recipient schools had been designated, he indicated the range of possibilities. Commenting on the successful integration of travellers' children in Aldcaster School, he noted that any relocation would have to foster the needs of these children.

From the village side, the 'official' version noted the points made by the Secretary of SAVE. These were:

1 The school is a centre and a focus for the community.
2 It would be unsound for young children to travel unsupervised on a bus.

3 Schooling at a distance is stressful, especially where a child falls ill and parents have neither car nor telephone.
4 Given closure, parents would lose informal daily contact with school.
5 The cost-effectiveness of school closure and transportation is questionable.
6 There is no evidence that children settle quickly following school closure.
7 Aldcaster School provided a good education for traveller children.

With the meeting thrown open to comment from the floor, village concerns were identified in the official version as follows:

1 Dissatisfaction with official interpretation of the concept of the peer group.
2 The possibility of cluster organisation.
3 Parental preference for low pupil-teacher ratio rather than a large number of teachers.
4 Parental preference for a secure and happy working atmosphere rather than for academic excellence *per se*.
5 The issue of transportation.
6 The permeability of catchment areas which could allow children from the overcrowded schools west of the village to attend Aldcaster School.
7 The notion of cost-effectiveness.
8 Doubts concerning official projections of pupil numbers.
9 The deleterious effect of intimations of closure upon school numbers.
10 The cost saving which resulted from village support for the school notably in the provision of resources.

The Aldcaster Version

The notes of the SAVE Group's version of the meeting are different from the official version in a number of respects. They include the comment that while parents and other interested persons had been invited to meet with the Advisory Sub-Committee, in the event only its Chairman, together with the Education Officers, attended. Moreover, although all members of the Sub-Committee had been invited individually to view the school, only one member had done so. Notes record that 'the general feeling was one of anger' for:

Their views had not been heard before the Sub-Committee's recommendations to close the school had been made ... the governors without prior warning, had been forced to defend the future of the school when they met with the Area Advisory Sub-Committee on 21 May. ... There was dismay that the meeting was not conducted by a neutral chairman. It was felt that this unbalanced the discussion that took place.

It was also pointed out that in the meeting a statement had been made that all parents in the Lordseat suburb wished their children to be educated within the Lordseat area development, whereas a Lordseat parent with children at Aldcaster school had refuted this assertion and had given as her opinion that other parents would opt as she had done, if they knew of the school's existence. The notes of the SAVE Group Secretary also assert that in the meeting the question was put: 'Was there any evidence that our children had suffered a disadvantage educationally when they moved on to other schools?' The Principal Education Officer, according to her notes, had replied that there was no evidence of this. Frustration that the meeting had closed before alternative schools had been discussed was noted, as was the failure of the official version to record a request for this omission to be minuted. The village version concludes:

'In spite of eloquent arguments from the Principal Assistant Education Officer that parents always opposed school closure, but were often glad once the children had been transferred to larger schools, nobody wavered in their determination to opposed the recommendation'.

The Aldcaster Defence

The Save Aldcaster Village Education Group, following the public meeting in July, identified three elements in the LEA proposal for closure around which they must construct their case. These were:

1 The present low school enrolment.
2 The issues of financial savings.
3 The educational advantages of closing the school.

In order to counter these three assertions, the Committee saw their main task as demonstrating:

1 That an increase in enrolment could be anticipated.
2 That the financial savings would be minimal in the short

term, and that retention of the school could, long term, save money.

3 That for the majority of children, the advantages of the school far outweighed the perceived disadvantages.

A glance at the enrolment figures furnished by the CEO to the governors in June 1982 indicates that while in the 6–9 age range the numbers were healthy enough for a small school, the youngest and oldest age groups were very small, viz:

Age group	4–5	5–6	6–7	7–8	8–9	9–10	10–11	
Number of pupils	3	4	7	5	7	3	2	(31)

Moreover, the CEO's forecast (based upon birth returns and existing numbers) anticipated little in the way of increased enrolment:

Year	Pupil Numbers
1982–83	37
1983–84	38
1984–85	36
1985–86	35

Faced with such a prediction, the Group set about demonstrating that increase in pupil numbers could be anticipated, that administrative anomalies were holding numbers low, and that predictions on building developments were inaccurate. The Defence Committee was able to identify five children who, with a spring commencement, would enhance numbers and they asserted that the successful integration of traveller children, together with increasingly effective liaison policies would encourage other traveller parents to enrol their children. Further, they found an anomaly in transportation arrangements in the Lower Aldcaster area of the school's catchment:

'The catchment area includes Lower Aldcaster and children from that village are transported to the school in a private car. This is financed by the Authority. There have been some Lower Aldcaster parents who have been informed by the Education Office that no transport was available. As a consequence they have reluctantly sent their children to other schools'.

Errors in the published predictions on house building in the catchment areas were also identified. While the authority had stated that only five new houses were anticipated by 1989 it was noted that at the public meeting an admission had been made that the figure was incorrect:

> 'In truth, there are five plots with planning permission agreed at present and the statistic excludes the village of Lower Aldcaster. It also excludes any gains that will arise out of the increasing trend of barn conversions and the modernization and extension of existing properties which will attract larger families into the area'.

The Group's assessment of pupil numbers concluded with the point that the Authority's forecast for the year 1982–83 was thirty-seven, whereas by January 1983, there would be forty on roll: 'To have improved on the Authority's forecast whilst the school is threatened indicates that Aldcaster School is still a viable proposition.'

Whilst the Group had demonstrated weaknesses in the CEO's enrolment predictions, some fast work was required to improve the numbers case, for the meeting of the Schools Sub-Committee at which the closure recommendation would be considered was to take place on 2 October 1983. On 30 September the governors received the report of the Area Advisory Sub-Committee detailing grounds for closure. In it, the predicted enrolments, amended from those of the CEO, were as follows:

Year	Pupil Numbers
1982–83	35
1983–84	39
1984–85	42
1985–86	47

In addition, the Advisory Sub-Committee report noted:

> '... three parents resident in the Lordseat development have expressed an interest in sending their four children to Aldcaster School in January 1983 and all, or some, may eventually choose to send their children to the school'.

The SAVE Group, moving with speed in the short time left to it, was able to show that five children from the Lordseat area, all covered by Education Authority letter of agreement, would commence at Aldcaster School, three in January 1983 and two in September 1983. On this basis, SAVE pointed out that the revised prediction would be:

Year	Pupil Numbers
1982–83	38
1983–84	44
1984–85	47
1985–86	52

Noting their predictions to be based on available fact, the Group went on to point out that if the assumption were to be made that, on average, three Lordseat children were to enrol at Aldcaster annually, the predicted enrolment would be:

Year	Pupil Numbers
1982–83	38
1983–84	45
1984–85	51
1985–86	59

Their assessment of numbers concluded with the comment:

'As a result of the public meeting, the Authority revised up-wards the forecast that it presented to the Area Advisory Committee. These new projections are already outdated and should be revised again. We submit that the rising trend is greater than predicted and will probably increase further'.

The Decision

In this account of the battle of the Aldcaster community to retain its school we have drawn almost solely from the document which the Save Aldcaster Village Education Group prepared and presented to the Schools Sub-Committee. Much of the Group's argument against closure has been left out. Their concerns over the dangers of the routes to proposed alternative schools have not been mentioned, nor have we depicted their efforts to chip away at the LEA assumptions underlying assertions of cost saving. Omitted altogether has been the press response to their campaign which gained them more than average coverage in the local newspapers. Their 'Leave Aldcaster Open' document, the sharp end of the community's attempt to retain the school, is a formidable presentation, fluent, detailed, well-organized and indicative of the village's capacity to deploy and orchestrate a variety of professional and community skills.

Nowithstanding the excellence of its document, the SAVE Group could, of course, anticipate a protracted battle with the decision-making machinery, first through the Schools Sub-Committee then, via the County Council, to the Secretary of State for Education and Science. (Their determination to proceed to the bitter end was expressed in their Chairman's assertion to the local press that if necessary, they would explore every legal avenue.)

Their preparation for the crucial first step, the Schools Sub-Committee meeting of 2 October 1982, was to present on 25 September, with full press coverage, a 374-signature petition to the Chairman and Vice-Chairman of the Education Committee. That done, they could only rest their faith upon the strength of their written case. In summary, SAVE's case against the closure of their school was based upon eight elements:

1 A view of the school as an interactive focus for the whole community and also as an important factor in maintaining a balanced age-structure in the village.

2 An appraisal of the village environment as a rich curriculum resource.

3 An evaluation of the school as constituting, by virtue of its size, organization and approach, a form of education academically and socially superior to that found in larger schools.

4 The recognition by educational researchers of the school's success in integrating travelling children.

5 The consequences which proposed alternative school placements would have in terms of fractured home-school links and difficult transport routes.

6 Scepticism as to the validity of assessments of financial savings stemming from closure of the school.

7 Criticism of the Authority's unwillingness to regard the boundary between Aldcaster and the Lordseat development as permeable, particularly with regard to the role the school could play in the easement of overcrowding in the schools to its western side.

8 Rejection of the Authority's projection of numbers and their own demonstration of anticipated increases in enrolment.

In the event, the Schools Sub-Committee was swayed by the Group's predictions of the increase of pupil numbers in the four years to 1986 to the extent that it recommended its Advisory Sub-Committee to reconsider the future of the school. In the parlance of death which invests consideration of small rural schools, Aldcaster had achieved a temporary reprieve or a stay of execution. That the recommendation did not represent a final victory is apparent from the subsequent comments of the Chairman of the Education Committee:

> 'Even with the new figures produced, the numbers are very small. The Committee will have to take account as well of the proximity of other schools and surplus of places in those schools'. (Local press)

It would seem, too, that the 'permeability of boundary' argument put forward by the Group was not, despite contemporary assertions of parental choice, to the liking of the Authority. This is apparent in the signal from the Chairman of the Education Committee of the consequences for Lordseat parents if they engaged in educational flirtations beyond their boundary:

> 'The Chairman also warned Lordseat parents that if they pressed for retention of Aldcaster it would weaken the case for a new school in Lordseat'. (Local press)

Beyond matters of numbers and boundaries, the Group had placed very considerable emphasis upon the merits of their school in terms of its educational and social benefits to both children and the community. Particularly stressed was the recognized contribution which the school was making to the education of traveller children from the Bloxton Yard site. Of this aspect, the Education Committee Chairman would seem to be simply dismissive for, confirming that he had read the Group's document, he is quoted as follows:

> 'It is not possible to ignore the fact that the school's numbers are swelled by children from the Bloxton Yard site'. (Local press)

All that said, the major theme in the Group's case was the high value which they placed upon the kind of education which a small institution made possible. This it would seem was the least cogent aspect in the eyes of the Education Committee Chairman. For him, financial saving and the potential inadequacies of small schools generally were dominant. Referring to the county's programme of small school closure as being incomplete, he is quoted as follows:

> '... we have quite some considerable way to go. ... It does seem to me that schools with two teachers or below can be highly successful schools and you can get some very talented individuals, but it is difficult for them to do well ... Small

schools [lead] to higher unit costs and this county's primary school costs are high'. (Local press)

Aldcaster then had won itself an extension of its existence.

The Battle for Ings Downton School

In accordance with instructions from the County Council. The former school of Ings Downton to be sold by auction. A substantial detached village primary school with outline planning consent for change of use from school to residential use. The school is located in the much sought after and attractive village of Ings Downton. The school commands fine views over the area and is within easy walking distances of village facilities and the river.

The auction sale in a hotel in the nearby town of Churningham ended a ninety-six year period of state education in the village of Ings Downton, and the final defeat of a group of villagers who had campaigned first to retain a school, and later, with that aspiration defeated, to preserve the building for communal village use.

Intimations of Closure

Three years before, almost to the day the auction notice appeared, an Ings Downton school parent wrote to the local education office to ask about the future of the village school. The number of children attending the school had dropped to seventeen and, via local press coverage of other small school closures, County Council policy relating to village schools was well known. Rumour was strong in the village that the school was under threat. The Area Officer's reply outlined county policy covering schools of under thirty pupils and indicated that Ings Downton School fell clearly into that category and would continue to do so for the foreseeable future. The picture was sufficiently pessimistic for the officer to add: 'I am sorry to have to write to you in such gloomy terms, but these are the facts.' Nevertheless the letter concluded with the assurance that no decision had, at that point, been made.

Three weeks later, the Chairman of the school's governors was informed by letter that the Area Advisory Sub-Committee would be discussing the possible closure of Ings Downton school at its next meeting in eight days' time. School governors were cordially invited to attend. This turn of events, of course, came as no surprise, for in the light of inexorably declining numbers, it had been anticipated for some time.

The meeting with the Sub-Committee was brief and uncontentious. County policy was articulated and the low enrolment at Ings Downton School set against it. The formal procedures of closure and the provisional transfer plans for the school's pupils were explained. The governors, it would seem, were resigned to the sadly inevitable end of their school. A week later, the Sub-Committee confirmed to the Chairman by letter their intentions to recommend closure and to circularize the parents of the school's pupils, prior to calling a meeting at which the decision could be explained.

The letter which the parents received the following month set out concisely the Education Committee's views of the small rural school:

'In considering this action, the Education Committee is not acting simply on ground of economy. The Committee recognizes the advantages of close pupil/teacher relationships and integration into the community which are possible in a village school, but feels that, in the extremely small school, these advantages are outweighed by the difficulties of the wide age range, the limited human and material resources and the isolation of children and teachers. In these circumstances, better educational opportunities are offered by grouping the pupils into larger schools'.

The letter further indicated that a meeting for parents would take place in the near future 'to discuss the proposal in more detail'. It concluded with an invitation to parents to visit the proposed alternative schools to which the children would transfer 'to meet the headteachers and to see the facilities available'.

Before the parents' meeting early in the following term, the headteacher retired and a temporary replacement was appointed. As is common practice elsewhere, the county in question often uses the occasion of a headteacher's retirement to review the future of a small school. This change in the teaching staff was subsequently to have some influence on the campaign to retain the school.

The Public Meeting: From Acquiescence to Resistance

Section 13 of the 1944 Education Act requires a public meeting in the event of a school closure proposal and strictly speaking, the meeting held at Ings Downton School did not fulfil that requirement for only the parents of existing pupils had received invitations. In the event, most parents and about a dozen others, including several parents of pre-school children attended. The closure proposal was explained by the local councillor (who was also a member of the Education Schools Sub-Committee) and a senior officer of the authority. In presenting the case, they stressed the educational advantages of a larger school and the restricted size of peer groups in very small schools. The cost savings that could be made by transferring pupils to existing larger schools were mentioned but in the meeting this aspect was not argued with any great force.

The reception from the floor of the meeting was distinctly hostile. The educational arguments were contested; the claimed financial savings were disputed; there was antagonism to the prospect of young children being bussed to school in the neighbouring town. The impression retained by some of the parents present that night is that the two authority representatives were taken aback by the depth of feeling, although both of them had much experience by this time of similar meetings. The meeting eventually closed with the councillor announcing that there was no point in further discussion and that they would take the tone of the meeting into account.

As the meeting broke up, a villager, who later was to play a major part in the campaign to save the school, recalled the councillor saying exasperatedly, 'You're not really going to make a fuss are you?' A hint was dropped that if the school closed without a struggle, the village would be able to retain the building for community use.

The KIDS Group and its Work

The nature of the meeting, it would seem, produced a determination in the village participants to defend their school and, characteristically, a group was formed to lead a campaign. As is the fashion in closure campaigns, an acronym KIDS (Keep Ings Downton School) was chosen. Not unusually, the time at their disposal to organize a defence was short, for the crucial date when the Sub-Committee was to meet was less than two months away.

A letter was written to all residents, calling for their support and advising them on how they might voice opposition to the closure. A petition was organized and attracted almost 230 signatures. A survey of the village and surrounding catchment area was made to provide information with which to challenge the authority's projected figures of future pupil numbers. Publicity for the campaign was sought via local television and newspapers and through car stickers distributed from the local shop.

Beyond local activity the Group contacted the national organization Defenders of Village Education (DOVE) and the Advisory Centre for Education (ACE). The ACE handbook on contesting village school closure, was as one person put it later, 'our Bible'.

The managers, initially acquiescent, were galvanized by the work of the KIDS Group and contributed to the campaign. The organization of the work was spearheaded by a group of relatively recent professional migrants to the village, but drew support from all sections of the local community: land-owning farmers, manual workers, and self-employed business people who had lived in Ings Downton for many years, all signed the petition. Support for the school was, as the Group was able to claim, virtually unanimous within the area. Encouragement and advice were also received from similar groups in the region and, via the national DOVE network, from other parts of the country.

The Group prepared a lengthy document which detailed the community's objections to the proposed closure and copies were sent to all members of the Sub-Committee and to television and press. Although only two Committee members acknowledged receipt, media interest was stimulated. The document, like many of its kind prepared as defences against closure, was a mixture of sophisticated educational theorizing with quotations from, and references to, educational research, and, on the other hand, local, almost homely, vignettes of life in the village and its school. It catalogued the advantages of the small scale of the school and its intimate connection with the community; it stressed the role of a school in village life; it requested councillors to take a broader view of the economics of rural schooling; it argued that numbers were likely to rise; it spelled out objections to bussing small children. Negotiatively, it suggested the possibility of a change of status to first school for the Sub-Committee's consideration. Additional to the document, and at the behest of the Group, many villagers sent letters to the Chairman of the Education Committee. The following extracts from a few such letters give some indication of the depth of local feeling against the proposed closure:

'(We) find it hard as a lot of imported officials attempt to deprive us of the school. They tell us, with no first hand knowledge of us or it, that we are depriving our children of a good education. Had they done the most elementary home-work, they would have abandoned that argument before they began'.

'... the likelihood of children being neglected in a country school is remote, particularly when parents and teachers are well known to each other and meet almost daily'.

'The child I have attending Ings Downton school at present is doing well ... My youngest child concerns me most ... I live two miles from the school it is proposed to bus her to. ... At 5 years old, I'll be expected to put her on to the bus with no supervision and no way of knowing if she actually gets to school. Should she be taken ill, or have an accident, I'll have a two-mile walk to reach her ... Can anyone in all honesty suggest that this is the correct situation for a 5-year-old?'

'The parents in the village should be allowed to choose the type of school that they prefer for their children. It would seem to be somewhat insulting to their intelligence to suppose that what they, the parents, choose for their children is inadequate'.

This last point was at the forefront of the KIDS document pre-pared for the Sub-Committee:

'It was suggested at a parents' meeting held at the school that the main reason for recommending closure was the belief that children would receive a better and wider education at Churn-ingham. It was claimed that facilities are limited in small village schools and that children are deprived of the compan-ionship and competitiveness provided by several others of the same age. In our investigations, however, we have heard no such criticism from the parents or the pupils and we may surely assume that no parent would sign a petition or lend us their support in order to preserve what they consider to be an inferior education for their children'.

The school, of course, continued to function throughout these two months of hectic activity, but an internal change contributed another energizing factor to the campaign against closure. The former headteacher who had retired after long service, was replaced by a temporary headteacher who set about her task with energy and imagination. Brought in, ironically to run down the school to its close, she gave added impetus to the campaign, for the Group did not miss the possible prospect which this turn of events held for increased enrolment. Coincidentally, the Group unearthed evidence that the education office bore some responsibility for the downturn in numbers, for its officials had been advising the parents of prospective pupils of the school's likely closure and, in at least one case, had stated this categorically. This latter revelation, together with the difficulties which the Group experienced in extracting needed information, for example, projected financial savings, from the Authority, caused Group members to feel that the game they were required to play contained elements of unfairness. Nonetheless, as the day of the Sub-Committee meeting approached, a feeling of optimism developed:

'I was feeling optimistic at this time, yes. I thought we had a good case. I thought we'd written it out quite well. We obviously had a lot of support, from everywhere. A lot of people were' phoning in from all sorts of places. Particularly once it hit the newspaper, I had all sorts of odd' phone calls from people, just people who wanted to say 'Good Luck'. From all round the county. I was optimistic'.

A question of stategy bothered the Group: Who should present their case to the Sub-Committee? Their own councillor was known to be unsympathetic. The Chairman of the Education Committee was consulted and argued that it would be a breach of good manners to bypass their own representative. This advice was taken, although retrospectively, the Group Secretary thought it was an error inasmuch as their case was presented with evident lack of conviction. A better choice might have been a member of the Sub-Committee who was a personal friend of the Chairman of Managers, for he was the only councillor to make a serious challenge to the proposal in the meeting.

Acting on advice from DOVE, the Group obtained permission from the Sub-Committee Chairman to send a deputation to Shire Hall on the day of the meeting. The Group called a special meeting to discuss tactics:

'We had a special meeting to discuss the deputation and to draw up exactly what we were going to do, what we were going to say and who was going to say it. And we expected to be ushered into a little office and sat down and listened to'.

The Sub-Committee Meeting: A Political Experience

The deputation of fifteen arrived at Shire Hall and, with their 'Keep Ings Downton School' banners, were photographed by the press alerted to the occasion. From there on, the gulf between their expectation and the experience was to widen:

> 'We assumed that we would be met by the Chairman certainly, Deputy Chairman and maybe a couple of others. Treated cordially, invited into an office and sat down and be allowed to make our points in a civilized way.

> When we got there, our councillor and one other met us in the entrance foyer. There were fifteen of us — eight parents or prospective parents, three parish councillors and four school managers, including the Chairman. One was an 86-year-old pensioner, another was eight months pregnant. Quite a good turnout and a very representative turnout — quite a few people had put themselves out to give up the morning to come. We were just kept standing in a little group in the corridor. They came out, obviously in a hurry, kept consulting their watches. They showed little sympathy for our case, and dismissed most of our questions and suggestions. Finally they hurried away, leaving us standing around, uncertain of where the meeting was to take place or when we might enter. When we did enter the chamber we just sat at the back, unable to say or do anything'.

It was all over in ten minutes and the group emerged in a state of considerable shock. Only the councillor who put the case and one other (the friend of the Chairman of Managers) questioned the proposal or indicated any interest in the case.

> 'The rest were doing their *Daily Telegraph* crossword, or coming and going, or were asleep. That's the way it goes I presume'.

For the Group Secretary, the experience was profoundly disturbing:

> 'It was my first encounter with officialdom at that level, and I was absolutely appalled. I came away almost shaking with rage and frustration. It was horrible, a horrible experience'.

It was in this ten minute encounter that the optimism which had buoyed up the Group evaporated:

'During the meeting, it became crystal clear that nobody was interested. They had got this recommendation and were happy to accept what had been said, one stage behind them'.

For the Secretary, especially:

'I was terribly upset after the Sub-Committee meeting because they were so dismissive. I felt I had put so much time into it and they weren't prepared to grant a fraction of that time'.

Aftermath and Appeal

The experience of the Sub-Committee robbed the group of its former drive, for after that, the campaign was never the same. Forward thrust became rearguard action. However, a new letter went out to the villagers:

'THE FIGHT, HOWEVER, IS BY NO MEANS OVER! No decision has yet been taken to close the school — it is still only a recommendation. It will now be discussed by the full Education Committee and then by the County Council. If, by then, the decision is in favour of closure, we shall appeal to the Department of Education and Science ... THERE IS STILL HOPE!'

A few days after the Sub-Committee meeting, the Secretary of the Group wrote in bitter terms to the Chairman of the Education Committee. She expressed the dismay of her Group at the education office's action in advising parents of prospective pupils of the likelihood of Ings Downton School closing, thus contributing to decline in enrolment. Further, she criticized the nature of the treatment accorded to the Ings Downton case in the Sub-Committee meeting and, whilst recognizing the busy schedule of Committee members, she deplored the fact that no member of the Committee had been sufficiently interested to visit the school. The letter ended with a plea for their case to be reconsidered: 'It is surely quite inconceivable that so many would fight with such conviction to maintain an inferior standard of education for our children.'

The Chairman, who had not been present at the meeting, replied courteously but uncompromisingly. He rejected criticism of the action of the local education office, declaring that not to inform parents of the likely closure of the school would equally have laid its officials open to criticism. He defended the behaviour of the Sub-Committee, affirming that county policy on closure was well known to them and that they depended on the detailed consideration given at lower levels: 'The amount of thought that goes into these matters is not necessarily reflected in the number of words that are spoken at the meeting.' His reply concluded:

> 'I certainly have no doubt of your conviction and, of course, small village schools have their advantages particularly for the younger children and they score some notable successes. At the same time, you must appreciate that the Committee receives advice from its officers who have long experience both as teachers and administrators about the disadvantages, particularly for the older children. Their advice, as I have said, is backed by the opinion of the teacher members of the Committee. We also cannot ignore the financial considerations because if very small schools absorb an undue proportion of our resources, they do so at the expense of other schools and other children in the county'.

Two events revived the flagging spirits of the Group. Against the odds, another county school facing closure won a last-minute reprieve and the local television company, initially uninterested in the Ings Downton case, after receiving the document, saw the events as sufficiently newsworthy to centre a documentary upon it. The Group now extended its search for support and received messages of encouragement from the Agricultural Workers Union, the National Federation of Women's Institutes and the National Council of Social Service. A more systematic survey of prospective pupils was mounted in the catchment area and this revealed a small enhancement of numbers for the September of the following year and for the subsequent year:

4–11-year-olds 24 and (28)
5–11-year-olds 20 and (21)
4–8-year-olds 18 and (19)
(Figures in brackets for subsequent year.)

The new figures were sent to the Sub-Committee with a request for a reconsideration of their decision and later, to the full Education

Committee which considered the case a month after the Sub-Committee meeting. No reply was received.

There was no KIDS deputation when the closure proposal came before the full Education Committee, although a few villagers attended privately. The Group had already shifted its sights to an appeal to the Secretary of State for Education. A month after the Education Committee's endorsement of the proposal, the closure notice was attached to the school railings and the Group formally submitted notification of appeal to the Department of Education and Science, accompanying it with their document and multi-signature letters of support.

The Appeal

Arrangements for the appeal meeting at the DES took considerable time and effort, a major cause of the delay being the prevarication of the local MP. Were he to signify his readiness to accompany the delegation, they would meet a minister. Without his support, only a meeting with a DES official would be possible. A veterinary surgeon, well-known in the county and local network and strongly committed to the community and the school, telephoned the MP. Promptly, he arrived, toured the school and met the Group's Secretary. During the entire campaign, he was the only elected representative so to do.

Six villagers travelled to the DES and met a minister. The contrast with their corridor experience in Shire Hall was considerable. They were listened to with courtesy and given ample time to outline their case. The minister was 'interested, asked questions and was very charming'. Although the group felt the odds of success to be slight, nonetheless, there was no sense of frustration or bitterness such as their meeting at county level had engendered. Five months later, a letter was received from the DES rejecting their appeal.

One last request was made to the Chairman of the Education Committee to reconsider, or at least, to defer closure for one year, in view of the delay resulting from appeal to the Secretary of State. This request was rejected.

Aftermath

With the last avenue explored, the school had only two more months of existence, and the village turned its attention to the future use of the building. The Parish Council and the Ings Downton Society contacted the Chief Education Officer to explore the means by which the premises might be retained for community use, for the village had no other public building. The CEO replied unambiguously. He observed that the Education Committee had no policy which permitted retention of redundant schools for community use, and transferred school buildings which were no longer required to the County Valuer and the Land and Estates Committee, who then had the purview of future action.

Acting on this information, the Parish Council sought the help of the voluntary Secretary of the County Association of Local Councils who campaigned actively on their behalf. She wrote several times to the chairmen of both the Education Committee and the Land and Estates Committee and circularized councillors, drawing attention to the effect upon rural communities of the loss of their schools, citing Ings Downton in particular. She advised the Parish Council on the long-term strategy of raising purchase money and the grant possibilities available in principle. For the short term, she advised renting for a period of three–five years. The critical issue, of course, was the level of rent which might be demanded. As on a previous occasion, there was a sense of optimism. The Leader of the Council indicated by letter that the possibilities of acquisition existed and that he had requested the County Valuer to enter into discussion with the Parish Council. He added:

> 'Please rest assured that the county councillors do not under-estimate the problems of the rural communities. We are, I hope, always sympathetic to practical suggestions as to how their difficulties might be mitigated'.

With future use of the building unresolved, the school term ended and the school, as a school, ceased to exist. Soon after, Council workmen arrived and removed fixed elements in the building including heating, sink, water heaters and all lavatory cisterns. The cisterns, the villagers learned from the workmen, were to be dumped. It was subsequent to this activity that the County Valuer provided an offered solution in the form of an annual rental for the building of £950 together with rates, insurance and maintenance — a figure obviously beyond the means of a small village, particularly if they were also to raise the capital sum needed for eventual purchase.

Not surprisingly, negotiations over leasing the building ceased. The County Valuer then informed the Parish Council of the County

Council's intention to sell the property and asked if they were interested in purchase. The Clerk to the Parish Council replied in the negative, adding:

> 'It was, however, unanimously felt at the public meeting that the conduct of the County Council throughout the sorry business of the school's closure and subsequently has been far from considerate or just'.

The final act centred upon a request that a fifteen-year-old climbing frame, still standing in the playground, might be left for the village children. The reply was that it was to be sent to the school in Churningham (already equipped with such apparatus). The local councillor was informed of the resentment which this reply had stirred in the village and arrangements were made for the climbing frame to be purchased by the village for the sum of £25.

Postscript

Since the school closure, the village post office and shop has closed. The owner (and parent of two former pupils) claims that the closure of the school led directly to loss of trade from mothers going to and from school each weekday. The bus company, for reasons of insurance, will not accept children under age 5. Therefore unless parents transport their children, they cannot start below age 5 nor can they attend on a part-time basis. The Ings Downton Society too, has ceased to function.

Two Perspectives

The two battles we have recounted are not grossly untypical of other closure conflicts which we have studied. Almost always, the combatants reveal deeply divided and passionate convictions centring on the values they place on the financial, economic and social aspects of schooling and the relation of school to community. Though both sets of protagonists focus upon the same phenomenon — the small rural school — the perspectives which they each create are almost completely polarized. The differences in the 'official' perspective and the 'grass roots' perspective may be summarised in Table 1, as follows:

Table 1: Main Features of the Two Perspectives

Feature	Official perspective	Grass roots' perspective
Economic	Village school seen as costly. Search for economy by closure.	Village school seen as virtually only major return to village ratepayer. Rejection of economic argument.
School's relationship to Community	Seen as contractual between school and parent element of community.	Organic. School seen as integral with community.
Curriculum	Curriculum regarded as inadequate in breadth and range of content.	Curriculum conceived as nutrient to feed acquisition of ways of learning.
Teachers	Staff size too small for requisite professional skills and curriculum expertise. Seen as isolated.	Personal/interpersonal qualities valued. Emphasis placed on caring and on fostering attitudes to learning. Isolation not seen as major issue.
Pupils	Size of single age peer group seen as inadequate for enhancing competition.	Total school population seen as peer group. Family nature of school stressed. Cooperation valued.
Transport	Pupil transportation essential if adequate sized schools are to be achieved.	Rejected as harmful to child and as fracturing informal home-school link.
Educational solution	Rationalise by small school closure and creation of larger units.	Retain and grant adequate resources.

Given the many problems in the urban areas of present day society, it is not surprising that rural schooling does not feature in the national context as an important and dominant issue. However, for those counties with a large number of small rural schools and for the villages in which the schools are set, the matter is important and dominant. For those participants in the rural education debate and in closure conflicts, it is easy to assume that the problems they confront have no history. This, we think is erroneous, for by placing the current issue in relation to the past, it may be possible to identify major patterns of thinking which illuminate the way in which rural education is and has been contemplated. With this thought in mind, we turn in the next chapter to tracing views of the rural school from the mid-twenties to the present time.

Chapter 2

Past and Present Perspectives of the Small Rural School

If all the criticisms which the official perspective levels at the small rural school are brought together, they represent summatively a charge that it represents a defective and inherently disadvantaging element in the national system. Further, if one studies an array of closure cases, what is striking is the apparent novelty of the charge, almost as if no history of the situation existed. Yet of course, rural schools like their urban cousins possess a past extending over a century. Hence, a question to be faced is whether the rural school has suddenly become a disadvantaging institution, or whether there have been times in its past when it has also manifested features which have caused concern to the national providers of education.

It is to this question that we turn now, principally to see whether any elements in the history of village schooling provide a thread or theme which can illuminate the contemporary official perspective. We do not propose to reach far back, for we have chosen to begin at the point when the 1926 Consultative Committee, led by Sir Henry Hadow, recommended in their first report, *The Education of the Adolescent,* that a change be made from the all-age elementary school to separate and distinctive primary and secondary stages. Although the process of transformation was not to be complete until the mid-fifties, it was as a result of this recommendation that primary schools, including the small rural primary school as we know it today, came into existence. Five years later, a second report by Hadow was published. Aimed specifically at the primary school, it yields evidence of a particular perception of rural schooling.

Hadow: Curriculum, Methods, Classification and the Small Rural School

Hadow's second report, *The Primary School* (1931), turned its attention to the needs and purposes of the primary school which his previous report had been instrumental in bringing into being. The Committee had a specific brief from the Board of Education:

> 'To enquire and report as to the courses of study suitable for children (other than children in infants departments) up to the age of 11 in elementary schools, with special reference to the needs of children in rural areas'. (Preface, xii)

The Report was, and remains, a remarkable document for the enlightened views which it put foward. An almost inescapable quotation from its pages is its assertion that 'the curriculum is to be thought of in terms of activity and experience rather than knowledge to be acquired and facts to be stored'. With this as its beacon signal, how did the Committee view the rural school?

Although the Report urged a more active interpretation of curriculum and some, albeit cautious, experimentation in the use of active project methods, it found little to quarrel with so far as the curriculum elements themselves were concerned. Its suggestions endorsed the staple, inter-war primary curriculum. There is no indication in the Report that rural school teachers, or indeed teachers generally, should find it beyond their capacity to cope with the range of curriculum that was considered appropriate for the primary stage. How teachers might teach, rather than the span of their teaching, occupied a more dominant place in Hadow's thinking.

The Report was concerned with ways in which teachers might diversify their approaches and, while not seeking to condemn 'well tried methods of corporate instruction', it cautiously urged some move towards more independent learning opportunities being provided for pupils. To illustrate what active learning and teaching might mean, Hadow drew upon William Cobbett's *Advice to Young Men*. Cobbett (1830), had forthrightly rejected didactic instruction in favour of engaging his children's interest in the work of his rural smallholding and allowing them to discover that 'book learning' could profitably be used in the search for solutions to the actual problems which they encountered in their daily activity. Hadow, circumspectly enthusiastic in advocating the adoption of the 'Cobbett Method', was able to indicate where the method was to be found already in action and where it had a natural fit:

'... schools, especially rural schools, may easily find, as the best of them already do, a good many opportunities for trying it'. (p102)

It was from the evidence concerning rural school practice that the Hadow Committee was able to typify the kind of individual and group methods of working that they saw as essential to any movement away from the dominance of class instruction:

'We have received a large number of interesting memoranda from headteachers of rural schools describing the internal organization and methods of instruction adopted. The impression gained from these memoranda and from our oral evidence is that the teachers in schools which have been converted into primary schools for pupils between the ages of 5 and 11 are developing a technique and a type of organization which are yielding good results ... In a small country school in the north with an average attendance of twelve children under one teacher, the pupils are grouped for different branches of the curriculum. The teacher makes full use of individual effort on the part of the children by training them from the very beginning to work for themselves and by allowing them to work at their own pace ... The scholars are allowed, irrespective of age, to proceed to other and more advanced work as soon as they can show their competency. ... In another primary school which is staffed with two teachers it has been found possible to make the work as individual and progressive as it has in small rural schools[1] ... Each pupil advances at his own pace ... and the older children help the younger children with their work'. (p81–2)

Methodologically, the small rural school emerged with credit from the second Hadow Report as an institution with much to teach larger urban schools. The Report, in fact, recommended the practice of young teachers spending an apprenticeship in such schools because 'in rural schools, and small schools generally, there are opportunities for gaining valuable knowledge of individual and group methods'. Hadow's principal concerns were the failure of training institutions to recognize rural school needs and also, the unduly high proportion of unqualified supplementary teachers in rural areas. (In 1929, 5565 unqualified teachers, out of a total of 7462 in the overall teaching force, taught in rural areas.)

The Hadow Committee called upon the very best psychological

evidence that was available at the time to assist its deliberations and, during the inter-war period, the central issues in educational psychology were intelligence and aptitude. The measurement of intelligence by objective tests was also establishing a legitimacy that was not to decay until the late 1950s. Drawing upon the contemporary views of its expert psychological witnesses, the Committee asserted that 'the mental capacity which is of most importance for intellectual progress is "intelligence"'. Thus:

> '... at the age of 5, children are spread out between the mental ages of about 3 and 7 or 8 years, a total range of about four to five years. By the age of 10 this range has doubled and it probably continues to enlarge till the end of puberty'. (p34)

Hadow, on the basis of this view of intelligence, claimed that pupils between the ages of 5 to 7 could be grouped together without too much regard to variations in their mental capacity, but that, by the age of 10, children should if possible 'be organized for teaching purposes in at least three distinct sections'. Thus prevalent psychological theory provided Hadow with an informing perspective on how the schooling of 7–11 year-old children could best be organized on the basis of their classification. What did Hadow's view of classification entail?

> 'In general, we agree with our psychological witnesses in thinking that in very large primary schools there might, wherever possible, be a triple track system of organization, viz a series of 'A' classes or groups for the brighter children and a series of smaller 'C' classes or groups to include retarded children, both series being parallel to the ordinary series of 'B' classes or groups for the average children ... In the smaller schools there might well be at least two classes or sets for each age group'. (p78)

If one summarizes the Hadow view of primary school organization, first, one can point to its firm recommendation that the infant school and the junior school should be separate entities. The Committee found little to support a break at the age of 7 in psychological terms but was concerned that an environment containing a 5–11 age range might prove daunting for the younger children. Secondly, convinced by the psychological evidence it had received on the intellectual characteristics of primary age children, and concerned at the wide spread of mental ages that could be found in a cohort of a given age, the Report commended age graded, streamed classes as the favoured means of meeting the difficulty. So, the best model for a junior school, from which infant children are precluded, is one of twelve classes, for this enables accommodation to the contemporary theories of intelligence and mental age by three class streaming. What is proper, as it were, in terms of size, type, internal organization and psychological fit is an urban junior school of around 320 to 400 pupils.

Given the Committee's view that the mental age of the child be so cogent a factor in organizing his learning, and its acknowledgement of the six-seven year spread of mental ages in a group of 10-year-olds, it might be asked why it is deemed natural that children be taught in single age bands. The question is not raised in the Report; the possibility that a 7-year-old might conceivably learn alongside a 10-year-old is not envisaged as a solution to the mental age problem; the Committee's thinking is absorbed by the conventional assumptions that a primary school is organized in age bands.

It is upon Hadow's preoccupation with pupil classification and the age grade — mental age axis, and its solution via streaming, that the small rural school in the 1920s and 1930s is depicted as a problem:

'... owing to the composite character of the groups or classes, it is not an easy matter to organize a small primary school effectively so as to maintain a progressive course of instruction. However small a school may be it may contain children who differ in age and in innate capacity as widely as children do in large urban schools, but so few children will fall within any particular age range or grade of capacity that it is quite impossible to staff the school on the basis of a separate teacher for each grade. The adoption of a rougher classification is inevitable ...' (p80)

While the issue of classification is clear enough, there is something peculiar about the reference to the small rural school's deficiency in maintaining 'a progressive course of instruction'. As we have seen, Hadow turned to such schools to illustrate how it was possible to enable children to work independently, 'to make their own pace', and 'to proceed to more advanced work as soon as they can show their competency'. All these features are central to an approach which emphasizes mental age rather than chronological age and takes a view of pupil progress as continuous rather than subject to administrative age graded arrangements. The only explanation it would seem, was that Hadow's view of a progressive course of instruction was the thoroughly urban one of progress via classified stream, age grade to age grade. Similarly, the Committee's insistence upon the need for a change of school at the age of 7 is developed largely on the basis of its understanding of urban school playgrounds. Even when the impossibility of this delineation in rural areas is acknowledged, the Committee's view of the rural school's internal organization is coloured by this same urban vision:

> '... we fully recognize that in most country schools, at the present time, it would be economically impracticable owing to the small number of children to establish separate departments for pupils between the ages of 7 and 11. We think however that ... even (in) small rural schools there should be a well defined line of demarcation between the younger and older children'. (p68)

What a study of Hadow has to teach us is the way in which educational theories (in this case relating to 'intelligence') interacting with highly visible practical concerns (urban primary schooling) can conspire to cast the small rural school as an abnormality. This is so even when the best of its practice appears to demonstrate both a commonsense application of the favoured theory and an espousal of methods which are commended as educationally valuable.

Handbook of Suggestions — The Invisible Rural School

On the eve of the 1944 Education Act, the Board of Education reprinted the 1937 edition of its *Handbook of Suggestions,* a document designed to advise teachers on appropriate organization, curriculum and teaching method. There was little in it to indicate that the rural school was a subject of particular concern to the Board; of its 570 pages, five were devoted specifically to what, borrowing from Hadow, it referred to as small 'decapitated' schools. In those five pages there was little to show that such schools needed to be considered as institutions with distinctive features of their own, still less that they needed to be taken especially seriously.

The Handbook noted that some rural teachers employed a technique of oral teaching to half the class while the remainder worked alone. Apparently ignorant of Hadow's commendation of the individual and group system of teaching and learning characteristic of good rural schools and the Committee's advocacy of individualized learning, the Handbook commented, somewhat resignedly:

> 'There are of course other variants of this technique possible, but in any case the child in the small rural school has through

force of circumstance to spend a considerable portion of his time in independent study'. (p46)

Two curricular problems were identified. The first was related to constructing syllabuses, especially in history and geography, which could meet the needs of a class containing three or four age groups. The advice offered, stubbornly attached to age-gradedness, and careless of Hadow's encouragement to experiment with project approaches, was to plan one course for younger children and one for older children and to vary them from year to year. Again fatalistically:

'This is the best perhaps that can be done in the circumstances'. (p46)

The second problem occurred in schools in which the junior teacher was female:

'In schools under a mistress, the question how best to occupy the boys' time when she herself is teaching the girls' needlework calls for her serious consideration. The principle should be that the boys are occupied with something which is as useful to the boys as needlework to the girls, for example scale drawing, surveying or certain forms of handwork'. (p46)

How far we have moved in one generation is nicely revealed by the comments of the 1978 HMI Primary Survey on this form of differentiated curricula:

'There is no justification for differentiation between the curriculum for boys and for girls because of traditional differences in social roles; such differentiation as does still occur, for example in craft work which limits girls to using soft materials, is unusual and should cease'. (para 8.29)

A problem in 1944 ceases to be defined as a problem in 1978. The solution advocated in 1944 becomes, by 1978, a practice to be deplored.

The Handbook, like the Hadow Report, was unenthusiastic about coeducation. Hadow had observed that there was no valid objection to it on educational or sociological grounds, but added that in populous areas it might be advisable to organize junior schools on a single sex basis (a further principle of classification to which the village school could not comply). The Handbook offered a similar view indicating the direction of its inclination with the comment that 'the mixed school is of course a necessity where the numbers are small'.

While the Handbook revealed no major concern with the capacity of rural schools to cope, other than their inability to employ the classificatory organization then enjoying a vogue in larger schools, it offers some fay visions of what teaching in such schools involves:

'... it is specially desirable that they (the teachers) should be interested in plant and animal life and have some training in drawing and simple handwork. The more interesting features and traditions of the neighbourhood should not be over-looked'. (p45)

The London view of what handicraft for the older rural boy might be is equally whimsical:

'The rural school has an advantage in finding opportunities that do not always exist in town schools for applying its handicraft to real needs, for example, in connection with the implements required for the cottage, the home or the farm. For them it may often be necessary to use materials that are ready to hand and to improvise. But though the materials used will often be rough, a boy who has been trained in the basic processes will suffer no undue handicap ... It would include such things for instance as hutches, beehives, coops, trap nets, or bins and fowl houses ... Occasionally opportunities may arise for little jobs in brickwork or stonework or thatching ... In some schools cobbling has been taught with successful results ...' (p271)

In 1959, the Ministry of Education published *Primary Education* which replaced its *Handbook of Suggestions* for teachers because, as the Ministry observed, 'the old title is no longer in tune with the status of the teaching profession, or with the broader view which we now take of what constitutes good education'. Professionalization of the teaching force was not the only change to have occurred in the immediate post-war years. The 1944 Act had, of course, established by statute the primary school as a valid and separate stage in the state education system. In many schools, particularly infant, that were sufficiently remote from the constraints imposed by the 11+ selection process, teachers had set about experimenting with more liberal methods involving active learning and curriculum reforms based upon project approaches to integrating subject matter. In-creasingly fostered by teacher training colleges, where it was linked to Piagetian theories of child development, the so-called 'progressive philosophy' became a modest presence not only in infant, but also in junior schools. Egalitarian in nature, and with a view that children's ability grew in relation to the richness and stimulation of their environment, this movement was opposed to the meritocracy of streaming and strong in its advocacy of teaching pupils in coeducational classes, mixed in terms of social origin, ability and, less certainly, age.

Primary Education reflected fairly these post-war changes: mathematics rather than arithmetic, free writing, discovery learning and concrete experiences all received more emphasis than formerly. Within this context, the document had little to say about rural schools, merely seeing them as dwarf varieties of the larger primary schools it was addressing:

> 'Where a school caters for more than one section of the primary
> age range and especially as in rural schools when it provides
> for comparatively few children between 5, or even under,
> and 11 years of age, and does with only one or two teachers,
> arrangements and procedures may have to be considerably
> modified to meet the varying circumstances ... But the basic
> educational principles hold throughout, and, where the
> teachers understand the needs of children at different stages,
> the resulting practices are not fundamentally different what-
> ever the type of school'. (p26)

By 1959, Hadow's recommended principle of classification by ability streaming was showing signs of erosion. *Primary Education* itself identified two disadvantages of streaming: the danger of a teacher failing to recognize the diversity of ability present within a stream and the demoralizing effect on the pupil of low stream status. Thus, movement away from an attachment to streaming appeared to have removed from the small rural school the stigma of being unable to employ this system of classification:

> 'In the small school, to the range of ability is added the wide
> age range within one class, though this is not necessarily a
> disadvantage if the numbers are small. Many devices are used
> in schools to give each child work which is suitable for him
> and to ensure progress in accordance with his rate of learning'.
> (p68)

Among the 'devices' which *Primary Education* had in mind was the flexible use of individual and group work. Here, apparently unwitting of the long history of the development of such techniques in the mixed age classes of rural schools to which Hadow had drawn attention, the authors present it as a recent innovation:

'One of the most remarkable developments in teachers' skill over the last decade or so has been that of educating in one class children of very different abilities. They do this by arranging the environment of the classroom and school so that the children learn a great deal for themselves, either individually or in small groups'. (p70)

What we can detect in this is the process whereby the decay in one theoretical position and the growth in another, influences the perspective applied to the rural school. The commitment in the 1930s and 1940s to theories of intelligence and ability, allied to the views of educational psychologists, had caused the Hadow Committee to recommend streaming by ability. Its implementation was dependent upon urban sized schools and consequently the small rural school was seen to be deficient because it was not large enough to conform to this prescription. With a decline of interest in that earlier view of 'intelligence', a realization of the problems inherent in ability classification and a shift of psychological interest towards how children learn, came a new focus — active learning procedures in heterogeneous classes. In the light of that new theoretical position, the small rural school ceased to be viewed as inherently problematic.

The Plowden and Gittins Reports: The Small Rural School as both Innovative and Deficient

The committees established in 1963 at the request of the Minister of Education by the English and Welsh Central Advisory Councils for Education 'to consider the whole subject of primary education and the transition to secondary education' and under the chairmanship, respectively, of Lady Plowden and Professor Gittins, published their reports in 1967. Both reports gave enthusiastic support to what had by then become firmly known as 'progressive education', as shown, perhaps most eloquently by Plowden's summary of the underlying principles of what it took to be the best of current practice:

'The school sets out deliberately to devise the right environment for children, to allow them to be themselves and to develop in the way and at the pace appropriate to them. It tries to equalize opportunities and to compensate for handicaps. It lays special stress on individual discovery, on first-hand experience and on opportunities for creative work. It insists that knowledge does not fall into neatly separate compartments and that work and play are not opposite but complementary. A child brought up in such an atmosphere at all stages of his education has some hope of becoming a balanced and mature adult and of being able to live in, to contribute to, and to look critically at the society of which he forms a part'. (para 505)

Notably, in terms of our interests, both reports devoted particular attention to rural schools and were indeed to prove influential in deciding the fate of many.

These two reports rang the death knell on classification by streaming. Plowden was especially emphatic:

'We welcome unstreaming in the infant or first school and hope that it will continue to spread through the age groups of the junior and middle schools'. (para 819)

The Gittins Report did not rule out homogeneous groups, but it warned sternly against the tendency for ability groups to become rigid — 'Streams have become glaciers', and it certainly removed any possibility that a small rural school's inability to arrange its classes in this manner could be considered a defect.

Both reports also paid warm tribute to the work of teachers in rural schools. Plowden, for instance:

'Acknowledgement must be made of the devoted work of many village school teachers. Often working alone and with few opportunities for discussion with their colleagues, sometimes heavily handicapped by their buildings, responsible for children of a wider age range than most junior teachers think practicable, they have created schools characterized by warmth, forebearance and an almost family affection ... Recent recruits to country schools have continued this tradition and, as we have seen for ourselves, have set an example for national progress in primary education, both in flexible organization of their schools and the excellence of their work'. (para 77)

Demonstrative though this testimony is, and despite its obvious congruence with Plowden's vision of what primary education ought to be, it is not difficult to detect between these felicitous phrases the signs of new concerns about the small rural school.

Both committees commented unfavourably on the generally poor state of village school buildings and their physical facilities. The major reason for this, the fact that for more than twenty years the overwhelming priority of school building programmes had been to create separate secondary and large urban primary schools, was fully acknowledged in both reports. Nevertheless, for the first time, the quality of rural school buildings was signalled as being a problem — a problem that is to say when these schools were measured against the superior standard of urban school provision.

Allied to this, because it relates to the cost-effectiveness of improving the fabric of rural schools, was the economics of rural schooling. Both reports drew attention to the higher costs, measured in terms of unit-costs per pupil, of providing a network of small schools across an area of low population density. Gittins observed:

'Where there is a large number of small schools needing very generous staffing, education is likely to be more expensive than in a compact area with a small number of larger schools. Our evidence shows this clearly'. (para 7.5.8)

The evidence produced in the Gittins Report revealed most clearly the association between density of population, teacher-pupil ratio, average size of schools and unit costs. The Report went on to affirm that there was nothing to indicate that the greater expenditure by the most rural authorities resulted in superior provision of better education. There was no evidence that it was inferior either and Plowden rejected any notion that the measured attainment of rural children differed from that of their urban peers, but another new problem had been identified with regard to rural primary schools, namely that they were more expensive than their larger urban counterparts.

With regard to the staffing of village schools, both committees were concerned at the difficulties of recruitment. This was, of course, a time of teacher shortage generally, but the reports argued that it affected rural schools disproportionately because, as Gittins put it, 'young teachers coming out of colleges of education are increasingly unwilling to accept first posts in isolated rural schools'. That was not all. The problem, merely hinted at by Hadow, of the depressing effect on a small school of one mediocre teacher, was affirmed in these reports and identified by a new term 'professional isolation'. The contrary effect, the influence of one outstanding teacher was also acknowledged; Plowden for instance spoke of the strength given to some small schools by keen, innovative teachers 'who often prefer headships in a country school, with responsibility for a class, to a deputy headship or graded post in a larger school'. Innovation and the spread of new, progressive ideas were major educational concerns in the 1960s and the situation in a small rural school in which teachers had few, if any, other colleagues with whom to exchange ideas and limited opportunities for contact with LEA advisory staff was seen as an intrinsic liability. Professional isolation, formerly hinted at, entered the lexicon of rural school problems.

It was on the question of the curriculum offered by the primary school that both Plowden and Gittins directed their main concerns about the small rural school. The curriculum, it will be recalled, had not hitherto been viewed as a problem. Neither in the Hadow Report nor in the subsequent *Handbook of Suggestions* were there any particular anxieties expressed about the village school teachers' ability to provide a sufficient and suitably varied curriculum diet. By the 1960s the definition of an appropriate primary school curriculum had altered, and as it did so, what had once been considered to be a perfectly adequate facet of a rural school's operation became deficient:

> 'The curriculum of the primary school is now much wider and richer than when many primary schools were first built. The goals proposed by modern primary education challenge the limited space and resources of the small school. Teachers must between them cover a wide range of activities and attempt to be equally effective in all fields. Some aspects of the curriculum, such as drama, physical education and expressive movement and science tend to be weak ... In the larger primary school, it is possible to use the special skills and interests of the staff by exchanges of staff or some 'specialist' teaching. Teachers with a particular interest or qualification can help to draw up schemes of work or advise their colleagues. The opportunity for this kind of cooperation is limited in a small school'. (para 7.5.6)

Even granted that many authorities made special capitation provision for small schools, both committees came to regard small rural schools as being inevitably under-resourced. Because a new emphasis was placed upon pupil interaction, tacitly assumed to be only valuable in age-graded peer groups, the small size of such groups in village schools meant a further restriction of a potentially important curriculum resource. But above all, it was the small number of staff and the assumption that this implied a narrow curriculum which provided the gravest concern. Plowden, less determinedly than Gittins recommended that 'schools with an age range of 5–11 should usually have at least three classes each covering two age groups', but noted that local circumstances would make exceptions inevitable. Gittins more emphatically recommended the minimum size of school as fifty to sixty pupils and three teachers. However the optimum solution for the rural area was to be found in the centrally located area school of six teachers, and Gittins, more readily than Plowden, was prepared to pay the price of this closer approximation to the urban model.

All of the difficulties mentioned above are, we will later argue, problematic issues in any school; the presence of a wide range of interests and skills among the staff gives no guarantees about the quality of the curriculum that any pupil actually encounters, for instance. In so far as these problems do relate to rural schools, they are amenable to positive and innovative thought which need not follow conventional urban channels. However, the most serious challenge to the continued life of the small rural primary school lay in the long-term view of the age of secondary transfer developed by both committees.

The Middle School Solution: The Problem of Specialization

The work of the two committees was influenced by government proposals connected with secondary education. DES Circular 10/65 (DES, 1965) required local authorities to submit plans for a comprehensive system of education. In the following year, Circular 10/66 (DES, 1966) announced the Government's intention to raise the school leaving age to 16 and permitted LEAs to change the age of transfer into secondary education to 12 or 13 if it could be warranted 'by reference to some clear practical advantages in the context of reorganization on comprehensive lines, or by the raising of the school leaving age or both'. This was the context within which both Plowden and Gittins were required to 'consider primary education in all its aspects and the transition to secondary education'.

Plowden pointed out that there was nothing hallowed about 11 as the age for transfer. Reflecting on the traditional point of primary/secondary division the Report commented drily. 'Practical considerations decided the matter; theory, so far as it came at all was used in support.' In considering the matter of transfer in the context of the time, both committees reviewed numerous and varied lists of advantages and disadvantages claimed for the retention of 11 as the age of transfer. One of the major concerns seems to have focussed on the long secondary span (11–18), if the transfer point was unchanged and the consequent difficulties secondary schools would experience in creating climates appropriate to both the younger and the older pupils. Such schools, it was argued, would be too large and the views of the Newsom Report (1963), on the need in deprived areas for small secondary schools, were quoted in support. On balance, both Plowden and Gittins favoured raising the age of transition.

But, if 11+ was to be abandoned as the age of transfer, what age should be substituted? There were disadvantages with 13: it would provide too short a secondary examination course; more tellingly, it would incur greater expense because the resulting (9–13) middle school would require extra resources and specialist accommodation in such areas as science, handicraft and PE. On the other hand, given transfer at 12, Plowden observed:

'Accommodation in a two-form entry junior school would probably be adequate for an 8–12 school provided that one or two general practical rooms were added'. (para 379)

Most serious of all, was the unconcealed anxiety felt in both committees about what might happen to teaching methods in the middle school if the age of transfer was delayed to 13. For Plowden:

'The danger of a two-year extension would be that the middle school would forget it was a primary school'. (para 384)

And for Gittins:

'We fear, however, that this kind school would tend to be drawn increasingly in its organization and teaching approaches, into the orbit of the secondary school'. (para 4.6.2)

Having surveyed the options, both committees recommended raising the age of transfer by one year, to 12. In so doing, they revealed that characteristic of groups seized with a strong ideological commitment, namely the urge to extend the range of their influence beyond the ground that they already hold. They saw an extension to age twelve as a means of enlisting children for a further year into the progressive primary school ambit. Thus, for Plowden:

'. . . the primary tradition of individual and group work might advantageously be retained for a longer period than at present and might delay streaming'. (para 381)

Most clearly in the Plowden Report, the 8–12 middle school was offered an evangelical mission:

'If the middle school is to be a new and progressive force it must develop further the curriculum, methods and attitudes which exist at present in junior schools. It must move forward into what is now regarded as secondary work, but it must not move so far away that it loses the best of primary education as we know it now'. (para 383)

The best of primary education, as the Plowden and the Gittins committees had seen it, was of course a system which, whilst it emphasized cooperation between teachers, nonetheless regarded the teacher and her class as a family unit of operations which celebrated the integration of curriculum. The price which both Plowden and Gittins were prepared to pay for extending primary education by one year was, necessarily, some form of compromise between the style of education that they cherished and the organization and character of secondary schools from which they proposed to remove the 11-year-old cohort. How these children were to be taught in the new middle schools was seen by Plowden in terms of a bridge which could be extended back to 9 and 10-year-olds:

'A school with semi-specialist accommodation shared between cognate subjects and teachers skilled in certain areas of curriculum rather than in single subjects could provide a bridge from class teaching to specialization and from investigation of general problems to subject disciplines. The influence of semi-specialist teachers primarily concerned with the older pupils might be reflected in more demanding work being given to nine and ten-year-olds ...' (para 381)

However, the two committees might argue their case for transfer at the age of 12, the system they were proposing involved a fundamental breach of the primary tradition out of which had grown a style of education of which they approved. Plowden:

'The newer methods start with the direct impact of the environment on the child and the child's individual response to it. The results are unpredictable but extremely worthwhile. The teacher has to be prepared to follow up the personal interest of the children who, either singly or in groups, follow divergent paths of discovery'. (para 544)

By advocating semi-specialist teaching and accommodation they laid the ground for a radically different form of school organization. For all the optimism and the progressive rhetoric, there could be no guarantees that the style of education could be preserved wherein, as Plowden so eloquently put it, 'the child is the agent of his own learning'.

For the small rural school, the long term prognosis was not encouraging. In the first place, the semi-specialist middle school, to be effective, needed to be of sufficient size to carry a non-teaching head and a number of teachers without traditional class responsibilities. For both Plowden and Gittins, the most satisfactory sizes for primary schools, reorganized along first and middle school lines were a two-form entry first school of 240 pupils and a two or three-form entry middle school of between 300 and 480 pupils. Only in urban areas could one expect to find existing schools of a size suitable for adaptation and redesignation as first and middle schools. The model was entirely applicable to urban settings. Used as a criterion in rural areas, it transformed the village primary school into an abnormal institution and a thoroughly questionable place in which to educate 12-year-olds because as Plowden put it:

'... it will be difficult to provide a sufficiently challenging curriculum for the older pupils who may become as one witness suggested "unwilling veterans"'. (para 481)

It was, of course, not only the education of the oldest pupils that was at stake within the Plowden and Gittins proposals. Given the middle school model, with its semi-specialist component reaching down to the 9 and 10-year-olds, the education of the youngest age groups becomes a dubious proposition if they were to be left in their village schools. They would fall prey to what the proposals were casting as an outmoded kind of teacher — the generalist primary practitioner. Effectively, both Plowden and Gittins, in persuading themselves of the appropriateness of twelve as the age of transfer, painted themselves into a corner, for whilst both reports celebrated progressive methodologies, they laid the foundations upon which later, tougher minded ideologists of subject specialization would build. So far as rural areas were concerned, both Committees gave their schools as hostages to political fortune.

Better Schools: The Rise of the Concept of Curriculum-led Staffing

The post-war faith in the capacity of schools to transform the lives of individuals and to contribute to the nation's well-being reached its apotheosis in the Plowden and Gittins reports. While the committees were deliberating, governments in the 1960s were placing an unprecedented emphasis on the primary sector which was manifest in the expansion of the building programme, and of teacher education and nursery provision. For a period of time after 1967 the impetus was maintained. As late as 1972, a government White Paper, *A Framework for Expansion* (HMSO, 1972), indicated an intention to 'bring about a shift of resources within the education budget in favour of primary schools'.

Subsequent events showed that document to have been expectacularly ill-named and ill-timed. The astronomic rise in oil prices in the following year triggered an economic crisis in which education suffered in the ensuing search for public expenditure economies. It was also the year in which the primary school population reached its peak before beginning its subsequent sharp decline. The following year, 1974, saw the clearest portents of the changes that were to come. The Assessment of Performance Unit (APU) was set up and, as Richards (1982) notes, it was in 1974 that the Permanent Secretary at the DES 'wondered aloud' in an OECD meeting 'whether the government could continue to debar itself from what had been termed "the secret garden of the curriculum"'. That most sacrosanct of professional properties, the curriculum, was to receive the increasing attention of central government.

Since the mid-1970s, curricula at all levels of the education system have become subject not only to more scrutiny, but only to greater centralized control. Lawton (1984) has identified key stages in what he dubs 'the tightening grip' as follows:

'1974, setting up the Assessment of Performance Unit (APU); 1976, the DES 'Yellow Book' and the Callaghan speech at Ruskin College, followed by the so-called 'great debate'; the 1977 Green Paper making references to 'core curriculum' and the Secretary of State not abdicating curricular responsibilities (DES, 1977a). The Green Paper was soon followed by Circular 14/77 (DES, 1977b) asking LEAs for information about curricula thus indicating the need for a national view on the curriculum'. (p8)

In 1979, the DES published its summary of LEA responses to Circular 14/77 (DES, 1979). It revealed substantial variation between authorities in the level of control which they exerted on the curricula of their school and on the extent to which they had articulated a currciulum policy themselves. It argued the need for a 'more coherent approach to curriculum matters across the country', and reported that 'the Secretaries of State believe that they should give a lead in the process of reaching a national consensus on a desirable framework for the curriculum'. Two months later, a consultative document, *A Framework for the School Curriculum,* (DES, 1980), was published.

Since that date there has been an unprecedented output of material from the DES and from HMI together with major policy speeches from the Secretary of State on the content and organization of the curriculum as a whole and on its specific components. Together they represent a thrust towards a national curriculum structure. For the purposes of this chapter, the main issue is not so much the movement towards stronger centralist influence itself, but the particular view of what the school curriculum ought to be and how it ought to be organized within the schools that is contained in this shift in the balance of control.

Lawton (1984) argues that there are distinct ideological differences in the proposals that have emanated from politicians, DES officials, and professional inspectors. Thus:

'On curriculum was should find evidence of the politicos' addiction to standards, the DES concern for specified objectives and the HMI support for a common curriculum'. (p17)

There is evidence of these three strains of thought in the White Paper, *Better Schools* (HMSO, 1985) and its attempt to manage the tensions between them. This is the most authoritative recent statement on what a coherent, nation-wide curriculum structure would look like, for it charts the route that schools are expected to travel into the next century. Because it has significant implications for village schools it will be considered here in some detail.

Better Schools, as its title implies, is essentially critical of contemporary schooling. It asserts that 'A weakness found to a greater or lesser degree in about three-quarters of primary and middle schools is in curricular planning and its implementation'. Moreover, not only are teachers' expectations seen as insufficiently demanding at all levels of ability, but able pupils are not stretched and less able pupils are given inappropriate work. As far as school organization goes, 'there are rarely effective mechanisms for ensuring that declared curricular policies are reflected in the day-to-day work of most teachers and pupils'.

The concern with educational standards and with enhancing them in a cost conscious climate is evident from the start. Paragraph Two of *Better Schools* begins:

'The government's principle aims for all sectors of education are first, to raise standards at all levels of ability; and second, since education is an investment in the nation's future, to secure the best possible return from the resources which are found for it'. (para 2)

Allied to this is a utilitarian purpose which recurs frequently throughout:

'Education at school should promote enterprise and adaptability in order to increase young people's chances of finding employment or creating it for themselves'. (para 9)

A prime element in the remedial policies developed by the Secretaries of State is the establishment of a set of nationally-agreed objectives for schools. This is to be achieved by appropriate consultation between government, local authorities, schools and other interested parties. Securing what the White Paper describes as 'greater clarity about the objectives and content of the curriculum' is seen as being a necessary action for tackling the current weaknesses in the educational system and a pre-requisite for improving standards. So: 'The objectives are intended to have practical effect by becoming the basis of the curricular policies of the Secretaries of State, the LEAs and the schools.'

The influence of HMI is apparent when the link is made between nationally agreed objectives and curricular content. Across the full range of schools it is intended that the curriculum that is offered to all pupils should reflect four fundamental principles. These are affirmed as:

(i) Breadth: pupils should be introduced to a range of experience, knowledge and skills in such a way that curricular areas are interrelated and not taught in isolation.

(ii) Balance: there should not be over-emphasis on any particular areas of experience.

(iii) Relevance: all subjects should be taught so as to point up their 'link with the pupil's own experience and to bring out their application and continuing value in adult life'.

(iv) Differentiation: differences in pupils' abilities and aptitudes need to be reflected in different teaching methods and curricular content.

A curriculum based upon these principles will, in the government's view:

'... serve to develop the potential of every pupil and to equip all for the responsibilities of citizenship and the for-

midable challenge of employment in the world of tomorrow'.
(para 46)

These are not new principles. They were as important to the
Plowden Committee's view of how a school could foster the all round
development of the child as they are to the authors of *Better Schools.*
What is new is the manner in which these principles are interpreted
and the strategy deemed necessary for the effective transmission of a
curriculum that unfolds from them. For a primary teacher working
within the model celebrated in the Plowden Report, these principles
pointed towards providing pupils with the widest possible range of
experiences inside and outside the classroom, a concern for practical
activity and for work differentiated through individualized programmes of learning. In short, they were pedagogical principles. Rein-
terpreted in *Better Schools,* they become principles for defining the
content of the curriculum, differentiated between 'brighter children',
'average' and 'less able'. In the context of nationally agreed curricular
objectives these principles are designed to specify what is to be taught.
Teaching method is subservient, as indicated in the assertion that in
the primary phase 'any given curriculum (can) be delivered in a
variety of ways'.

With this content-driven view of primary education, *Better
Schools* consistently argues the necessity for the introduction of curriculum specialization into the primary school.

> 'Teaching the broad curriculum ... and doing so with the
> necessary differentiation, places formidable demands on the
> class teacher which increase with the age of the pupils. Older
> primary pupils (including those in middle schools) need to
> benefit from more expertise than a single class teacher can
> reasonably be expected to possess; this has consequences for
> staffing and the deployment of staff within a school, including
> the use of teachers as consultants'. (para 62)

The consequences for a school composed of generalist class
teachers, however skilled they might be in creating conditions for
active learning, are that it can no longer be considered to be adequately staffed because:

> 'In the government's view, older pupils in the primary phase
> should begin to be systematically introduced to teaching by
> members of staff with expertise in an area of the curriculum
> other than that which the class teacher can offer'. (para 64)

What is required, according to the perspective in *Better Schools,* to raise standards is 'curriculum-led staffing', that is to say an application of the principle of staff selection which ensures that each subject or curriculum area of a national curriculum structure is represented by a teacher with that expertise. Their deployment in the school will involve both specialist teaching and a consultancy role to support other teachers who lack their specific expertise. In the short term this might be achieved by retraining existing staff (or surplus secondary school teachers). In the longer term it would be achieved by new forms of teacher education and recruitment to bring about a match between teachers' qualifications and their teaching duties:

> 'Each new primary school teacher should be equipped to take a particular responsibility for one aspect of the curriculum, (such as science, mathematics or music), to act as a consultant to colleagues on that aspect, and to teach it to classes other than his own'. (para 162)

The principle of curriculum-led staffing is regarded by the authors of *Better Schools* as applicable to the great majority of primary schools, for the White Paper states as a main aspect of the managerial responsibility of LEAs 'the need to see that each school has a staff of teachers as well matched as possible to the curricular needs of the pupils'. The constraints, of course, are obvious — the existing qualifications of the staff, finance and the size of the school. 'The smaller the school, the more serious these constraints are likely to be.'

What then is considered to be the minimum acceptable school size? To create better schools, the 7–11 junior school should be of two-form entry, while the 5–11 primary school should be no less than one-form entry. We can see here the curriculum-led rationale plainly at work, for, given a staffing allocation of no more than a non-teaching head and six class teachers, it becomes just possible to acquire the range of specialist expertise deemed necessary to cover the defined areas of the curriculum.

Better Schools, in virtually its only recognition that British society contains a rural element, acknowledges that factors of geography, population sparsity and the need for denominational choice may result in the maintenance of unusually small schools which require more generous staffing than that found in larger schools. But ominously,

> 'Since the resources available to the LEA are limited, it is in the interests of pupils in both these categories of school that the former should include only those schools which for valid

educational or practical reasons cannot be included in the latter'. (para 272)

The issue is not only one of limited resources, but also of educational criteria. Except in some isolated communities:

'The number of pupils should not in general fall below the level at which a complement of three teachers is justifed, since it is inherently difficult for a very small school to be educationally satisfactory'. (para 275)

This is the bluntest assessment yet of the problem of the rural school — quite simply it is inherently difficult for it to be educationally satisfactory. Education is defined in terms of a nationally agreed set of objectives surrounding a common curriculum; a satisfactory education is therefore reduced to the satisfactory transmission of this formal curriculum; a pre-requisite for that is held to be a satisfactory pattern of staffing of each school whereby the constituent elements of that curriculum are matched against the subject knowledge of the teachers. Demonstrably, the small rural primary school cannot be educationally satisfactory because it cannot provide teacher experts in each area of the curriculum.

Better Schools invites no room for manoeuvre on this logic. Previous reports and DES publications have invariably endeavoured to weigh the relative weaknesses and strengths of rural schools, as their authors have perceived them. Problems such as teacher isolation and peer group size for example have been set against the benefits of the sense of security which small schools provide for young children or the close contact they engender between teachers and parents. The White Paper pursues a single target and with a tougher minded determination. Thus, the rural schools commended by Plowden and Gittins for providing a fine education, however excellent they might be, fail automatically under the present criteria of curricular specialization and curriculum-led staffing.

A few small and inadequately staffed schools will remain because the facts of geography leave no feasible alternative, but they will do so at the expense of larger, urban-based schools. To indulge the ruralite is to deprive the urbanite. To many rural inhabitants who have, in recent years, witnessed the progressive decline in the range and quality of public and commercial services available in the countryside, that judgment may strike as grossly unfair. For all that, it remains the current view, not only in London but also in many Shire and County Halls.

When we review, as we have done in this chapter, the images of rural primary schools that have been portrayed in governmental reports and Department publications over the last sixty years, several themes start to emerge. It is clear that rural schools have been examined in the light of the currently prevailing preoccupations with the state system as a whole, but of course, these concerns have not remained static. Whether the focus has been upon the length of compulsory education, the administrative structure of schooling, the aims and appropriateness of what is officially provided in schools, or standards of achievement, public and professional views have changed over the years. New theories, new expectations, new evidence, together with broader societal changes have caused periodic redefinitions of the dominant educational issues. Revised aspirations for state education (and anxieties about its performance) have replaced previous ones and in so doing have ushered in educational reforms. Against that fluctuating background, rural schools have been judged and ususally found to be wanting.

'Never run after a bus, a woman or an educational theory; another will be along soon.'[2] Cynical that remark might be; sexist it certainly is, and for those familiar with rural bus timetables, it is a hollow joke. Teachers in rural schools might, however, be forgiven for endorsing it. For Hadow, the major issues centred on the classification of pupils and how schools could be organized to reflect their intellectual differences. The rural school was a problem in as much as it was not able to offer different courses of instruction to distinctive categories of pupil. There was no hint that teachers could not cope with the curriculum, and the teaching methods the Committee encountered, even in some very small schools, were judged to be exemplary; but the rural school was too undifferentiated to respond to a theory which demanded that pupils be organized in three distinct ability streams.

In the period immediately after the war, rural education disappeared as a national issue; rural schools were not so much problematic as invisible. The priorities were formulated around the demands of implementing the 1944 Act and the massive task of post-war reconstruction. Set against those urgencies, rural primary education was a small affair. The indifference was shown in the neglect to the fabric of its buildings and in the almost feckless passing references to rural schooling in the reports.

By the mid 1960s, the situation had altered. Education's priorities had been reformulated; new teaching practices were in evidence. Educational theory and research were casting doubt on previously held assumptions. Rural schools were under scrutiny once more. Their inability to stream was no longer a deficiency because streaming itself was no longer in favour, but the Plowden and Gittins committees identified new causes for concern. Despite their often cramped and inadequate buildings, rural schools were expensive; teacher isolation emerged as an obstacle to professional development; small peer group size was seen as restricting opportunities for pupil interaction; the capacity of teachers to offer a wide curriculum hitherto never felt to have constituted a problem, now became identified as a limitation in the small rural school, all the more serious when the implications of raising the age of transfer were spelled out. And yet, like Hadow before them, both Plowden and Gittins testified to the professional skills of many rural school teachers.

Today, judgment relates to a single issue — the inability of a small school to contain the requisite number of teachers to match the number of separate elements in the formal curriculum. Securing this match in all schools is seen as a *sine qua non* of educational quality and raising standards throughout the system, and, by definition, small schools fail against this criterion. Any claims that might be made for the teaching talents of generalist classroom practitioners are ruled out of court as mitigating circumstances. While it is acknowledged in the White Paper that some small schools will need to be retained because of the peculiarities of the rural terrain, LEAs are instructed to keep their number to a minimum. Not only are they viewed as an educational liability, they are also a financial burden. In the current economic climate, a more generous allocation of limited resources is tantamount to extravagance.

Throughout these fluctuations in the fortunes of rural primary schools whereby various characteristics have been singled out as deficiencies at different points in time, there has been one common factor. The rural school has been judged by comparison with the large urban school. Whether the comparison has been implicit or (increasingly in recent years) explicit, it has been urban schooling which has been used as the norm, the indicator of what schools can be and should be like. Measured against a yardstick which is derived from urban practices, rural schools have often been defined as 'a problem' to which the recommended solution has been that they should be closed, or that the pattern of rural schooling should more closely approximate to that found in urban areas. The possibility that urban models are not particularly appropriate in rural contexts is an idea that has been rarely entertained in official reports.

This argument will be explored more fully in the following

chapter; here we will seek simply to illustrate it by reference to the Gittins Report. This came from an enquiry which not only examined the position of rural schools more thoroughly than any report before or since, but which contains passages which are lyrical in their praise of these schools:

'The small rural school has made and continues to make a fundamental contribution to the life of the countryside. One of the most stimulating educational experiments recently reported took place in a one-teacher school, but this has since closed'. (para 7.5.1)

The irony there seems to have escaped the Committee completely. The paragraph continues:

'One of the liveliest rural schools we have seen is a one-teacher school. Its work illustrated how the rural school can be like a family, with close and friendly relationships between children and teachers. Children can work as individuals or in small groups. If the school is prepared to allow the children to learn through activity, there can be a true integration of learning, within a completely flexible timetable. Environmental studies and science can begin at the doorstep of the school, in field, forest or mountainside. There can be lively discussion and easy movement from one area of study to another. The younger children can learn from the older, groups can be flexibly re-arranged for different aspects of work, and children can learn to live and work in a community'. (para 7.5.1)

All of this in a chapter which repeatedly insists that the solution to the rural school problem lies in the creation of area schools with an optimum size (for a junior/infant school) of 100–150 pupils. The point is not that the proposal is necessarily wrong, only that the catalogue of observed educational virtues is automatically dismissed in favour of advantages which are presumed to stem from larger scale organizations. To put it in a different way, it is scarcely conceivable that an enquiry concerned with primary schooling in urban areas would define the schools as making a fundamental contribution to life in towns and cities, report so fulsomely on the qualities of some of those it had actually encountered, and then recommend a reorganiza-tion which eliminated them. If one of the most stimulating education-al experiments recently reported had occurred in an urban school, committees of enquiry would beat a path to its door. Finding it boarded up, they would, at the very least demand an explanation of the educational vandalism inherent in that act.

It is, of course, quite possible to envisage a different set of priorities and policies than those which stem from urban experiences. Sher (1981) invites us to do so in his OECD/CERI report, *Rural Education in Urbanized Nations*:

> 'Imagine for a moment a developed nation which regarded its rural schools as its elite and as models to be envied and emulated by metropolitan schools. Imagine a system in which rural schools were the prime beneficiaries of educational research, the recipients of a steady stream of the nation's best educators, and the bastions of the education world's power, prestige, and resources'. (p4)

Not a single OECD country could, as Sher reminds us, make such a claim for the educational provision in its rural areas. Nonetheless, without demanding so elevated a status, we can conceive of those characteristics encountered by the Gittins Committee in that liveliest of one-teacher schools being identified as the hallmarks of quality to which all schools might aspire. If that were the case, the problem of small rural schools would need to be addressed very differently; not only would we cease talking about them as if they were merely inadequate versions of urban schools, we might also find ourselves questioning some of the assumptions about the benefits of education in large-scale institutions.

The presence of conflicting sets of educational values impinging upon rural schools is what we will consider in the next chapter.

Notes

1 It should not pass unnoticed that Hadow tended to reserve the term 'small' for the one teacher school
2 Quoted by King, R. (1978) from Clark, B.R. (1962) *Educating the Expert Society*, Chandler.

Chapter 3

The Small Rural School and Ideological Conflict

> When rural schools die, they die alone. There is no ideology which justifies them or condemns them.

It is unlikely that Thomas would feel able to make that remark now quite so easily as he did in 1972. The school, whose bitterly contested and protracted death was traced in chapter 1, did not die alone. Far from there being an absence of ideological commitment, the struggle was characterized down to the final squabble over its tiny legacy of a fifteen-year-old climbing frame by competing educational idologies. The same opposing beliefs clashed in the first case we considered where the school was kept open precisely because it did not stand alone. In both instances the opposition to the closure proposal was conducted through well organized, hardworking action groups which had access to a range of professional skills, knew how to use local press and television, and could draw upon the experience and support of national organizations. These are the features of campaigns against closure in recent years which distinguish them from the tacit acceptance, muffled resentment or the purely parochial hostility which have often accompanied closures in the past.

Our purpose in this chapter is to consider the changing strategies which have attended rural school closure over the past two decades and the perspectives of those involved. It is obvious that we do not regard Thomas's view as applicable to the period we are to consider and it will be evident too that we see the conflicts which have developed over this time as increasingly ideological in nature.

Before going any further it is necessary to be clear about the concept of educational ideology. 'Education', asserts Kogan (1978) 'more than virtually any other activity is concerned with what *ought* to be rather than with what *is*'. To listen to people discussing education is very often to listen to people revealing deeply held beliefs about the nature of society and the individual, the social order, status and equality and so on. The discussion may have started with some fairly concrete aspect of schooling (the curriculum or standards of achievement for example) but the sets of prescriptions for what schools ought to do are informed by those underlying convictions. That is why educational discussion so often proceeds by the assertion of tenaciously held ideas rather than by examination of evidence. If you stay on the fringes of the discussion, you are likely to detect inconsistencies in the sets of ideas that participants present; you are also likely to notice that what holds together a set of ideas are the deeply felt convictions of their advocate as much as any rational coherence. In short, you have been listening to the expression of educational ideologies.

We define an educational ideology as a collection of ideas, beliefs and emotions which express a conception of an ideal institutional arrangement together with a pattern of underlying values. Its principal tenets go beyond that which can be validated by the evidence which is publicly available; they are pre-eminently a set of 'ought' statements. They may not necessarily be logically consistent but they have an emotional unity which points unambiguously towards a certain social action. If we apply that concept to rural education, we would say that an ideology which either justified or condemned small rural schools would articulate a set of beliefs about the educational quality of such schools and a commitment which legitimated their maintenance, or their closure. Given the determination with which some LEAs have, at times, pursued closure policies, and the fervour with which, again at times, they have been opposed, and given also the paucity of evidence about the educational merits of either case, it is fairly clear that the rural school issue has been strongly infused with ideological conviction. And, where closures have involved direct conflict, it has been unabashedly ideological in nature. We can note too, that educational ideologies change with the passage of time. They fluctuate not only in the way particular ideas in their repertoire receive different emphasis at different times, but also in the manner by which they are expressed. During periods marked by rapid change, they are usually overtly proclaimed; at other, more stable times, they tend rather to take the form of mere tacit acceptance of a collection of implicit assumptions which are rarely articulated because they are rarely challenged.

With these thoughts in mind, we propose to examine the shifts and turns which have accompanied small school closure in rural areas. To do so, we will consider the national scene briefly and then, in closer focus the recent history of the closure issue in the county of Norfolk.

The General Scene

Rural school closure is not just a recent phenomenon. It has a past which goes back a very long way. As numbers have fallen, as buildings have been declared unfit for educational purposes, there have been closures almost from the time when the network of rural schools began to be established. The expansion of educational provision in the countryside in the decades after 1870 often entailed the demise of schools founded half a century earlier. The School Sites Act of 1841 contained sections designed to regulate claims to the ownership of land released by the closing of a school that had been built upon it. The period between the two world wars saw many more schools closing in the aftermath of the agricultural depression and population drift towards the towns. Partial implementation of the Hadow Committee's (1931) recommendation on the separation of primary and secondary stages also, via its decapitating effect, resulted in the disappearance of village schools.

After the Second World War, a new set of factors placed more rural schools at risk: the 1944 Education Act and the establishment of separate secondary education had, by the mid 1950s, finally removed the 11–14 pupils from the many remaining all-age village schools. More recently, the fall in the birth rate from its peak in 1964, the Plowden Report's recommendation of the minimum size of rural school as three teachers and the fiscal constraints imposed on rural authorities by central government have all given further impetus to closure strategies.

It is impossible to say with any certainty how many rural schools have closed in the post-war period. Many education authorities simply do not possess accurate data in an accessible form (especially where boundaries were changed through local government reorganization in 1974). On the basis of a very incomplete survey of English and Welsh authorities in 1977, by the Advisory Centre for Education, Rogers reported:

'Since 1945, there has been a massive programme of closing schools. Our 1977 survey established that at least 500 rural primary school have been shut down over the last ten years.

Otherwise, no figures (official or unofficial) have been available to reveal the extent of the loss'. (Rogers 1979, p3)

The Aston University (1981) research, while confirming the absence of official data, suggested that this figure was an underestimate. It calculated that approximately 1000 rural schools were closed in the period 1955 to 1967, and a further 660 between then and 1974 in the wake of the Plowden Report, and about 275 from 1974 to 1980. Only since 1978 has the DES compiled accurate data on rural primary school closures, and between then and 1984, there have been 508 such schools closed.

There can be little doubt that very many of these schools which have been removed from the educational map of rural districts have indeed died alone. Depopulation had left them with few children or the education they provided had not been highly regarded by local parents. In other cases the community had been convinced by the pragmatic, balance of advantages argument of LEA officers that, sad as it might be, the school ought to close. Whatever the reason, schools went out of existence because apparently, in the end, they were not wanted. We were told by one LEA adviser of a headteacher who, when the numbers in his school had fallen to a mere five pupils, had recommended to their parents that the children be transferred to another school. On the opening day of the following term, he arrived to find himself the only person in the building. If you are a rural school, you cannot die more alone than that.

Normally, of course, LEAs do not wait upon such an extreme event; the future of the school comes under review when its numbers drop below a defined minimum threshold. Decline in enrolment may happen not only because of national population movement or falling birthrates, but also because parents have signalled their dissatisfaction with the school by transferring their children to another school. There are clear indications in the study of rural schools in North Yorkshire by Mordey and his colleagues (1984) and in a larger investigation in Scotland (Forsythe, 1983) that the degree to which parents are willing to support small schools, and to oppose whatever closure proposals may be put, is strongly related to the academic reputation of the school. That in turn appears to be a function of the personal qualities of the headteacher and the way he is judged by local opinion. Schools which have lost that parental support, and found their numbers dwindling as a consequence, have, so to speak, died before they have been officially closed.

When the village school is valued for the education it is providing to a small number of local children, parents are less likely to accede easily to the LEA's view that it is in the best interests of their children that they be transferred to another, larger school. The history of village school closures is littered with stories of education officers and councillors facing angry groups of villagers in public meetings on wintry evenings in remote country areas. McWilliam's (1978) history of a two-teacher school in Devon contains a vivid account of just such a confrontation with a despairing Deputy Director of Education failing to move his audience with the declaration: 'You may not want it, but your children may one day regret that they were not educated in modern surroundings.' To talk to education officers who have repeatedly been through these struggles is to talk to people who often manifest something resembling battle fatigue. It would, however, be quite false to suggest that every proposal for closure, the considerable majority of which up and down the country have been successful, has resulted in a public row. The Chief Education Officer for Somerset reports the public meeting in a small settlement on the top of Exmoor as comprising 'a blunt statement from the local member that the school must close, followed by a single comment from a spokesman from the small audience, "If it's all right with you Mr. Matthew, it will be all right with us".' (Taylor, 1978)

The story is perhaps apocryphal, but it is certainly the case that parents who are in no way deferential can be persuaded by the education committee member's argument in favour of reorganization, 'for the good of the children'. The school passes away amid some nostalgia, to be remembered perhaps with affection, but it dies alone as its former pupils are bussed past it to a newer, larger school with modern facilities.

It may often have been the case in the distant past that, as Thomas (1972) says, rural schools died alone. Some died because they could not be sustained by adequate population density, others because parents voted with their feet in search of a school more in keeping with their ideal view of education. The obsequies of others have been attended by villagers who accepted the advice of experts that a peaceful end with a better heaven was more appropriate. More recently, however, the metaphor has not been that of the terminal ward but of death on the battlefield with, in at least one case known to us, threats of appeal to the European Court of Human Rights substituting for the Geneva Convention. These schools did not die alone.

Setting aside the schools which closed their doors because they found themselves in a rural desert, it is possible to observe that an ideological component was present in all the other cases. For those decapitated village schools which disappeared in the pre-war and immediate post-war years, Hadow's view of the ideal education system as composed of separate infant, junior and secondary stages was both the measure of their inadequacy and the rationale behind the political force which removed them. In the case of the happy Mr. Matthew, his prized set of ideas was accepted deferentially as more appropriate than the unarticulated views within the village hall. For the Deputy Director, angrily warning obdurate village parents of the future wrath of their children if they did not accept his preferred form of education, the clash was, for him and the villagers, between national and local values. Here, we may appear to be presenting a linear view of a steady shift from an earlier time when villagers accepted the closure of their school in deference to the prevailing and dominant ideology, to a contemporary position of sharp ideological conflict. Although we see the trend in this direction, it is far from even paced and its path is anything but straight. In order to illustrate variations in the development of ideological conflict, we turn to an examination of the history of post-war education policy in the rural county of Norfolk, which has one of the highest proportions of small schools in England.

Norfolk: Ideology and Small School Closure

Between 1948 and 1965, sixty-three rural primary schools were closed in accordance with a clearly defined strategy to eliminate all-age schools and to establish a network of secondary modern and grammar schools across the county. In applying their strategy, Norfolk planners were doing no more than following the dominant meritocratic prescription which flowed from the 1944 Act. The Norfolk development plan of the time actually envisaged discarding substantially more of the stock of Victorian buildings that were deemed to be wholly unsatisfactory, modernizing others and building a number of new schools. In the event, the urgent priority of setting up the new secondary system prevented much of this from happening, but the important point to make is that all of the closures took place within a coherent, county-wide framework of reorganization of the entire educational provision. By 1966, the principal features of the development plan had been accomplished. For the next eight years, primary schools continued to be closed in various parts of the countryside, not as a systematic element of a plan for educational reform, but as reaction whenever a school became unacceptably small. Reviewing that period, the Chief Education Officer observed: 'There was no vision of rationalization; it was just ad hoc.' (Edwards, 1985). There was no plan for rationalization to produce larger area schools as occurred in a few other authorities; thirty village schools were closed in response to population movement. The lopping, as it were, was more in the nature of economic and administrative tidying than a response to an ideologically driven rationale.

Local government reorganization in 1974 brought forth a new development for the period 1975–90, which proposed a three-tier system of schooling incorporating 8–12 age middle schools. These were intended to be located in towns and key villages and to draw in pupils from the 4–8 age first schools (each with a minimum of thirty pupils) that would be located in the smaller surrounding villages. Edwards explains: 'At the heart of the plan was the middle school — large, educationally powerful, commanding resources.' It was acknowledged that reorganization would not be immediate and that the all-through primary school would be retained in rural areas for some considerable time. Nevertheless, there was a clear horizon and a plan for arriving there which was drawn from the recommendations of the Plowden Report. Here, the effect of a major ideological shift can be seen. The familiar 5–7 infants' school and the 7–11 junior school were no longer regarded as ideal. New forms of age-grouping were coming into favour in terms of 4–8 first schools and 8–12 middle schools. Particularly troublesome were the village schools, because they could not provide, as could existing urban schools, adaptable foundations for the desired change.

There was some substantial opposition to the plan, whose major effect would be to remove the 8–11-year-old age group from their village schools. Teachers in the rural areas, as well as parents, claimed that the programme did not fit the requirements of their locations, but, for a period of time, reorganization proceeded. The development plan had been drawn up on the assumption of a slight increase in population, but the error of this assumption soon became apparent and with it, the realization that viable schools in the countryside could not be supported if the top three years were removed. A rational plan which had articulated a significant new educational ideology was arrested and there was a gradual reversion to an ad hoc policy of recommending individual closures as numbers happened to fall below the thirty pupil threshold. Seventy-five schools were closed between 1974 and 1984, of which sixty-seven had less than thirty on roll at the point of closure. It was during this time and perhaps owing something to *The Godfather* genre of films that the term 'hitlist' appeared in closure language, denoting target schools which the local authority was suspected of favouring for closure.

Before the end of this period, there were some slight movements which signalled not a return to the 1975 blueprint, but rather a recognition that the furtherance of a master plan directed towards conversion to middle and first school organization was not possible in the foreseeable future and that many village schools would remain open. This movement was manifest in explorations of ways in which small schools, though remaining where they were, could unite with others. Here, for example a 'cluster' of schools under one headteacher was established and some advisory support provided for the federation of a group of small schools and one secondary school.

All that was left of the former ideological thrust was the latent conviction that small schools were inappropriate economically and educationally. The pragmatism of minimum size took over to initiate ad hoc closures. And minimum size can be a pretty arbitrary device as is illustrated by the variation that can be found between one authority and another. Between the minimum size of twelve to fifteen in Devon, thirty in Norfolk and eighty in Nottinghamshire, that were reported to the ACE survey (Rogers, 1979) there is a greater diversity than could be rationally accounted for by topographical differences alone.

Arbitrary it may be, to a degree, but how is a figure arrived at? Edwards (1985) explains a process which must be common to all local authorities:

'That figure back in 1976 was seen as the lowest level which could attract two full-time staff but that was not based on some sophisticated assessment of curriculum or indeed of financial viability. It was to an extent therefore an arbitrary figure. Behind the choice, however, was a range of important perceptions based on member and professional experience — some educational, some practical and financial'.

It was, of course, during this 'rule of minimum size' phase that political and professional members of the local education authority articulated their perceptions of the educational disadvantages of small schools. Largely derived from the Plowden Report, such disadvantages may be summarized as:

1　Teachers may suffer professional isolation.
2　A wide age range in a single class may prove too difficult for some teachers.

3   The range of curriculum to be taught may be daunting for a small staff.
4   Small peer group size does not provide adequate stimulation and competition, particularly for the older children.
5   Small schools are costly.

However, the application of the rule of minimum size was not uniform during the phase under consideration. Familiar strategies were to target schools where parental discontent was manifest, the headteacher was on the point of retirement or, ideally, where the headteacher himself recommended closure. It must be stressed that such strategies were not necessarily based upon political deviousness. As one respected political leader, deeply involved in school closure emphasized to us, such strategies inflict fewer human and professional wounds in what is always a hurtful business. That said, the fact remains that during this phase of administrative pragmatism, a school defended by an elite panzer of parents was rarely the ground chosen for capture.

1985 it would seem is probably a change point marking an end to the ad hoc phase and the beginning of a new ideologically-based reform of rural primary schooling. In the previous chapter, it was argued that since 1979 an increasingly interventionist central government ideology has been formulating and pressing upon local authorities a particular system of ideas. These are articulated in the government publication *Better Schools* (1985) Five of its features are of particular significance for small schools:

1   The definition of the areas which are to constitute the school curriculum.
2   A managerial perspective of schooling.
3   A specification of the primary teacher as one possessing a specialism.
4   A conception of the primary school as staffed so as to inform each area of the curriculum by means of specialism.
5   A determination of minimum size to meet 1 to 4.

These features, drawn from the contemporary and dominant official ideology, are apparent in the Norfolk structure plan first published in October 1985. The relevant educational section (Development Plan Guidelines for Primary Schools), revised to a final draft in 1986, asserts:

'Primary schools can no longer be said to require just teachers in front of classes and heads in front of schools'. (para 4.1)

With that familiar primary teacher model declared redundant, the development plan goes on to emphasize:

1   The need for teacher leadership in the curriculum: 'Few teachers are experts in all parts of the curriculum.' The development plan asserts the need for teacher consultants who possess expertise in aspects of the curriculum. It draws the attention of schools to those areas of the curriculum to be considered in this respect. These are: language development, mathematics, scientific/environmental, aesthetic/creative, physical and ethical/personal.

2   The need for management: 'The complexity of modern organization and management techniques, the establishment of teacher leaders and the delegation of organization and management roles require a response in staffing terms if advances in the standards of educational opportunity are to be realized.' Six management functions are identified — curriculum development, monitoring of standards, staff development, home-school contact, inter-school liaison and relationship with LEA officers. (para 4.1)

The primary teacher then, within this set of ideas is transformed. No longer a generalist teacher whose identity solely rests upon pedagogic expertise, she becomes part specialist, part manager, part class teacher. More importantly, the change in specification has very considerable implications for the size of school. If it is to contain all the curricular specifications and all the management functions then, in the terms of the development plan:

'. . . it has been concluded that a minimum of seven teachers would normally be required for a primary school, suggesting a minimum school size of 150 pupils . . .' (para 4.2)

Here of course, the ideal prescriptions of the Norfolk plan, the 'ought' of its desires, encounters the realities of the Norfolk context — quirks of terrain, difficulties of lines of communication and eccentricities of population distribution. Even the ideal minimum is not achievable in the face of such vagaries. Whilst obviously, anything smaller than the prescribed minimum size cannot meet the curriculum specialisms and management functions required by the plan, it concedes:

'Although it will always be necessary to assess very closely and carefully the particular circumstances, current evidence suggests that normally a permanent establishment of the equivalent of three full-time teachers would be required to justify the retention of a 5–11 primary school on educational grounds'. (para 4.5)

In setting its bottom line of pupil numbers (sixty for a 5–11 primary school and forty pupils for first/infants' schools) the report stresses the need for additional peripatetic support. Any school falling below these numbers, in the report's view, becomes an even greater abnormality:

'As it is not expected that 5–11 schools of less than sixty pupils would be common, the retention of schools below the suggested sizes will need to be strongly justified'. (para 5.2)

What this brief account of the educational fortunes of small schools in Norfolk shows is that there are periods marked by an explicit and clearly annunciated set of beliefs about what constitutes good education, and about what institutional arrangements are necessary prerequisites for bringing that about. These definitions are endorsed by professionals and elected representatives in County Hall and from this consensus emerges a rationally planned programme of educational reorganization which includes, and justifies, the closing of some rural schools. At other times, there is no apparent vision which positively informs the authority's policy on rural schooling. The thrust of an earlier set of established principles becomes exhausted or is halted by unforeseen external constraints such as a rapidly dipping birthrate. Nothing resembling an ideology is then articulated and a more pragmatic policy ensues for a time until a new formulation of ideas energises educational activity and reform. In the case of Norfolk, the drive to implement the meritocratic ideology of selective secondary education informed its post-war strategic plan in terms of what must happen to village schools. That thrust accomplished, subsequent decisions on small school viability moved to an *ad hoc* basis. In the late sixties, a dominant egalitarian ideology, driving towards comprehensive education and eventually coinciding with local government reorganization, yielded a plan embracing first and middle schools based upon Plowden recommendations. Plowden too, provided the criteria upon which village schools could be seen as educationally inadequate. This plan, part implemented, and foundering as it did upon the reefs of a national economic crisis and a falling birthrate, yielded its ideological prescription to an administrative doctrine of minimum school size. Subsequently the rise of a central interventionist ideology provided a core of new ideas which were then utilized as the basis of a new strategic plan.

With respect to this new informing ideology, we must notice one feature of particular significance for small rural schools. In the post-Plowden era, the rhetorics justifying closure were, in principle, refutable. Given an articulate action group, the arguments to do with teacher isolation, and inadequate breadth and range of curriculum could be countered by local evidence. It could, for example, be demonstrated that the teacher was of high quality and that the children were receiving a worthwhile curriculum in a stimulating classroom. Under the new ideology, these arguments become irrelevant. The test for the small school is the same as that for the large urban school namely: Are all the curriculum areas informed by specialism? Are the six managerial functions informed by the principles of the division of labour? Where previously supporters of the small village school might vigorously counter, via local evidence, an attack based upon negative assertions, they are relatively powerless in the face of an ideology whose system of ideas is framed upon criteria of structure principally achievable only in urban areas.

The Development of a Counter Ideology

So far, we have concentrated primarily upon charting the way in which ideologies recommending small school closure have changed and developed over the post-war years and we have made only passing reference to the voices of opposition. It is to these that we now turn.

Identifying the point at which anything resembling an oppositional ideology emerged is difficult. It is probably true to say that such village school closures as occurred in the immediate post 1944 reorganization provoked little active organized opposition. That time did not coincide with any denudation of other village services. However, across the late 1950s and increasingly during the following two decades, school closures ran parallel to other important social changes in rural England. First, there was the decline and removal of rural services and institutions on a scale and at a speed never experienced before. The Beeching axe, wielded in the quest for railway profitability, removed many branch lines; similar policies by local bus companies left many rural areas with no more than a skeleton service. Mergers between breweries and their resulting rationalization policies frequently removed public houses from villages and the general spread of car ownership, together with the rise of urban supermarkets, placed the village post office/shop at risk. Reorganization of policing often took away the policeman from all but the largest villages. Even the Church of England rationalized its placement of rural clergy. As the Standing Conference of Rural Community Councils (1978) pointed out, there was growing evidence of the progressive erosion of the central institutions of rural life.

At the same time, there were the beginnings of what Scandinavians refer to as the 'green wave'. Some people, rejecting urban values altogether, moved to rural areas to enjoy, as they saw it, a 'more natural way of life'. Others, less extreme, continued to work in urban occupations, but chose to reside in rural areas, often in new housing developments, preferring a pattern of living which incorporated something of the values and amenities to be found in the countryside. Many sought for their children the small-scale intimacy of education which they thought a village school could provide. Their mortgage, as it were, included the village school while, for the native villager, the school came to represent the only return they received from their rates.

More generally, we can see during this period many instances of resistance by local groups to decisions taken by elected members in local and national government. They concerned road development schemes and power station plans as well as school reorganization. Baron (1977) referred to this movement as:

> '. . . a dissatisfaction with representative democracy, that is the affairs of countries and localities being run by a few elected people. Increasingly, it is being felt that more people should be involved with the affairs of the areas in which they live'.

To the extent that such changes as these were well developed by the beginning of the 1970s it is probably near this time that a counter ideology, one that was opposed to the closure of village schools, began to be articulated.

The initial growth of oppositional ideology may be likened to the isolated growth of spores in a culture dish. Villages, widely separated and unwitting of each other, found themselves confronting the prospect of their schools closing. The crisis which that represented for each individual community flushed out deeply held, almost unconscious assumptions of the values which their school represented and which, if it was to be defended, must be articulated and made coherent.

In villages lacking the capacity and the skill to organize an articulate defence, the schools succumbed swiftly to official decision. In others, where organizing capacities, professional skills and resources were to hand, coherent defensive campaigns were mounted. In these latter contexts, opposition was no longer limited to protestations at the required public meeting, but was sustained over several months of well organized community action, usually spearheaded by a small group of energetic individuals. One indication of this development can be found in the Case for Retention documents produced over a period of years by these action groups. They have become increasingly sophisticated in their presentation of the arguments for small schools in general, and their own school in particular. It is now not unusual for them to have drawn upon the advice of professional specialists; architects have furnished alternative remodelling plans for the threatened school in line with the most recent building regulations; quantity surveyors have costed redevelopment; academics have undertaken opinion surveys in the villages, or researched local population trends, to produce alternative sets of enrolment projections. Copies of the document, often polished in their format, are run off in somebody's office in the nearby town and distributed by an energetic team of campaigners to all education committee members. In appearance at least, they are decidedly more impressive than the two typed pages often submitted in support of closure by a hard-pressed LEA official.

What has characterized the change since 1970 has been not only the much greater organization and skill deployed by individual community defence campaigns, but also the increasing coalescence of rural voices creating a general system of ideas amounting to an oppositional ideology. The resentment, sometimes bitterness, of local people that has often in the past accompanied the closing of a popular school has become more than a series of isolated local dramas, however skilfully they are now fought. The creation of wider associations out of the atomized village school support groups appears to have begun independently in several counties at about the same time and, characteristic of rural dwellers across history, a village Hampden, or rather several such, were necessary to trigger a move to stimulate unified action.

A Norfolk vicar[1], Chairman of the Managers of a voluntary-aided primary school, which had successfully fended off a closure proposal, wrote to the local newspaper inviting anyone who was concerned about the declining number of village schools to attend a meeting on a Saturday afternoon in late 1976.[2]

About seventy people attended, and out of that meeting emerged the Friends of Village Schools. Its Chairman and Secretary had occasional meetings with education officers and councillors, and the group provided some help and encouragement via the telephone to others in the county who, almost invariably taken by surprise, found themselves facing the likelihood of seeing their local school closed.

The following year, the Friends of Village Schools changed the name of the organization to Defenders of Village Education. Whether or not it was intended to indicate a more combative stance, it proved to be a clever publicity stroke; the acronym DOVE appealed to press and television editors. A number of short articles were published, regular newsletters and information sheets were produced and it began to be known beyond the county. The Secretary started to receive a regular flow of phone calls requesting advice from other parts of the country, many of them forwarded by the London office of the National Council of Voluntary Organizations.

At about the same time, and the other end of England, and again with what seems like an eye for the power of acronym, CARE, the Cumbrian Association for Rural Education, was founded. One of its initial members, a headteacher who had twice in her career experienced school closure, recollects:

> 'It became apparent at a course held for teachers in small schools at Higham that rationalization meant that few one and two teacher schools would survive in Cumbria, and that the future was indeed bleak. Fourteen concerned people met on a very snowy February evening in Kendal and decided to form CARE before facing a hazardous journey home ... Since then CARE has grown rapidly because many people feel that the small schools play an integral part in the countryside, because the children are receiving a good education in their own surroundings, and because the emphasis on individual needs is near the true heart of education. In the past, we have had a raw deal — after all one cannot have a much rawer deal than annihilation'.[3]

Simultaneously in Staffordshire, another county in which a substantial number of small rural schools had been axed, the Moorland School Action Group had been formed with a similar purpose of resisting further closures. Its Chairman was to have a critical influence, since it was on his instigation in 1978 that representatives from the other associations, together with less well established coalitions in Oxfordshire and the West Country, and individual campaigners from other parts of England met in Staffordshire to discuss the possibility of a more coordinated national effort.

The result was the formation of the National Association for the Support of Small Schools (NASSS), which held its inaugural meeting in September of that year. It was an appropriate moment; the previous month, the Standing Conference of Rural Community Councils had published *The Decline of Rural Services* and, for a brief period, this document appeared to touch a national nerve. It was reviewed in a sympathetic editorial in *The Times* which argued that the local school was the single most significant public service for sustaining the quality of village life. For several weeks there was a continuing correspondence on the subject, including one letter from Lady Plowden which indicated a change of mind since her Report of eleven years earlier had recommended a policy of closing small schools. Scarcely a single Case for Retention document has been written since then which does not quote from, or refer to, that letter.

The NASSS acts in the characteristic fashion of a pressure group; its Committee (and especially its Secretary) speak for the rural school lobby at meetings and conferences in various parts of the country as well as to television, radio and the national and local press. In addition, the Association publishes regular newsletters and information sheets about events, trends and Parliamentary questions that are pertinent to closure issues. Above all, it offers specific advice and encouragement to groups endeavouring to contest individual closure proposals. In that sense it runs, so the Secretary puts it, 'a fire fighting service'.

An ideological stance underscores all of its publications and is explicitly asserted in many of them. For example:

> 'We are concerned about the dangers of centralization, which weakens links between parents and schools. We seek to advance the case for the small 'community' school, and to affirm our conviction that it is not only educationally sound, but offers a supportive environment for our children. We believe infant commuting to be harmful, and assert that the flexibility within a small school tends to encourage the development of a broad curriculum rather than inhibiting it'. (Information Sheet No. 0)

and

> 'It is therefore not for sentimental or nostalgic reasons that NASSS seeks to help the small school. There is a strong

feeling among members that something of value to the nation will be lost if rationalization leads to the end of a vast number of our small community-based schools'. (Information Sheet No. 13)

Membership numbers about 800 at any one time, but is highly volatile; the solid, permanent core is much less than this figure. Individuals and groups, such as parish councils, tend to join when a school is threatened and to leave when the issue is settled one way or the other.

Very recently, the Committee of the Association has endeavoured to persuade its members to adopt a more proactive resolve, in particular to examine the primary school provision in an area and to carry forward suggestions to their education committee. The Secretary claims that there are instances of these moves having had some success, but for the most part, the transitory membership appears to remain preoccupied with the fate of an individual school. The dilemma is expressed in a 1984 newsletter:

'Today we have an organization used increasingly as a lifeline when a school is threatened. It is that, but it is also an association of those who consider that village schools have both educational and social advantages which in most cases are too precious to lose ... If this is true ... then NASSS must work hard for positive policies like the Northamptonshire model, and appeal to all who join to support our general aims on a long-term basis, not just for a time of trauma when a school is threatened'. (Spring newsletter, 1984)

In part, the inspiration behind this shift of policy has come from speakers at NASSS conferences, a senior adviser from Northamptonshire detailing support programmes in that county and the Secretary of State's mention of education support grants for groups of rural schools, when he addressed the annual conference in 1984. But it remains to be seen whether parents and village school governors who are prepared to devote hours of their time over a period of months, in some cases years, to wage a campaign to retain their school will be induced to spend time examining alternative proposals for the provision of primary education across a wider catchment area than that of their own school.

In sum then, drawing from the documents produced in closure conflicts and from the unified view of the National Association for the Support of Small Schools, it is possible to identify several core values which are at the heart of the oppositional ideology. Notably, high value is placed upon the qualities of intimate teacher-pupil relationships and pupil cooperation which can serve as the foundation of learning within an experientially-based curriculum. Another quality which the ideology stresses is that of the informal, as opposed to the contractual, links which a small school can establish with parents and other community members, given that the community is small enough to be characterized by face to face relationships. These features form the core of almost all the 'Case Against Closure' documents which we have studied. The NASSS not only formalizes such ideas, but also adds a further dimension to the ideology in urging the governors of adjacent small schools to come together in the formulation of cooperative policies. This last may, in fact, represent a discernible weakening of a key symbol in its ideology.

The Nature of the Ideological Conflict Considered

At a simple level, the conflict between official closure ideology and oppositional ideology could crudely be seen as no more than a clash between those who believe the delivery systems of education must be large and those who believe they should be small. Such an assumption would be in error on several grounds.

First, absent from oppositional ideology is any belief that post-primary children should be educated in small-scale institutions. Second, their argument does not involve a critique of large primary schools in appropiate settings. In this respect, the ideology of small school supporters is unlike many other ideologies which seek to foist their prescriptions upon the wider world. Their view, straightforwardly, is that education is not only possible in a small school embedded in a small community, but also something to be prized.

Official ideology, similarly, is not simply focused upon the idea of large schools *per se*. True, there is a not entirely supportable idea within the dominant ideology that large schools must necessarily be more economic than small schools, but its ideological assumptions go deeper than that.

Ideologies, as they grow, are often unwittingly influenced by the past history of the situation they seek to influence, and also by the assumptions buried within the contemporary context. With the genesis of the Industrial Revolution, the United Kingdom changed from a society containing a rural majority to one containing an urban majority. Increasingly as rural populations have declined and as urban populations have increased, the issues and problems in society have been defined more and more in urban terms and the perceptions of those confronting such issues and problems have been shaped within the urban context.

Thus, when a politician, or an education officer, recites the disadvantages of small rural schools: teacher isolation, small peer group, absence of competition, restricted curriculum — the measures which are employed are construed from models which are urban in character and in scale. Effectively, the use of such models of what education ought to be like yields what may be called a tacit ideology which depicts the small school in a rural setting as an institution which works intrinsically, because of its size and setting, to the social and educational disadvantage of its pupils.

It is our contention that what is defined as the proper curriculum to be learned, the appropriate techniques of teaching and learning, the most efficacious organizational setting and the valid tests of achievement are defined in terms which reflect urban assumptions. When the criteria that are drawn from them are applied beyond the urban boundary, the rural school is revealed as deficient. When policies are built upon them and applied uniformly across urban and rural environments in a genuine concern to improve the educational opportunities of all children, the result is an attempt to urbanize rural school provision.

This point was illustrated briefly in the previous chapter when we noted the Gittins Committee's willingness to close outstanding small schools to create the area school, an institution which more closely approximated to an urban conception of what a school ought to be. Of course, not all rural schools are outstanding. They can be, as Gittins observed, 'among the dullest and most dispiriting'. So too can urban schools. The difference is that when deficiencies are detected in an urban school, the instinctive response is that something should be done about rectifying them. Send in a team of advisers; establish an in-service programme; transfer the teachers if necessary. Even in the most notorious case of an urban school problem, that of the William Tyndale School, closure was not the solution. When, however, deficiencies are noted in a rural school, they are defined from an urban perspective as being endemic. Closure thus becomes a prime solution.

Thomas (1972) identified the same take-for-granted urban bias in the Gittins Committee's recommendations for establishing teacher-parent links:

'There seems to be a special kind of educationist's madness which rules that you close a school where parents and children meet the teacher outside school, belong to the same community, probably went to the same school, but insists that home-school relations are important and tries to formalize this by setting up a PTA in the new distant area school'. (p169)

It is not madness so much as the consequence of applying urban standards to rural schools and urging them to adopt urban models of school organization. That is not so extraordinary as it may seem. As we have said, this is a predominately urban society in which urban culture has naturally acquired the status of the dominant culture. This phenomenon, the National Association of Local Councils (1979) referred to as, 'the ingrained belief that rural problems are now the same as urban problems but set in a rural context'. The Association argued that it was one of the basic causes of the decline of all public and commercial services operating in the countryside:

'The belief that rural and urban problems are the same leads to national policies and national administrative arrangements being framed for the whole country without regard to the differences between rural and urban areas'. (para 6)

Britain is not unique among urbanized nations in this respect. The assumption that urban solutions to social problems can be applied uniformly to rural problems has underpinned the massive programme of rural school consolidation in America. In 1950, there were 128,000 elementary schools in America, of which, astonishingly perhaps, almost one half (60,000) were one-teacher schools. By 1972, the total figure had been reduced to under 65,000, and the number of one-teacher schools to a mere 1475.[4]

Sher and Tompkins (1977) comment:

'The movement to consolidate schools was merely one part of an urbanizing, modernizing trend that affected everything in America. ... Modernization dictated new values and new organizational forms that emphasized large size, specialization and professionalization'. (p72)

Those are the values and organizational forms which are emphasized in contemporary British accounts of the deficiencies of rural primary schools, and give rise to recommendations such as area schools and other more recognizably urban answers to the question of rural schooling. Edwards' account of the prevailing image of the middle school when the redevelopment plan was being discussed in Norfolk in 1975 — 'large, educationally powerful, commanding resources' — fits exactly.

It might be supposed that, in an authority so obviously rural as Norfolk, which (together with North Yorkshire) contains the highest proportion of small schools in England, urban definitions of educational problems could not prevail. The previous Chief Education Officer, Coatesworth (1976) reflects:

'Yet the reorganization of local government by bringing together in Norfolk a predominately rural county and two urban county boroughs, brought into sharp focus the difference between town and country and prompted urgent consideration of the question how to achieve equal educational opportunities for the children in both situations'. (p275)

Again there is a clear parallel with the American pattern. As Tyack (1974) describes, 'the models developed to reform city schools became educational blueprints for consolidation of rural education' in the pursuit of what he calls 'the one best system'.

With respect to the Norfolk context, as we have shown, the endeavour was to provide an identical educational experience to all children in all areas.

However well suited the middle school model may have been to urban areas, it is far from obvious that it represented an ideal in the villages. Had the considerations been less urgently conducted, and the plan that emerged not been so soon halted, it is possible that the question Coatesworth isolates might have provoked a more sustained debate. After all, equality of educational opportunity is a profoundly different concept from identical educational experience. A debate which did focus on what educational opportunity (and educational experience) might mean in completely contrasting social locations would certainly need to examine something more fundamental than the size or internal organization of school. It might also conclude that equality of opportunity is best furthered by responding to the real differences which inevitably exist between schools because of the different communities they serve, rather than endeavouring to create a standardized form of schooling. But the more pessimistic view is put by Thomas:

'In an industrial and urban country it is unlikely that the small rural school will ever be the subject of a major educational debate'. (p168)

That not least because for different reasons, the major political parties feel no call to attend to the rural voice.

We are left, therefore, with ideologies which either justify or condemn small rural schools. The former rests its case upon the educational and social merits of the small scale institution; the latter, applying urban scale and definitions of education, condemns it as pathological in a predominately urban society. The gulf between them is understandable.

If one is a ruralite by origin or by choice, then the features of one's personal and social life shape one's views of how institutions ought to be. Thus to prize a social network in which personal, familial, occupational and friendship patterns are characterized by their overlap and lack of anonymity is to subsume a preference for institutions, particulary developmental ones, which affirm and utilize such a network. Forsythe's (1983) survey in rural areas of Scotland contains implicitly this perspective in its findings on parental opinion:

'Overall half the respondents associated larger schools with poorer teaching/education and/or lack of individual attention for the pupils. This problem was reported by 70 per cent of the respondents in (one school) where several small schools had been incorporated into a large area school. Nearly a quarter of the respondents mentioned that the atmosphere and relationships were poorer in the larger school'. (p101)

At the heart of that finding is a dislike of the relatively greater anonymity and the diminution in the quality of relationships perceived to be present in the larger institution. Not surprisingly perhaps, when rural parents make judgments about the quality of local schools, they do not do so upon the basis of 'objective' data to do with staff size, specialisms, curricular structure or organization, but upon what they know of the personal qualities and skills possessed by teachers with whom they and their children relate. Forsythe's sample contained schools that were considered locally to be excellent and others that were regarded as poor, but, as she observes:

'. . . the most important explanatory factor is not school size, condition of building, community type, geographical or cultural area or regional policy but rather the identity and nature of the headteacher concerned'. (p132)

That this is not mere Scottish whimsy is shown in Dunne's (1977) review of the situation in American schools when she comments:

'Teachers in the small rural school remain accountable to the community in ways virtually unimaginable in cities and suburbs, where they tend to be viewed as specialists whose personal lives are separate from those of their students' families'. (p92)

What both of these studies indicate is that in rural contexts, teachers and schools are evaluated and held accountable through the informal day to day, person to person and person to community contacts which are possible in a small social setting.

Teacher and school acccountability, of course, constitutes a prominent idea in contemporary educational ideology, and central to it is a component affirming the need for schools to render an account of themselves to the area they serve. In characteristically urban fashion, the accountability formula seeks to create rational structures whereby nothing is left to the chance of informality. The school must present itself via the publication of a school brochure and through a formal managerial structure.

Here we can see the dichotomy between urban and rural perspectives at its most vivid. The urban scene is inevitably a place wherein large numbers of parents, pupils and teachers face the problems of overcoming personal and institutional anonymity and social distance. Because of the scale of the urban enterprise, such problems must be mediated through contractual rather than personal relationships. The defeat of anonymity must be achieved through the managerial functioning of year-group coordinators, year-group tutors and formal structural arrangements to guarantee school and parent dialogue. The new Norfolk plan, for instance, sets down 'home school contact' as one of its essential managerial functions for primary schools and, within a large urban school, such a requirement makes good sense if face to face parent-teacher conversation is to be achieved. However, the imposition of such structures and functions upon small institutions which find it difficult *not* to discharge that task informally, in their day to day working, looks more like the rigid application of an ideological tenet than good sense.

If the absurdity of implanting a formal managerial structure into that setting is self-evident, as it was to Thomas more than a decade ago in his comment on a similar Gittins' recommendation, the issue of parental participation takes us to a fundamental problem in the school closure debate. The chapter on 'Parents and Schools' in the Government's White Paper, *Better Schools* begins:

> 'It has long been a principle that pupils should be educated in accordance with the wishes of their parents, provided that this is compatible with good education and the reasonable use of public funds'. (para 194)

The chapter continues by detailing ways in which the 1980 Education Act was intended to give greater practical effect to that principle. But, as we have seen, in rural areas there are radically divergent views as to what constitutes 'good education' and they lead, not infrequently, to opposing conclusions as to whether this can be achieved in small local schools. So, when the elected members of an education committee propose the closure of a particular school, they are forced into the position of asserting that it is their definition of good education that is the correct one and that it is incompatible with the continued maintenance of the school in question.[5] However well intentioned parents and others in the community who oppose the proposal might be, and however much they are supported by bodies such as the NASSS which articulate an alternative view of what education ought to be like in rural areas, they are held to be misguided. Furthermore, the children need to be protected from the consequences of their parents' wishes. That is the logic of the affair.

One chief education officer, even prior to the rise to prominence of the current ideological conflict, identified just that problem. Counselling greater caution, not out of pusillanimity, 'to avoid a fight for better educational standards simply because the going will be much tougher and the outcome increasingly uncertain', but because the evidence about educational standards is itself increasingly uncertain, he commented:

> 'I believe we should contemplate the closure of the smaller primary — or secondary — schools with the greatest possible caution. There must be a limit in a democracy to the extent to which educational policy can be pursued in the teeth of public opposition'. (Taylor, 1978, p299)

Notes

1 It is not altogether surprising that the initiative came from an Anglican clergyman since Norfolk, like most predominately rural counties, has a

high proportion of Church of England primary schools. A survey by Gay (1985) shows most clearly that the smaller the school, the more likely it is to be a Church school. So, for example, although such schools represent only a quarter of the total stock of primary schools in England, they constitute 62 per cent of schools with thirty pupils or less.

2 The school's reprieve was not to last. It has since closed.

3 Craig, G.M. (available from CARE)

4 Sher, J. (1978)

5 The argument about economic use of public funds is usually one factor in the debate but rarely is it presented as being the major factor.

Section II
Educational Concerns

Chapter 4

The Peer Group in the Small Rural School

In the primary school years, especially from 8–12, the child moves increasingly into social groups composed of children of the same age and maturity. In this 'peer' group he learns how to play and live in cooperation and competition, how to control his feelings, establish roles and social techniques, and become accepted for what he is and can do, outside the close relationship of his family on the one hand and the more formalised relationship and values of the school on the other. Group membership in work and play within the school fosters this social and emotional development, the process of defining oneself as an individual through the reflected appraisal of the group. (Plowden, para 72)

Not long after the Plowden Report was published, one of the authors had cause to visit a two-teacher village school[1] and, business completed, he was invited to stay for lunch. After the mealtime bustle, the children were dismissed to the playground and, over a post lunch cup of tea, the headteacher suggested that he might like to watch the children playing cricket. Mildly surprised at the suggestion, he nonetheless complied, went out to the top of the short flight of steps leading down into the playground, and settled to watch the game. About twenty boys and girls, ranging in age from 6 to 11, were participating in that well-known primary fashion where all but the batsmen field.

The scene was familiar enough. The bowler bowled, the batsman made his stroke and fielders and wicket keeper filled their roles impeccably. The style of play was polished. Occasionally, a spectacular diving catch despatched the batsman, at other times, mere snicks earned a cheeky single and full-blooded strokes had fielders hard put to cut off a boundary. On two or three occasions, the batsman sportingly deemed himself or herself to be out and walked from the crease. The game was very interesting to watch, not merely because of the players' absorption in it, but also because it was being played without a ball. Put in stark terms, the bowler bowled an imaginary ball, the batsman played at an imaginary ball and the fielders caught or pursued a ball which was not there. The fact that no ball existed did not diminish commitment. One fielder, in pursuit of a sturdy drive, ran up the three steps to retrieve the non-existent ball from near the watcher's feet.

A little shaken by the experience, the visitor returned to the headteacher, who had plainly anticipated his bewilderment. It transpired that, because of the road alongside the playground and the danger of retrieving balls from it, she had made a rule that cricket could only be played when she was present.

Frequently, she took her lunchtime cup of tea outside and so made cricket possible. One lunchtime, determined to complete marking and administration, she had resisted pleas for the usual game of cricket. In answer to a final deputation from the playground, she had said jokingly, 'Of course you can have cricket. Play without the ball'. A little later, her work completed, she had gone outside to find the children doing exactly that. The practice had survived for two years, assimilating newcomers to the school, who somehow overcame sensations of the Emperor's new clothes syndrome. Though, as the headteacher observed drily, the children much preferred to play with a ball.

The game which the children had devised was highly unusual and one is tempted to lay the claim that it could only have happened in a rural school. That temptation must be resisted — it was simply seen in that setting. If one reflects upon it in the light of Plowden's valuation of 'the peer group', then, in an activity of their own devising, the children were learning how to 'play and live in cooperation and competition ... outside the close relationship of [the] family on the one hand and the more formalized relationships and values of the school on the other'. It may also be the case that participation in the game enabled the children to experience 'the process of defining oneself as an individual through the reflected appraisal of the group'.

A nice question, however, is whether, in Plowden's terms, it was members of a peer group who were participating in the game, for as we have seen, Plowden saw a peer group as composed of 'children of the same age and maturity'. The answer is almost certainly in the negative, for when Plowden came to consider the disadvantages of small schools it listed their inability to provide peer groups of adequate size for '. . . the older children and particularly the abler ones may lack the stimulus of their peers'. Time, of course, has passed on and much of Plowden thinking has withered in the blast of a tougher ideology. What has, however, survived is a concern over the inadequacy of the peer groups to be found in small schools. If we recall our two case studies, the restricted size of peer groups was referred to in the Ings Downton conflict, whilst with regard to Aldcaster School, the CEO observed that:

> 'The size of the peer group in a school of approximately thirty pupils limits that part of the learning process which arises from the stimulation and competition between pupils. The authority believes that peer group interaction is important for the learning process and that children should have a sufficient number of children of similar ability in a year group'.

Such thinking is, of course, subsumed in current central government initiatives to achieve, as a base line, schools organized in single age classes. Insofar as the assertion of the deleterious influence of the small peer group is a factor which influences the fate of small rural schools, it is necessary to explore the basis upon which it is made. If a small peer group depresses stimulation and competition and a large peer group enhances them, it would seem to follow that the difference would be reflected in a disparity between the levels of pupil attainment in large and small schools. A factor to consider then, is the relationship between small school size and pupil performance.

To What Extent Does the Small Size of Rural Schools Influence Pupil Attainment?

It would be an act of extreme irresponsibility to criticize the right of committees of enquiry and educators to articulate their concern, when they identify features of schooling which impede children's attainments. However, if the existence of an impediment is formally identified, a reasonable expectation is that evidence of its effects will be provided. In the matter of the small rural school size and its alleged disadvantaging effect upon pupil attainment, little beyond rhetorical assertion is used to support the claimed relationship.[2] This is not surprising, for unequivocal evidence does not exist.

The Plowden Committee, when it confronted the issue of pupil attainment in small rural schools, encountered the familiar absence of research into rural matters. Drawing upon Barr's (1959) study, they observed:

'Enquiries into the measured attainment of children in rural and urban schools have tended to show lower mean attainment for country children than for urban children ... Yet a summary of the evidence in 1959 suggested that when socio-economic class is taken into account, the differences between town and country children disappear'. (para 478)

This observation is mirrored in Sher and Tomkins' (1977) overview of American studies directed to the same question. They note that, in the period from 1930 to 1965, the bulk of research which focused upon the relation of school size to pupil attainment made little attempt to take account of the effect upon attainment of pupils' socio-economic backgrounds or IQ levels. The evidence from such studies indicated that small school size depressed pupil performance and hence, provided valuable ammunition for American policy makers anxious to develop larger consolidated schools. Subsequently, the use of more sophisticated research techniques yielded evidence which was markedly different. Sher and Tomkins comment:

'... in recent years, researchers have begun controlling for IQ and social class. The effect of this development has been nothing less than a complete reversal of the traditional conclusions about correlation between size and achievement. In fact, of the recent controlled studies, there is not one that records a consistent, positive correlation between size and achievement, independent of IQ and social class'. (p63)

The Inspectorate's analysis of test scores for classes of 9 and 11 year-olds, reported in *Primary Education in England*, which did not attempt to control for the effects of IQ and social class, reported these to be significantly lower in 'inner city' than in either 'rural' or 'other urban' localities. Further analysis which was carried out within each type of locality indicated that 'these differences were not accounted for by the size or type of school'. This was in line with the results obtained by Nash (1977), on a much smaller sample of Welsh rural primary schools. Comparing reading scores of pupils in two teacher and larger (three to six teacher) schools he reported:

'... the reading abilities of pupils in very small schools are neither significantly better nor worse than those in larger schools'. (p79)

An inevitable feature of the organization of small schools is that each class contains within it children whose ages span more than one year. In fact, in HMI's 1978 Primary Survey, schools of one form entry or less constituted a very substantial majority of schools in their rural sample. In spite of the fact that neither size nor rurality was linked with reduced pupil achievement, the presence of mixed age classes was. It was reported that the 11-year-olds and (to a lesser degree) the 9-year-olds in single age classes 'produced better NFER scores for reading and mathematics than children in "mixed age" classes'. It is difficult to know what this finding properly indicates. In the first place, the locations of the mixed age classes are not given and hence, there is no way of knowing to what extent the location factor is associated with the lower scores that were obtained in 'inner city' localities where there have been sharply falling rolls. As Bennett *et al* (1983) subsequently remarked:

> '... there is an increasing adoption of mixed age grouping as a direct response to falling rolls and associated staff cuts. The change is not usually by choice since headteachers prefer a twelve-month age span and hold negative attitudes towards its implementation'. (p55)

A second cause for caution is that the HMI survey is the only study which reports such an association between achievement and internal school organization. Galton and Simon (1980), were not able to identify any significant differences in pupils' progress with respect to reading and mathematics between single age and mixed age classes. Much American research which has focused on the effects of mixed age or multi-graded classes upon children's performance similarly points to there being no significant difference; several studies do in fact claim positive advantages for pupil attainment from mixed age classes. So, Marshall (1985) in his survey of recent North American research, although pointing out that some of the evidence is equivocal, observes that overall, it is 'somewhat conclusive in at least suggesting that multi-grading does not affect achievement adversely'.

In addition to the matter of pupil attainment within small schools, we might also ask how well the children perform when they move on to secondary schools. The Plowden Committee raised this concern, and given the paucity of relevant information, they did little more than note the finding of Cross and Revell (1957) that rural Cambridgeshire children who obtained places in selective secondary schools, 'fulfilled their promise more consistently than those from the towns'.

Our present state of knowledge on how the children from small rural primary schools fare academically at the secondary stage is little better than it was at the time of Plowden. Certainly it is not uncommon for secondary schools who receive pupils from large schools and from small rural schools to report no detectable difference. Johnston (1981), at that time, HM Chief Inspector for Schools (Scotland), commenting upon the Scottish scene, offers both a note of caution on the difficulties inherent in making straightforward urban and rural comparisons, and also, a positive view of the performance of rural pupils at the end of their schools careers:

'Such evidence as has been produced about the educational performance of young people who have attended small schools in sparsely populated areas shows, first, that there are many variables to be taken into account before true comparisons can be made with other categories of pupil; and second, that in external examinations girls from sparsely populated areas often do considerably better than girls in urban areas and boys slightly better'. (p26)

Lewis (1980), contemplating the issue of alleged differential achievement between children in town and country, comments:

'. . . it has still to be shown that standards of attainment recorded in small rural schools are on the whole lower than the achievements recorded in larger town schools, and that they do not approximate to either regional or national averages'. (p21)

To the extent that the alleged connection between small school size and pupil attainment is, in the light of present knowledge, of doubtful validity, it follows that the implication of the small peer group as a factor depressing pupil performance is similarly dubious. Moreover, it should not pass unnoticed that both higher education institutions and the independent education sector assert exactly the counter thesis to that of small school critics, namely that learning is enhanced by the provision of small teaching groups. Recently, with a fine irony of timing, an edition of a local daily paper[3] carried both accounts of protests over proposals to close small village schools and a two-page spread of advertisements for private schools in which the virtues of small group teaching were proclaimed.

The gap between the grass roots' perspective and the official perspective is very wide on the matter of school size, attainment and peer group. Confident in its belief that small school size does not affect attainment, the grass roots' perspective stresses the social benefits which the small school, because of its size and the intermingling of age groups, can confer upon the child. The official perspective, confident in its belief that small school size does depress attainment, points to the obvious target, the small single age peer group and cites its disadvantaging effects. It is apparent that each perspective possesses a different interpretation of the nature and the effect of children's relationships upon the educational process. Yet, given that difference, both have little difficulty in assenting to the view that the peer group is a very important part of the socialization process, occupying the interstitial space, as Plowden puts it, between 'the close relationships of [the] family on the one hand and the more formalized values of the school on the other'.

Two questions are central to the matter of the peer group and the rural school:

1   What is the socialization process and how does the peer group relate to it?
2   What is a peer group and how might it differ according to its context?

The Socialization Process and How the Peer Group Relates to It

That no-one is born possessing a personal and social identity is at once obvious and yet necessary to state. The child, indeed all of us, until the day we die, face the question: Who am I? It is the steady supply of information, which our many interactions with others provide, that enables us to construct a sense of who we are. That line of thinking inspired Cooley (1902) to coin the term 'the looking glass self'. By it, he meant that just as a person uses his reflection in a mirror to judge how he appears physically to others, so also he uses the way in which other people react to his behaviour as a mirror with which to compare their view of him with his estimate of himself. This perspective is evident in the quotation from Plowden with which we opened this chapter.

George Herbert Mead (1934), when he contemplated the relationship between man, the individual, and man, the member of society, produced a similar, but more elaborate view. Mead regarded the human being's greatest possessions as those of communication, the capacity to engage in social interaction and the ability to reflect upon it. Those three assets, he saw as vital in enabling the child not only to come to grips with the many roles which surrounded him, but also to use them in the construction of his own identity. Yet what might the constructional process be like? Mead held as crucial the phenomenon which he called 'taking the role of the other', and this can best be illustrated by how infant children employ the Wendy House in their play. At various times the Wendy House is home, hospital, school, shop and office and, if one observes children engaged in their play, it can be seen that they are assiduously taking on the roles of mother, father, doctor, nurse, patient, teacher, and so on. Via such routine activity, Mead would argue, children try out and internalize a variety of roles and form understandings of how people act within their social world. Even more fundamental is the fact that once the roles of others are internalized by the child, he can, in contemplating his own be-haviour, call up their roles in his head as a means of judging how, in pursuing particular courses of action, he might be seen by others. Here, we have the intersection of two powerful forces, namely the individual egocentric desires of the child and his understanding of the expectations of his social world, interacting to create his sense of who he is and how he relates to others. As Hargreaves (1972) puts it:

'. . . the self is not inborn, nor could it appear in the individual isolated from his fellows. The self arises from the social ex-perience of interacting with others . . . In interaction, a man learns to respond to himself as others respond to him, he acquires a self by putting himself in the shoes of others and by using their perspective of him, to consider himself'. (p11)

Mead further argued that the people whose roles a child chooses to internalize are not randomly selected but are those whom he per-ceives to be important, because they are influential in his life. Such people, 'significant others', as Mead called them, are, in the early years of life, those most intimately bound up with the child: his mother, father and immediate family. As mobility and maturity in-crease, other significant others appear in the shape of other children and, of course, eventually those who comprise the world of school.

Our account of Mead's view of the process whereby the human infant achieves a sense of self and of his social context, by its brevity, has not done justice to his own complex and elegant elaboration. Our purpose, in describing his view, has been to underline something on which unamimous agreement is possible, namely the important role which a child's social context (and hence his childhood associates) plays in his construction of identity. If one accepts Mead's perspective, it also follows that the social contexts which children encounter, and the interrelation of significant others, will differ from place to place. In one setting the significant others of the child may be closely interconnected, whilst in another, they may be only loosely related. For example, the social experience of a child in a large family, surrounded by kin and possessing the same friends in and out of school, will differ from that of an only child living with his parents on a residential estate remote from kin and travelling to a distant school. Plainly, the particular circumstances of family, friendship group and school will combine to provide a particular range of socializing experiences. With Mead's view of the socialization process in our minds, we turn to a consideration of the peer group and the ways in which it might differ from context to context.

The Peer Group and How it Differs According to Context

Strictly defined, 'peer group' means 'a group of people of the same age and status who meet and interact continually', (Frankenberg, 1966). A definition of that kind is tidy, but of course, the social life which it seeks to label lacks an equivalent neatness. Unless some extraordinary constraint exists, it is almost always the case that the informal group associations which people create are somewhat mixed with regard to age and contain, however unobtrusively, slight differences of status. (Here, readers may care to reflect on how many of their 'peer' affiliations, formed via work and leisure activities would meet the strictness of Frankenberg's definition.) Children's friendship groups too, where the voluntary principle is evident, show a lack of precise fit with the definition. As this paragraph is being composed, a regular assembly of seven children has come together in the road outside for their evening play. The group, aged between 7 and 10, consists of two girls and five boys. A 10-year-old girl, dressed in Brownie, uniform, her arm laden with badges, is masterminding the construction of a roller skating slalom course on a tarmac incline. The others are bearing various objects from a nearby building site and, amidst agreements and differences of opinion, are setting out the course. The 7-year-old is passably accepted in the activity of the group, so long as he complies with instructions. Soon, the Brownie will go off to participate in the activities of her pack in which, its single gender character and its particular form of hierarchy will shape the kind of relationships she makes within its defined age structure.

Both the slalom making gang and the Brownie pack represent elements of her peer group life, yet neither would be recognized as such if we stayed rigidly within the peer group definition.

What characterizes the playgroup outside the window is that it is entirely voluntary in nature and, based as it is on shared interests and the desire to engage in common pursuits, can be regarded as a freely arising or organic peer group. The Brownie pack, as a peer group, is a little less organic. Although membership is voluntary, the constraint of gender and limitation of age range to three or four years influence the peer group structure which the pack contains. Where the organic quality is likely to be least evident, is in those circumstances where the constraints are so severe that a social group can do little else but match the sociological definition exactly. Such circumstances, exceptionally difficult to find in the social life of adults and children are, of course, present in the single age class which forms the unit of organization of the larger school. The single age class, of course, unlike the Brownie pack, is not organized to tap the organic peer group structures which exist when a degree of voluntary choice applies. Its organization rests upon the single assumption that if children are classified strictly by age, then the members of the class will be so alike in so many other characteristics that education can be delivered to them more effectively than by other, more mixed, systems.

It is obvious, of course, that if children are closely and compulsorily confined to a single age class, they will, through its intense interactive conditions, forge strong and often life-long relationships. That, however is not the same thing as asserting that their class group is necessarily their peer group. Whilst the single age class may be a powerful influence upon children's voluntary associations, it is not the only possible influence. Observation of how children shake out into activities when the voluntary principle is dominant, indicates that more than their age graded school categorization can determine relationships. (The bizarre game of cricket, for example, could never have been created, had the children, like educators, identified their peer group with their single age group.)

From Hadow onwards, the single age class group has been the emphatic unit of primary school organization. From Plowden onwards, the single age class and the peer group have been firmly linked. Yet, the Plowden Committee, lukewarm to the idea of vertically grouped classes, had difficulty when contemplating the process of learning in the single age class, for it noted: '... how much children of the same age differ in their powers of perception and imagery, in their interests and their span of concentration'. (para 754).

In the end, the Committee, after considering the possible ways of dealing with such diversity, in terms of individual, group and class teaching and, trapped as it was, in the conventional age organization of primary schools, could find no set of principles to act as panacea. Resignedly, it observed, 'There are no infallible rules.'

Perhaps the only infallible rule, is not to confuse a conceptual definition, such as that of the peer group, with an organizational artefact such as that of the single age class. By doing so, one may confer upon the former the unwarranted rigidity of the latter. We do not make this comment in the spirit of petty-minded academic point-scoring, but rather because, if one becomes attached to the view that class group equals peer group, one may be blinded to the educational merits which different forms of peer group possess. Relationships with other children form such a vital part of their lives, that children can be very adept at shaping their peer group structures to fit the social contexts which adults impose upon their freedom of choice. We make this point, particularly with the small rural school in mind, because what it seems important for educators and policy makers to do, is not to condemn outright the size of a child's age group in a small school because it does not rival that in a larger school, but rather to consider the social contexts of these two different kinds of institution, the peer group relations each particularly fosters and the value which they offer to the social experience of the child. To exemplify this line of thinking, we propose to consider first, peer group relations in a large urban school and second, those to be found in several small rural schools.

Peer Group Relations in an Urban Middle School

Meyenn (1980), conducted a study of peer group relationships in an urban, 9–13 middle school over a two-year period and focused upon four mixed ability classes in their final two years in the school. The children were observed in a variety of settings, the classroom, playground, lunchtime events, coming and going from school and so on. The children's views were solicited in interviews and their teachers' observations gathered. Sociometric techniques were used to discern the pattern of their relationships and additional information was derived from school records. One of the classes (4F) consisting of fifteen boys and sixteen girls was subjected to intensive study.

The school served a new town estate whose residents were predominantly working class and 80 per cent of the children lived in rented council housing. Most of the estate's residents had been re-housed there as a consequence of inner city redevelopment and clear-ance schemes. The estate was modern and well served with shops, facilities and public transport. Employment was to be found in many local light industries. When interviewed, many of the residents said that they enjoyed living on the estate but did feel 'somewhat isolated'. The school was organized on a four-form entry of mixed ability classes and, in the final year, utilized some ability setting across the four classes for maths, English, French and some science.

Meyenn made considerable use, in his study, of the children's private responses to three questions which were aimed at eliciting from them their play and work associates. The questions were:

1   Who do you play with after school? (evenings and weekends)
2   Who do you usually play with in the playground? (at breaks and lunchtimes)
3   Who do you usually work with in class?

Meyenn developed sociograms based on the children's responses. Sociograms are diagrammatic representations of relationships in a group. Obviously, if one asks individual members of a group the kind of questions Meyenn used, there will be instances where one person names another person but is not named in return. This is an unre-ciprocated choice. Equally, in many instances, two people will inde-pendently name each other and this circumstance is known as a reciprocated choice. In constructing his sociograms, Meyenn used only the reciprocated choices which the children had made. The sociograms of class 4F, which he uses as the basis of his discussion of middle school peer group relations are set out in figure 1.

As Meyenn observes, the sociograms of the relationships of the boys and those of the girls differ markedly. Effectively, the boys form a virtually undifferentiated class group. Only one boy, Tom, tends to stand a little on his own, and this is perhaps explained by the fact of his transfer, the previous year, from another class. He, like Richard, has made choices outwards to other children in the year group. The girls however, have characteristically organized themselves into tight cliques which, with one exception, that between the 'PE' girls and the 'Science lab' girls[4], are not interconnected. Three of the girls' groups possess affiliations with children outside their class group, and the largest number of these 'out of class' affiliations is possessed by the 'PE' girls. Noticeably in Meyenn's discussion of his results, all of the out of class affiliations are confined to the single age year group of which class 4F is a part. These depictions of children's peer relations

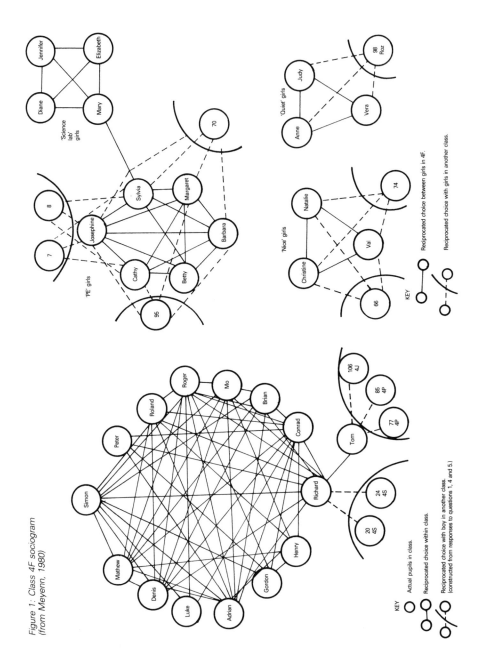

Figure 1: Class 4F sociogram
(from Meyenn, 1980)

show a similar pattern to that noted by Blyth (1960) in the social relationships of 11-year-old primary children.

Speaking of the children's relationships, Meyenn observes of the girls:

> 'Any attempts to break up the group by other girls are resist-
> ed. The greatest "disaster" that can befall a group is for another
> girl, or group, to take one of "their" girls away from them'.

Of the boys, he comments:

> 'The boys spent most of their time and certainly saw them-
> selves as one big class group. Their school lives remained
> within the bounds of this class group, and boys in other classes
> were classed almost as strangers ... The two most obvious
> features of these pupil peer networks were that they were
> formed largely within class group boundaries and were almost
> entirely of the same gender ... Peer networks were almost
> exclusively single sex in character and there tended to be
> very little interaction between the boys and girls'. (p275)

What is striking about these children's peer group relationships is the influence which the school's organizational structure has upon them. Blyth and Derricott (1977), in commenting upon this phe-nomenon in 8–12 and 9–13 middle schools generally, assert:

> '... in school, with its age-graded organization (nowhere more
> underscored than in middle schools) all children earn their
> annual increment of status ... Because of their close associa-
> tion with the school as an institution, the children's informal
> relationships mirror the formal organizational structure sub-
> stantially ...' (p79)

Effectively, the latent function of the social structure of the school is to constrain markedly the individual's relationships and his pupil identity within *single age graded frameworks*. What it becomes important for the child to grasp is that his personal qualities are not to be deployed and tried out in interrelationship with older or younger children, or with people who are more or less mature than himself. Rather, in order to achieve an approved identity in the eyes of the school and his fellows, he *must* take on a social hue characteristic of a given age grade. Blyth and Derricott indicate the pressure towards age grade identity:

> '... the children's relationships suggest that they follow some-
> thing of a learned pattern of expectations, handed down from

each set of incumbents of the age-position to its successor. This may well take place partly from the school's situation and partly through what is mediated from older and younger children in neighbourhood peer groups. In this way they manifest an age pattern doubly, both because they extend their network of social relationships primarily among their coevals but also because they develop ideas and expectations about how 9-year-olds, or 12-year-olds do and ought to behave in their particular context. All this further emphasizes and is reinforced by, the age graded structure of the school'. (p81)

So strong is the tradition of single age grading in schools, that when educationalists ponder factors which might influence how children relate to one another, their thinking, like the peer groups they describe, is constrained by the limit of the social context which the single age class and year group provide. Thus, Blyth and Derricott:

'There is also another division in which informal relationships can reflect the formal organization [of the school], namely the horizontal interaction within each age group. Where a rigid classteacher pattern exists ... then it is likely that informal relationships will crystallize within each class ... but in an open plan situation in which a year group is only partly differentiated then the scope for regular informal contacts is wider and friendship groups can also be wider'. (p82)

In short, so far as the formal organization of the school is concerned, what the child can anticipate, and is expected to anticipate, is that his relationships are to be found either within his class, or his year group. To be seen playing with, or associating with, a younger or older child, could be good cause to be regarded as odd.

It is important, at this point, that we emphasize our position, which may appear critical of the effect of the larger school upon a child's peer relations. We do not wish to be condemnatory. What we seek to note is that the socializing experience which a large primary school provides is of a particular kind in which the significant others of the child's peer group are very closely tied to his own age. Also, one can observe that it is within the large school organization that one finds children's relationships which match the strict sociological definition. It is not surprising, therefore, that when educators turn to a consideration of the small primary school, they carry with them the mental image of what a 'proper' peer group should be like: large and uniformly aged. Overall too, study of the social relationships of pupils has been mainly conducted in large schools, especially secondary schools, e.g. Hargeaves (1967), Lacey, (1970) and Willis (1977). So far as knowledge of pupil relationships in the small rural school is concerned, little exists beyond the amusing and affectionate accounts of Miss Read. We can, however, illuminate something of children's relationships in small rural schools by drawing upon a study made by one of our students, Finch (1986).

Children's Relationships in Five Small Schools

The staff and pupil sizes of the five schools which Finch studied, are given below

School*	Number of staff	Number of children
Wrettingham	4	82
Northby	3	55
Erdby	3	49
Cailey	2	49
Halton	2	32

* The schools have been given pseudonyms.

Finch used a variety of enquiry methods including classroom and playground observation, a pupil questionnaire, and informal interviews with teachers and pupils. The questionnaire, designed to yield information on children's friendships, workmates and views of school, was completed by 134 children, all in the 7–11 age group. In addition, 103 children, including fourteen infants were interviewed informally in groups of three or four, to elicit their views of life in school.

Via her questionnaire, Finch had asked the junior children to name their best friends in school. (The infant children were excluded from this part of the study because of the difficulty of gathering such data from them.) As in Meyenn's study, some of the choices exercised by the children were reciprocated by other children, whilst others were not. Finch employed both reciprocated and unreciprocated choices to construct her sociograms in order to identify not only mutual choices but also the lines of attraction between children. The sociogram of the friendship choices exercised by the thirty-three junior children of Erdby school is set out in figure 2. It is reasonably representative of the other schools.

In one respect, the pattern of the children's choices is similar to that commonly made by junior children when given 'best friends' as

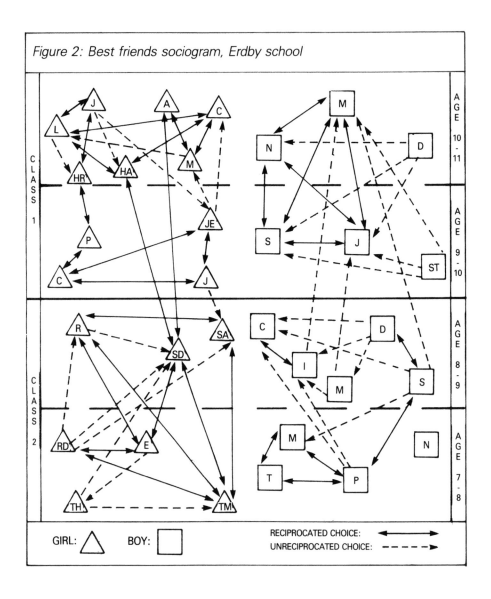

Figure 2: Best friends sociogram, Erdby school

the criterion of choice, for it is rare that cross-sex friendships are nominated. This holds true for the Erdby juniors, for no link extends between the boys and girls. The usual tendency to make choices within class boundaries is also evident. However, the junior classes at Erdby are each composed of two age groups, and as can be seen from the sociogram, lines of attraction, reciprocated and unreciprocated, cross the internal age group boundaries within the classes. In addition, six lines of attraction cross the formal demarcation line between the two classes. (Three friendship claims exercised from the lower junior to the infant class are not shown because, in the absence of infant information, it was impossible to know whether they were reciprocated.)

Obviously, a sociogram developed on the simple factor of 'best friend' choice can provide only a limited view of the relationships which children possess. Whilst one can be fairly certain that a reciprocated choice betokens a friendship link, an unreciprocated choice provides little information for it does not necessarily imply an absence of friendship; it may mean no more than that the person chosen has exercised a different order of priority in nominating friends and has merely overlooked the person who chose him. What a 'best friends' sociogram cannot do, is to convey anything of the complexity of relationships which stem from the interactions of classroom life and of play activity in and out of school. Meyenn, as we have seen, sought to capture just those relationships in his sociogram of class 4F. Drawing upon her questionnaire information, Finch too, constructed what she called positive interaction sociograms, based upon the junior children's statements of those they worked with in school and played with at break, lunchtime and out of school. The positive interaction sociogram for Erdby School juniors is given in figure 3.

It can be seen that in two major respects, its pattern of relationships differs markedly from that of Meyenn's class 4F, and also from those found commonly in larger primary schools. Firstly, reciprocated links between five boys and eight girls cross the gender boundary. Secondly, whilst it is apparent that the seven 10–11 year old girls form a particularly densely knit network, they, like the other children, do not confine their relationships to their own age group. Discounting the unreciprocated relationships, twenty links cross the boundary between class 1 and class 2, and of these, six extend from the oldest to the youngest juniors. Within class boundaries, nineteen relationships link the two age groups which compose them.

Sociograms, of course, are somewhat chilling representations of social relationships for, using as they do, nothing more than lines,

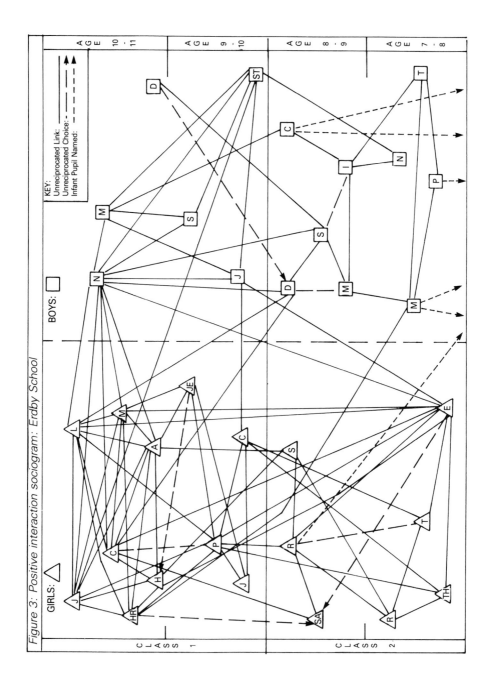

Figure 3: Positive interaction sociogram: Erdby School

triangles and squares, they convey nothing of the warmth of interaction. In an attempt to move closer to the flavour of the children's relationships, Finch devised what may be described as a snapshot technique whereby she attempted to map very quickly the composition of children's groups as they engaged in lunchtime play. The technique is fraught with difficulties, not least because children's play groups can break up and change composition very rapidly. Problematic as it may be, it gives an impression of the children's playground relations. The snapshot of Cailey, one of the two teacher schools is given in figure 5.

Of the eleven groups mapped in the snapshot, five contain one or more members of the opposite sex. Two of the four paired groups consist of children of the same age, whilst the remaining groups all show some mixing of age, from two upper junior boys interacting with four upper infant boys to, more commonly, groups of children within two years of each other. Finch, in commenting on the groupings she observed, notes that, whilst interactions occurred quite frequently across age groups, territorially, the infant children tended to remain close by, or within the small play area outside their own classroom. She also notes how groups containing older and younger children can be transient in character, citing the group of four junior and three infant girls where, after a time, 'the younger element was no longer welcome'.

With sociometric and snapshot data complete, Finch set about eliciting the children's views of life in school, and interviewed 103 of them, including fourteen infants, in informal groups of three or four.

The Children's Views of School

Finch aimed, first of all, to find out how the children perceived the mixed age organization of the school. In this respect, she notes something of the difficulty which her questions provided for some of the children:

> 'I was perhaps the first person who had ever questioned them about the situation, and some children were quite puzzled by my questions. It seemed that they had never really thought of their class as being made up of different year groups'. (p12)

Certainly, the children's reponses to Finch's questions indicate that age graded distinctions are not of manifest concern to them. As the following quotations indicate, they take a pragmatic view:

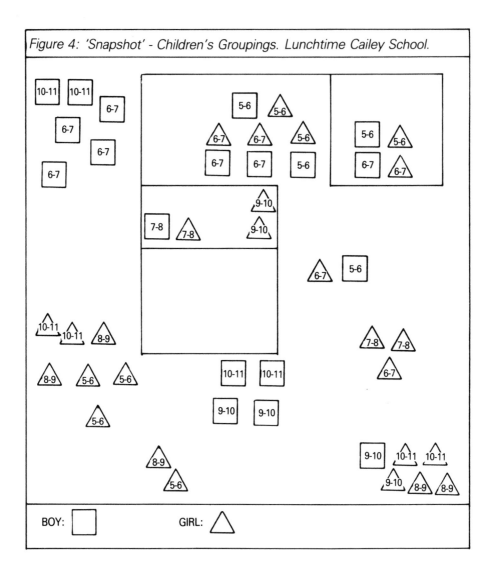

Figure 4: 'Snapshot' - Children's Groupings. Lunchtime Cailey School.

'We all mix, you don't really notice. We're not sort of separate from them'. (Boy, 10–11, Northby)

'They're just the same as 3rd years. Everybody is like everybody else'. (Girl, 10–11, Northby)

'I like the children who are any old'. (Boy, Infant, Northby)

'We're all together really. We get away from the tables and go and talk to each other. We all mix up'. (Boy, 10–11, Cailey)

'You have less people of your own age so you mix with younger children. It doesn't matter'. (Boy, 10–11, Cailey)

'There's more variety to play with'. (Girl, 8–9, Cailey)

'I play with my friends Ian and Mark and they're 4th years'. (Boy, 8–9, Cailey)

'We all get into groups to make things and that'. (Boy, 9–10, Wrettingham)

'The 4th year girls are brainy and they can help us, though sometimes they tell us to go away'. (Girl, 9–10, Wrettingham)

'Sometimes the 4th years boss us about'. (Girl, 8–9, Cailey)

'They (2nd years children) are quite noisy and naughty'. (Boy, 7–8, Erdby)

Finch observes that all the 103 children interviewed claimed to know all the other children in their individual schools, although she did not put the claim to the test. However, the friendliness which the grass roots' perspective attributes to the effect of small scale is evident in the views of the children whom she quotes:

'I prefer it when they all get together. Then you're all together as one school. 'Cos when they're all separate, its like more than one school'. (Girl, 10–11, Erdby)

'Here's a lot more friendly. You know everyone'. (Boy, 9–10, Wrettingham)

'I like small schools. There's less people to know'. (Boy, 8–9, Wrettingham)

'I like a small school, you talk to more people. You know everyone'. (Girl, 10–11, Northby)

'You meet up with people more quickly'. (Girl, 9–10, Northby)

'I remember when I first came here. The first day I made about ten friends and in a couple of days, I knew everyone in the school'. (Girl, 8–9, Northby)

'It's really cosy here'. (Girl, 8–9, Halton)

To some extent, the absence of a press of numbers and of noise was signalled by several of the children as a benefit:

'In a big school there's too much crowd'. (Boy, 9–10, Erdby)

'I like it here 'cos you don't get squashed in the playground and crowded everywhere'. (Girl, 7–8, Erdby)
(in a larger school) . . . 'There'd be too many children and too much row'. (Girl, 7–8, Halton)

'There's less people running around'. (Girl, 7–8, Halton)

'If this was a bigger school there'd be even more noise than there is here'. (Girl, 9–10, Halton)

Finch found that across her interviews, pupil comment about the social climates which the schools provided was almost wholly positive. Negative perceptions were very few and were confined to several older girls who tended to find the fourth year boys immature. Here, two fourth year girls, talking of two male class-mates, who were one-and-a-half years their junior, are quite passionate in their dislike:

'They're like babies, they get on your nerves'. (Girl, 10–11, Wrettingham)

'I mind it. I hate it'. (Girl, 10–11, Wrettingham)

However, those two acid observations apart, the dominantly positive tone of the children's interview comments reflects that of the opinions expressed in the responses of the 134 children who completed the questionnaire. Of them, 126 claimed to like school, fifty of them liking it 'very much'. Only eight claimed not to like school and of these, five were from the largest school.

Urban Peer Groups and Rural Peer Groups

In the five schools represented in Finch's study, the largest single age group of boys and girls numbers only thirteen pupils, whilst the largest single sex age group contains only eight. At the other end of the scale, in one age group, a single boy represents his sex. It is apparent that, if one holds to the view that a 'proper' peer group must consist of children of the same age and status and must approximate to the size of an urban class, then the children in all of the five schools are seriously disadvantaged. The chief implications of their circumstances are that they suffer both socially and academically, because there is an insufficiency of significant others, all of the same age with whom they can interact. Yet, as we have seen, whilst the children in Meyenn's study built their relationships in almost exact conformity to both the boundary of their class and to the sociological definition of peer group, the relationships of the rural children ignore both. Because the size of their schools, the size of their age groups and the mixed organization of their classes provide them with a different context, the pattern of their relationships is different. The children both recognize the feature of age group and ignore it. They recognize the division of interest between the sexes, yet can cross the line when shared interest requires it. Status may accrete with age, but is no barrier to mixed age friendship, nor is a mixed age relationship regarded as a departure from the norm. The context of their relationships is not first and foremost *their class,* but rather, *their school.* The relationships they form within it produce an extended peer group which, poor fit as it might be to the definition, resembles much more the organic social groups which people develop in the everyday conduct of their lives.

With all that said, the fact that the extended peer group of the rural child is much more akin to an organic social group is, by itself, no answer to the charge that the rural school is deficient in the number of significant others of the same age which it can provide. The charge, as it stands, may be true, for quite how many significant others of the same age a child must possess, in order to develop satisfactorily, is simply a matter for conjecture. Where the error lies, is in the assumption that only those of the same age, or perhaps older than oneself, can be beneficial significant others. That is not an assumption which informs adult education, nor the many mixed age educational and leisure pursuits, such as the cycling clubs, writer's circles, and historical societies, which people create informally. When an older and a younger child engage in a joint activity, it is not simply the case that the older child is *the* significant other. To the extent that the older child must learn to appreciate the younger child's limitations of stamina, knowledge and appreciation of rules, and to the extent that he must learn to appreciate what the younger child is capable of contributing to their relationship, then the younger child is also a significant other to *him.* The circumstances where significant others bring most educational and social benefit, are not necessarily those where similarity of maturity and intellect are the only ruling criteria. A context which provides a range of significant others, interdependent, yet differing in maturity and status may be of equal of greater worth. It is substantially this view, subsumed in the term 'family atmosphere', with which the grass roots' perspective opposes the claim of inadequately sized peer groups. In the next section, we seek to do no more than illustrate from observations and fieldnotes which we have made, several ways in which the extended peer group can support and enrich the work of the small rural school.

The Extended Peer Group and the Small Rural School

A prime claim which the grass roots' perspective makes is that the intimate atmosphere of the small school enables a beginning infant to make the transition from home to school easily and rapidly. Although this claim goes uncontested by the official perspective, it rarely involves consideration of the peer group's role in such adjustment. Gregory (1975), provides a contrasting picture of the nature of home-school transition in small and large school settings:

> 'Another advantage in a small community is that only two or three new children will be starting school at any one time and the teacher has plenty of time to help them to settle down and overcome initial difficulties'. (pp79–80)

Of the larger school she observes:

> '[The children] may even be in a reception class where all the other children are as bewildered as themselves. Children are resilient and most will survive this upheaval but it may take longer to achieve the sense of stability and security which is an essential condition for learning to take place'. (p80)

The point to underscore in Gregory's comment is that, in the larger school, it is frequently the case that beginning children necessarily need to pass *en masse* through that process known in reception teacher language as 'getting them settled', without the benefit of existing role models in their class to assist them. By contrast, the rural infant enters as a novitiate to an extended peer group which already encompasses her own class group. Something of that process is captured in the following observation of Gillian, who at 4 years and 3 months was just beginning her life as a pupil in a four-teacher village school:

'... in the playground, Gillian did not always play with her classmates. On some occasions, she was observed playing with a female classmate and with junior girls who, because of Gillian's small stature were appearing to mother her which she seemed to enjoy. Although Gillian appeared to play with the full age range of girls in the school, it was rare that she played with boys'. (MA student's observation)

Although the influence of the extended peer group in a small school is most easily observed in its accepted domain, the playground, it extends also into the classroom and across the working life of the school. How children may take account of each other when the pupil group is small, yet possesses a wide age span, is illustrated by a fieldnote made in a two teacher school:

Fieldnote. The juniors (7–11) have gathered in an alcove and sit on benches around its edge. Items from diaries are read and discussed. The teacher fills a gap in her local knowledge: 'Terence — does your cousin live in the house I saw you at last night?'. The infants come in and the juniors make gaps so that they sit between knees. Teacher asks two older juniors if they are ready with recorders. One is not — 'Haven't got it right'. The other gives out the hymn and accompanies the children's singing. The teacher reads a story '*The Nail Soup*' and offers a brief prayer. More news. An infant tells excitedly about the local ford flooding. The teacher is doubtful (little recent rain). A lower junior corroborates. Another infant tells of his birthday party. Teacher: 'I know, you had sausage and chips.' Infant: 'No Mrs — chips and sausage.' Grins all round. A junior boy: 'Yes Mrs — chips and sausage.' It is now five minutes to break. Teacher: 'Is anything happening at one o'clock?' (She is thinking about the space walk.) Juniors are ready to offer answers. Teacher reminds the infants of the space drama she has been building with them. One infant has the idea — can't articulate it — mimes with his hands and by rocking — an older junior offers the space walk requiring a rocket-assisted pack. Several juniors invoke a *Tomorrow's World* programme on satellite repair. The teacher nods to three of the older girls. They organize a game for exit to the playground: Anyone six can go. Anyone with a watch may go. Anyone wearing blue may go.

The most obvious feature of that observation is the easy physical intermingling of infant and junior children, but other aspects are also apparent. The teacher fills in a gap in her community knowledge; both older and younger children can contribute because they share local knowledge and because, in their different ways, they have been attending to the topic of space; the junior children do not seem to feel that their status is diminished if they lend support to infant contributions; a joking relationship binds infants, juniors and headteacher together. Finally, the younger children witness the behaviour of those whose roles they will ultimately fill.

Gregory broadens the conception of what is possible within extended groups of this kind:

'... both younger and older children benefit from learning side by side. The younger children learn a great deal from watching the older children do things. They try out the ideas for themselves and they also aim higher in their activities. ... The older children also benefit in many ways. They watch the younger children reaching stages that they remember going through themselves ... Children love an appreciative audience, and a mixed age group provides a ready-made audience to listen to stories, admire works of art, watch plays, and enjoy many other activities. The, largely uncritical, younger children help particularly to increase the confidence of the rather shy older children and give them a sense of successful achievement'. (p80)

In some respects, the small rural school mirrors the small community of which it is a part. Frankenberg, speaking of differences between urban and rural forms of life observes of the latter that 'Communities ... suffer a shortage of actors to play all available roles.' By that, he means that there are fewer people than there are tasks to be undertaken and hence, each person possesses a variety of overlapping roles. It is not simply that you are village postman, but also caretaker of the parish hall, village goalkeeper, darts player and horticultural society committee member. A rather similar phenomenon influences the life of the small school and its extended peer group. For example, if netball or football is to be played, or a school play produced, a constant problem centres around how the group is to fill the necessary roles in the team or cast. Where such activities are held to be worthwhile, conventions to do with age and gender break down and allow children to experience roles which a larger context could deny to them. The following fieldnote is illustrative:

> *Fieldnote.* Two teacher school. It is games time for the 7–11 junior class. Netball and football. They divide up. Nine girls and three boys elect to play netball. Nine boys and one girl opt for football. I take the football group and they choose teams. The 8-year-old girl is no mean player — her four team mates give her a full share of the game and lay off the ball to her when she is better placed.

The infants teacher of the school commented:

> 'At least they (junior aged children) accept that 6 and 7-year-olds and maybe girls are going to join in on the football pitch — and they are into it just as much as the others — so whereas in a larger school those of a certain age will be on the football pitch and no one else must play — here it is natural for them to mix. Joan — who was playing football with you yesterday — she is fully accepted. Generally that happens all the time — girls will be in on the football. And the boys too — if they get a netball game going they are in on it as much as the girls. And if you think about it that's in agreement with present thinking — that you mustn't discriminate'.

An alternative way in which gender stereotypes may be weakened by peer group involvement, is suggested by the headteacher of Wrettingham, the four teacher school in Finch's study. She told us that she regularly uses a group of boys to provide practice competition for the girls in the school's netball team.

A feature of the urban stereotype of rural children is that they are 'biddable', and implicit in that view reposes an almost feudal conception of the rural environment and its effect. Our perception is quite different. Two features, those of cooperation and a sense of taking responsibility, constitute two of the strongest impressions we possess of how the extended peer group of rural children can, in a healthy climate, relate to the life of the school and actively transmit its values. The following extracts from fieldnotes convey something of the grounds for our impression:

> *Fieldnote.* Infant class, two-teacher school. A 5-year-old is adrift without his pencil. He looks towards the teacher. She is busy. He stands a little lost. A 6-year-old boy asks him the

problem. A 6-year-old girl announces, 'I have a spare.' She gets it from her locker ... The older sixes return from recorder tuition. The lower sixes are to go. One boy slightly panicky looks in his bag. He has recorder book but no recorder. An older six girl stowing her recorder notices and asks. She gives him her recorder.

Fieldnote. Infant class, three-teacher school. Various activities — painting, using crayons, simple needlework, constructional materials. A 5-year-old needs a crayon. Begins to call 'Crayon! Crayon!' A 6-year-old puts down his work and goes over — 'We don't shout for things.' Finds him a crayon. The teacher does not intervene.

Fieldnote. Two-teacher school. Lunchtime. At my table, mixed juniors and infant group. An infant (6) embarks on the beginning of a smutty rhyme. A lower junior girl silences him with the remark, 'Thank you, we want none of that.'

A rural teacher, commenting on the positive attitudes of the school's children also conveys something of the way in which the children's peer group relations can support the values of the school:

'Joan (the welfare assistant) saw a lovely case the other day which I think is very representative. Two boys were having a little difference of opinion — an altercation — and she was about to go over to them when one of the older girls went over to them and said, 'Come on, what are you doing?' And Joan said the girl sorted them out so competently and it really does seem to represent that family feeling that there is here. They don't tolerate one another to behave badly ... It's just natural to them. Not because they're doing a teacher act but just because it's the right thing to do'.

It is obvious, of course, that a critic of our position could argue with complete justice that any one of those events could have been witnessed in an urban school. We have no defence against such criticism, beyond the evidence of our own experience of urban and rural schools and that of teachers possessing both urban and rural experience with whom we have worked, which indicates that the kind of instances we have cited are more apparent in the small rural school. In this respect, the headteacher of Wrettingham School who had previously taught in a London school commented to us:

'In seven years there, I don't recall a very slow child being supported like they are here. It was far more competitive. Here there is less 'arms around your work' and pupils are more likely to help each other out'.

What can be based upon empirical evidence is a connection between the small rural school and beneficial personal and social effects for the children.

Mixed age grouping is, of course, a major feature of small schools. Milburn (1981), reports of his comparison of Canadian multi-age classes and single-age classes, that pupils of all ages in multi-age classes had a stronger self-concept and 'had a more positive attitude to school'. With respect to school size, the most sophisticated and detailed set of studies was that carried out at the University of Kansas and published under the editorship of Barker and Gump (1964). Two hundred and eighteen high schools, ranging in size from eighteen to 2287 pupils were studied. One of the researchers in that cluster of studies was Campbell (1980) who concludes:

'In summary, students from the large schools *were exposed* to a larger number of school activities and the best of them achieved standards in many activities that were unequalled by students in small schools; on the other hand, students in the small schools *participated* in more activities — academic, inter-school, cultural and extracurricular; their versatility and performance scores were consistently higher, they reported more and 'better' satisfactions, and displayed stronger motivation in all areas of school activity'. (p119)

Similarly positive findings were obtained by Edmunds and Bessai (1977). Their investigation, which took place on Prince Edward Island, involved a comparison of the attitudes of children in forty-seven one and two-teacher schools with those of children in larger schools which had been produced by a policy of 'consolidation'. Significant differences were found; most especially the children from the small schools reported higher levels of 'satisfaction' (they enjoyed their school work and school experience) and of 'cohesiveness' (they played well together and cooperated well in school work). The pupil questionnaire was then given to pupils in twenty-one two-teacher schools in Cheshire and a further five similarly sized schools in the Pennines. The results obtained were remarkably similar to those from the small Canadian schools, although, for the English context, their significance is reduced by the fact that no data were obtained from larger schools in this country.

Clearly, the findings of North American research cannot be translated directly to the British school scene, although, that of Edmunds and Bessai establishes a bridge. However, the message of a connection between school size and pupil attitude is also to be found in a purely British study.

The University of Aberdeen conducted an investigation of pupils' attitudes towards school and of their own self-concept (socially, personally and academically). The sample was drawn from pupils in 'small' (one and two-teacher), 'medium' (three and four-teacher) and 'large' (up to eleven-teacher) rural schools and the survey was conducted shortly before the end of their primary schooling. On four of the measures of attitude and self-concept, it was clear that size of school was related. Shanks and Welsh (1983) summarize these findings as follows:

> 'In no case did these differences favour "large" school pupils. Compared with pupils from "small" schools, the "large" schools group exhibited greater apprehensions about transfer to secondary school, and poorer personal and academic self-concept. "Large" school pupils also had lower scores on the academic self-concept sub-scale than those from "medium" schools. On the "attitude to primary" variable, the results showed them better disposed to primary school than either the "small" or "large" groups'. (p190)

None of these investigations involved study of the pupil peer group as a factor.[5] Yet, to the extent that, in a small school, the extended peer group virtually represents its pupil population, one can suggest that it is a factor influencing the development of the positive personal and social attitudes which these studies indicate.

The Rural School and its Peer Group:
A Concluding Comment

At the outset of this chapter, we saw that the peer group is recognized as an important influence upon children which schools can harness. We also saw that limitation of peer group size in the small rural school could be regarded as a factor which depressed competition and intellectual stimulation. To the extent that such evidence as exists cannot support claims that children in small schools perform less well, it is difficult to see how the size of the single age peer group could be implicated. By comparing children's peer groupings in both large and small school settings, it was possible to observe how children adapted to their contexts. In the urban setting, the peer group which emerged was characteristically single sex and single age and its boundary showed virtual conformity to the class-based organization of the school. In the rural setting, the children's relationships were more extensive in terms of mixed age and cross sex relationships. It was also apparent that the rural children found the context of such relationships congenial. Such research as exists, and indicating as it does, the more positive personal and social attitudes of pupils in small schools, supports, rather than condemns the quality of interpersonal (and by implication, peer group) relationships which such schools can generate. Rather than suffering from the lack of competitive stimulation, it could be, as the headteacher of a small rural school suggested to us, that the pupils benefit from the fact that they are less liable to be stigmatized by others in their peer group for working hard. To the extent that a climate of that kind is achievable within the more intimate relationships of the small rural school, another benefit becomes possible. Given that the classteacher, that very important significant other, is sufficiently skilled, the more worthwhile challenge which arises from a child's personal interaction with the learning task, otherwise known as self competition, becomes more realisable than it might be within a larger context.

In a society, where legislation is necessary to regulate the conflict which may arise out of the differences which people perceive between themselves and others, it seems distinctly odd that the extended rural peer group, which proves capable of taking differences of age, sex and status and of fashioning them into a satisfactory way of life, stands condemned as inherently disadvantaging.

Notes

1 The school has since closed.
2 It should be noted that, with respect to this allegation, it is employed only at a general, rather than a specific level in closure cases. For example, when the Principal Education Officer was challenged on the matter with regard to the attainment of the children in Aldcaster School, SAVE group notes record that he said there was no evidence.
3 *Eastern Daily Press,* 4 February, 1986.
4 The titles 'PE' girls, 'Quiet girls' etc., are used by Meyenn to distinguish the different groups.
5 One intriguing study which does, is that of Twine (1975). His study reports the familiar finding that pupils in rural schools have better

academic and personal self-images and more positive attitudes to school than do the children from the more urbanized parts of the area from which his sample of twenty-nine schools were drawn. He endeavours to relate these findings to the structure of peer group relationships found in the schools. Unfortunately, his account gives little detail of the size of the schools or from which pupils in the schools the peer group data were obtained. Moreover, unlike Meyenn and Finch, Twine's study restricted the pupils' friendship choices to their own classroom.

Chapter 5

Teacher Isolation and
the Small Rural School

It is rare for any discussion of the small rural school to travel far before the topic of teacher isolation is raised and, of course, in closure conflicts, it is invariably cited as one of the major disadvantages of the small rural school. Teacher isolation (or professional isolation as it is interchangeably called) is a serious charge to bring against any individual teacher or institution, for it implies that children may be receiving an education which is less than it should be. A teacher who can not, or will not, engage in professional exchange with her colleagues is likely to be one who, in the absence of stimulation, will settle for a few favoured methods and go down the same royal road year after year. A school which isolates itself from the mainstream of educational development will lack awareness of new moves in curriculum and resources, so that its pupils will receive an education more fitted for yesterday than for today or tomorrow. Teacher isolation then, merits serious attention and cannot be left merely as an item of argumentative rhetoric to be bandied about in the cut and thrust of closure debates. However, if teacher isolation is to be considered, care is needed in how it is approached, for it is conventionally conceived as a peculiarly rural phenomenon. That such an assumption comes ready made should be warning enough, for as we have already suggested, in a predominately urban society, rural matters tend to be viewed from the standpoint of the majority. A little story may illuminate and reinforce this problem of perspective:

Some years ago, at the end of a day's walking on the Cumbrian fells, one of the authors dropped in at a village pub for a beer. The innkeeper had known him as a wartime evacuee and, after a period of reminiscence, talk turned to the increased flow of urban holiday-makers into the area following the construction of the M6 motorway. 'There are three questions I must answer a dozen times a day', said the landlord. 'First, they ask me what the weather is going to do because country people are supposed to be weather experts.' 'Next', he said, nodding towards a stuffed wild cat in a glass case, 'they look at that and ask "Is that a fox?".' 'Last', he said, they say to me "What do you do in the winter?" He smiled ruefully and commented, 'It's pointless to tell them that there is so much going on here in the winter that just getting the drama club togeher for a rehearsal is a nightmare.'

The landlord was, of course, recounting and reacting to a common rural stereotype, often deeply held by urban dwellers who, when they compare what they see of the rural scene with the experience of their own lives, conclude that rural living must be extremely isolating, especially in the dark months. Forced to reflect upon urban living, they might admit to the fact that for some people, town and city life can be disturbingly lonely, yet that admission, by itself, would not dissolve a general conviction that rural life must embrace a much greater degree of isolation.

This same general stereotype of rural isolation which our Cumbrian innkeeper identified in his urban customers has, of course, been applied to the teachers who work in small rural primary schools. The view presented below is characteristic of the many assertions made about the isolation of rural teachers:

> 'Teachers in small rural schools may not suffer from the stresses and problems of inner city schools, but may appear to feel a sense of professional isolation and can lack the stimulus of a staff of reasonable size with every access to in-service education and to facilities for further study'. (Skinner, 1980, p56)

We should note that this comment rests not just upon a rural stereotype, but on an urban stereotype as well. Rural teachers, by virtue of where they teach and the size of the school in which they teach are held to be vulnerable to the effects of isolation, whereas by implication, urban teachers again by virtue of the size and location of their schools are not. To adapt Lady Bracknell's famous observation;

> 'To base an assertion upon one stereotype may be regarded as unfortunate: to base it on two looks like carelessness'.

It is this careless transportation of stereotypes in our mental baggage which we must avoid if we are to make a serious examination of the problem of teacher isolation. This not least because easy use of stereotypes may obscure the exact nature of barriers which stand in the way of teachers, wherever they teach, engaging in worthwhile professional exchange and development. A first step in breaking away from the shackles which the familiar stereotypes provide, is to consider the features by which one could identify an isolated teacher, wherever he or she practised.

What Might be Regarded as the Characteristics of an Isolated Teacher?

A positive way to approach this question is to ask what the profile of a non-isolated teacher might be like. At a direct personal level, one can suppose that she would be intrinsically interested in her work and sufficiently intrigued in the problems and dilemmas which it threw up, not merely to reflect upon them, but also to share them with other professionals practising in the same field of work. Additionally, she would welcome observation of her work and the comment which other professionals could offer her about her activity. She would be keen to learn about new ideas, new techniques and new developments relevant to her practice and would be happiest working in an organizational setting which was sufficiently open to allow their cooperative and critical trial. However, she would not be satisfied simply with these conditions, for she would wish to reach beyond her immediate working environment in order to tap national and international professional networks. She would be what Hoyle (1974) terms an *extended professional*.

By contrast, the isolated teacher would be one who preferred to work in privacy and, whatever her thoughts were about her practice, she would wish to keep them to herself. The prospect of someone watching her in action would be uncomfortable and hence, she would discourage other adults from entering her classroom. Given a choice, she would prefer a school which allowed people to plough their own individual furrows and where professional conversation affirmed a comfortable state of affairs rather than provoking the destabilizing contemplation of new ideas. It might be that over time, she had reached the conclusion that her initial training had provided her with a professional kit for life and so she felt no need to reach out to the professional world beyond her own insitution. Although she might be a hardworking and competent classroom practitioner, the narrowness of her outlook would cause Hoyle to regard her as a *restricted professional*.

In portraying the restricted and extended poles of a professional's view of his or her task in the way we have, there is, of course, a real danger of seeing an orientation to one or other extreme as no more than a matter of personal inclination. Whilst personal attitude is obviously a powerful force in determining how an individual sees her professional task, other influences, both social and physical, also play their parts in determining whether she builds a wall around herself and her task, or whether she creates doors and windows. Not least among such influences is the nature of the work to be done, the traditions, hierarchy and working arrangements within which it is to be done, and the culture of the social group which helps her to interpret how the work should be done. To begin at the beginning, it is necessary to consider whether the nature of teaching is, of itself, pre-disposing to isolation.

Is the Nature of Teaching Predisposing to Isolation?

Teaching is an uncertain activity. Despite years of research and classroom experiment, teaching, is devoid of any sure-fire certainties of method. Unlike medical men, teachers cannot quote the statistical odds of success for the methods which they use. All that they can do is to proclaim faith in the approaches which they employ. There are, of course, in education, an abundance of ideologies, each claiming to possess the one right way, yet unable to furnish strong proof for their claims. Moreover, teachers are at the centre of contradictory advice as to what they should be about, from governments, universities, industry, parents and the like. For teachers, the classroom can be a solitary world in which external exhortations surround the dilemmas of personal classroom practice. Teaching, in the absence of any certainties of method, and informed as it is by contradictory advice, is predisposing to self doubt. Lortie (1975) summarizes the teacher's position in relation to that of other professionals as follows:

> 'People in other fields of work also have occasions to doubt the professional efficacy and the value of the service they offer. In fields where people perceive their knowledge (and their ignorance) as jointly shared, the individual burden is reduced. A person can take comfort from his compliance with normal expectations within the occupation; he can feel he did everything possible within 'the state of the art'. (Physicians so argue when they are charged with malpractice.) Then the individual can cope with unpleasant outcomes by sharing the weight of his failures; his inadequacy is part of the larger malignancy of the field. Teachers derive little consolation from this source; an

individualistic conception of practice exacerbates the burden of failure'. (p81)

To engage in a form of work where certainty of method and outcome is elusive is obviously to expose oneself to the possibilities and effects of self-doubt and the ideal medium for its development is likely to be individual teaching closely confined to a classroom. That said, an obvious solution is to share one's practice and thinking about one's practice with fellow practitioners. By so doing, even if nothing more is achieved, the 'malignancy of the field' can be recognized as common property. Yet, it would seem that, in general, teachers do not take this route. As Webb (1981) observes:

'... with all the pressures they face in the classroom, one might think that teachers would work to establish strong relationships with their fellow teachers. Such relationships could serve to alleviate self-doubt, and re-establish self-worth ... It would help to establish the educational aims of the school and facilitate the sharing of workable methods and worthwhile ideas. Yet most studies of teacher-teacher interaction emphasize the insularity of teaching and the superficiality of teacher interaction'. (p253)

Here, we face a considerable puzzle, for the old saw that a problem shared is a problem halved does not seem to have much purchase. The majority of teachers wish to do well by their pupils, yet appear to insulate themselves from professional exchange. Self-doubt, which could be the starting point for creating professional openness appears to be a condition which fosters professional solitude. A tendency to classroom isolation then, may be more than just a feature attributed to the rural teacher; it may be bedded in the general nature of teaching, wherever it occurs. Moreover, particular features of teaching, its organization and its cultural context may work for or against isolation. Two questions need to be addressed. These are:

1 How do the organization and the traditions of primary schooling influence tendencies towards teacher isolation?
2 To what extent do the informal staff cultures which teachers generate affect teacher isolation?

How do the Organization and Traditions of Primary Schooling Influence Tendencies Towards Teacher Isolation?

Setting aside limited excursions into architectural designs such as the open plan school which render teachers much more visible to each other, the vast majority of primary school buildings celebrate and emphasize through their spatial arrangements the right of a teacher to conduct her teaching in private. Common school design, almost unchanged since mediaeval times and found standardly in the capitalist West and the Communist East, seems to be predicated on the assumption that the best physical environment for teaching and learning is cellular in character; each cell containing one teacher and one class, masked off so far as possible from surrounding cells. Whether such an arrangement is the most appropriate for the education of children is immaterial to our purpose. However, the consequences for teachers are considerable. Space speaks, and the message across the years is that teaching is an activity to be conducted behind closed doors and out of sight and earshot of similar activity. Moreover, the conventional timetable of the school day enhances such insulation, for its effect, by and large, is to confine teachers to their classrooms at the same time. A major consequence is that, even if willing, teachers are largely denied sight of each other at work and hence do not possess a shared knowledge of each other's practice as a basis for professional dialogue. What they can know of each other's work is mainly derived from elsewhere than the classroom — for example, listening in to children's talk, observing colleagues taking assembly, or watching them controlling the playground or the mid-day break. Webb summarizes the isolating effects as follows:

'Because teachers do not see one another at work and because they often devalue the self-reports of colleagues, they are deprived of constructive evaluations of their own accomplishments and professional support for their methods. Teachers' professional self-confidence is largely self-constructed and is therefore quite vulnerable. A few bad experiences or a couple of mediocre days may throw them into self-doubt. Even when things seem to be going well, there is lingering suspicion that they are fooling themselves, that they are really not as good as they pretend to be. This insecurity encourages isolation'. (254)

It is, of course, not possible to quantify the proportion of teachers who fall prey to the insulating effects of the physical arrangements in which they teach. Ross (1980) indicates his view of its generality as follows:

'There is ample evidence that classroom teachers find their spatial isolation desirable ... the isolation of classroom teachers is a pervasive phenomenon that manifests itself in myriad boundary maintenance activities all of which function to reduce the influence of the [headteacher] upon their individual practices'. (p220)

Although the isolation of teachers may be a pervasive phenomenon which is fostered by the physical structures in which they teach, the fact remains that, in urban eyes, teacher isolation is seen largely as a rural problem. Saville (1977) in his discussion of rural teachers refers to their 'rustic reclusiveness', by which he means their tendency to turn inwards to the work of the school rather than outwards to wider professional matters. There may be some truth in his view. However, what it overlooks is the possibility that the small size of the rural school and even, in some circumstances, the eccentricity of its spatial arrangements may work against the kind of classroom isolation about which both Webb and Ross express concern. A study of three small rural schools by one of the authors, Sigsworth (1984), indicates how the teachers' awareness of each other's activities sprang naturally from the settings in which they taught.

The observed schools, consisting of two three-teacher schools and a two-teacher school, were all housed in Victorian buildings in which glass and wood partitions separated the teaching groups. Additionally, the schools had incorporated the vacated headteachers' houses which, attached to their main buildings, provided additional teaching, storage and office space. In all three schools, the teachers worked for most of the time as individuals in their own classrooms and, in this respect, were no different from teachers working in larger urban schools. However, two factors operated to reduce classroom privacy and to increase the teachers' awareness of each other's work.

Firstly, although the classroom partitions served as visual screens between classes, they were insubstantial barriers to sound. Very obviously, in the ordinary practical sense of classroom privacy, this architectural feature could be seen as potentially disturbing. However, the teachers had adjusted to it by cooperating in the timing of 'quiet' and 'noisy' activities and by commonly placing considerable emphasis upon individual and small group modes of teaching. What the inter-classroom permeability did was to erode classroom privacy involuntarily. An example of such permeability is caught in the following field note:

Lower Junior Class, 11.40
The adjoining infants engage in a rumbustious singing game. The noise carries through. A pupil, momentarily distracted, looks up, catches my eye, smiles and shakes his head as a mature knower.

This feature of interclassroom audibility appeared to be significant in its breaching of classroom privacy because of the way it allowed teachers to know something of the work of their colleagues. As Joan, headteacher of the two-teacher school pointed out

'We feel very comfortable working in front of each other and that includes our part-timer. We know exactly what is going on even though we are in separate classrooms. There is only a glass partition and, if I am quiet, I can hear Elizabeth perfectly well, and if she is quiet, vice-versa. So we know exactly what is happening in the school'.

Joan had previously taught in the more private circumstances of a large urban primary school and, as her subsequent comment indicates, a professional reorientation was needed when she took up work in her small rural school:

'That was something that I had to adjust to, because normally you go in and close the door and you're completely by yourself'.

The second feature in all three schools was that routinely across the day a traffic of teachers and children through and into classrooms occurred. This arose partly because no transit corridors existed and teachers passed through one another's classrooms to reach other facilities, notably those in the headteacher's house in each school. Classrooms were also exchanged to service aspects of the curriculum, for example, art, craft and PE, and in relation to a small degree of specialist teaching. As described, the traffic of other teachers through one's classroom sounds intolerable yet, the modes of working and an acceptance of the building's eccentricities seemed to minimize the problem. Latently, such transit and exchange served to increase professional visibility and familiarity with colleagues' work. As Neil, headteacher of one of the three-teacher schools observed:

'I think we move around each other's rooms more (than in urban settings). While we are teaching — working — in

Victorian classrooms — we see much more what is going on. I don't think you positively look. It's more you can't help seeing'.

Sylvia, the infants' teacher in his school, independently contributed a similar view:

'It is possible to know more about your colleagues because you. mix more together. And of course to watch television — to get to another room — you have to walk through other classrooms and so you see what is happening. It seems natural. I don't remember discussing things as we do here when I taught in X (a large urban primary school)'.

It is not possible to generalize from this microcosm of rural primary schooling to *all* rural primary schools. The three schools were satisfactory and ordinary examples of their type. The teachers, it seemed, shared a knowledge of each other's working practice partly because the buildings they worked in offered little choice in the matter and partly because the teachers perceived a need for interdependence in terms of classroom and class exchange. Pragmatic as the circumstances were which substantially prevented professional privacy, there was no indication that the teachers yearned for the reclusiveness which their former urban experience had granted them. Nor did they manifest any sign of the insulating and boundary maintenance activities which both Webb and Ross identify as central contributors to teacher isolation. Teacher isolation, however, is not merely a matter of architectural effect, powerful as that might be. Because it is also influenced by the traditions which inform both the teacher's view of her task and the organizational structure in which she performs it, necessarily the effect of such traditions must be considered.

The common and reasonable view which parents take of the primary teacher is that she will give priority to the education of children in her class. It is also one to which the majority of primary teachers would assent, not least because it is within the classroom that they see children develop as a result of their efforts and it is there that they find their prime reward. Taylor, Reid, Exon and Holly (1974) point out in this respect the relative lack of interest which a teacher may have in school-wide matters compared with the private world of the classroom where the teacher 'secures to himself a personally manageable set of transactions with his pupils'.

Leese (1978) who writes movingly of his daughter's commitment to her classroom also indicates the psychological bond which a teacher can develop with her pupils:

'A teacher's real gratification comes from what her pupils learn from her … There is I think no greater reward for my own daughter — a first grade (i.e. reception) teacher — than the evidence that those who have come to her unable to read can do so when they leave. There is a strong interpersonal transaction and subsequent bond between her and each child. It is her individual influence upon her client which makes her professional … consequently, she deeply resents and resists those who would stylize and interfere with that intimate art upon which her ego rests'.

That American observation is echoed in the study of ninety-nine English infant and junior teachers by Nias (1984) who observes:

'Over and above the self-confessed "crusaders" in my sample were the two thirds who regarded the "pursuit of principle" (as one put it) as a crucial part of their job. As one teacher said, "the key to the way I try to do my job is my inner conviction about what's right". Another claimed, "I'm not going to let my principles go, no matter how much (the other staff) get at me"'. (p271)

One of her teachers summed up her professional perspective vividly in the statement, 'I live in my own world, make my own standards.'

Long-standing traditions, too, underline and support the professional privacy of the classroom. 'English primary education', observes Blyth, 'grew mainly, if tardily, out of English elementary education … and in some ways it still bears the marks of its ancestry'. (Blyth 1965). One of the major features of English elementary education, with its simple organization of headteacher and assistant teachers was its foundation upon the one class-one teacher principle. This part of its ancestry, carried into the newly created primary school of the thirties, formed the basis of its organization. Although subsequently, the progressive movement and the Plowden Report were zealous in their efforts to remove the narrow instructional outlook of the elementary tradition, they too, in emphasizing the worth of the small intimate classroom community, under-wrote the sanctity of classroom privacy. It should also be noted that the hidden curriculum of teacher training, with its focus upon individual classroom performance rather than inter-colleague cooperation conveys the 'teacher in the classroom' tradition.

The psychological bond then, which the teacher forges with her class reinforced by traditions of training and schooling, can act power-fully to affirm classroom privacy and, by implication, the insulation of one teacher from another, at least so far as daily practice is concerned. A further reinforcing insulator so far as the conventionally sized primary school is concerned is to be found in its organizational structure and the roles which it contains.

In primary schools large enough to sustain a non-teaching head, the headteacher is distinctively separate. He is marked off by possessing his own non-teaching room and he can choose the amount and kind of teaching he undertakes. More important than these practical features, his role and its power are buttressed by the English head-teacher tradition and by official assertions that the philosophy and the style of the school are his to mould. These official comments, spaced across thirty years, convey an unchanging view of the head-teacher:

> 'It will be an important part of the headteacher's duty to direct the work of his assistants ... He will himself set them an example of professional craftsmanship worthy of their emula-tion ... It will be his privilege to show them ...' (*Handbook of Suggestions* 1937, p55)

> 'The overriding responsibility for planning and supervising the life and work of the school rests with the headteacher — though he usually makes his staff feel that their views have had due weight in the decisions taken'. (*Primary Education* 1959, p92)

> 'The independence of the headteacher within his own school is great'. (*Plowden*, 1967, para 929)

Alexander (1984) comments:

> 'The according of massive responsibility to the primary head is a constant in all recent writing on primary schools ...' (p161)

Alexander notes too the strong possession syndrome manifest not merely in the 'my school', 'my staff' content of headteachers' talk, but also in the proneness of official documents to employ 'his school', 'his staff' when referring to the primary head. He observes:

> 'This personalization of the senior management function is extensive and of considerable significance. For heads thereby become the keepers not merely of a school's organizational arrangements, but of its entire value system. The school be-

comes an extension of their personality and their beliefs (or what heads tend to term 'their philosophy')'. (p162)

The considerable power which tradition offers to the headteacher is, of course, partly counterbalanced by the relative lack of formal power which it offers to the classteacher. Indeed, tradition endowed the classroom practitioner with the title of 'assistant teacher' a term we continue to use with the implication that the classroom teacher will assist the headteacher to fulfil his, rather than a collective, purpose. But of course, a dilemma faces the teacher. On the one hand exists an expectation that she will contribute to the school, sustaining and supporting its organizational life, its climate and its curriculum style. On the other hand, she possesses both her own view on how children are to be educated and a classroom in which both tradition and architecture have granted her privacy of practice. Her dilemma lies in how she reconciles the 'my school' of her headteacher with the 'my class' of her professional commitment.

Such research as exists to illuminate how teachers reconcile the dilemma indicates that largely, they yield the school to the head-teacher in return for rights to classroom privacy. The study of Taylor *et al* (1974) indicates that the primary teachers whom they studied dichotomized the classroom and the school into what the researchers termed 'zones of influence'. So far as the school zone of influence was concerned, the head was seen to be dominantly placed. So far as the individual classroom was concerned, the shaping influences upon it of pupils, headteacher or colleagues were regarded as much less than that of its teacher. This, it would seem is not simply an English phe-nomenon, for Scrupski (1970), on the basis of his investigation of American elementary schools, describes how the classroom teachers he studied were compliant to the school principal's requirements insofar as he was prepared to grant them autonomy over their class-rooms. Pollard (1985) in one of the most recent studies of primary schools confirms the findings of both Scrupski and of Taylor and his colleagues:

'Another important concern of the teachers was the protection of their personal independence and autonomy ... the teachers wanted to control their work situation and classroom auton-omy ... Two main threats to classroom autonomy routinely emerge: the headteacher and parents ... [headteacher] visits to classrooms could be seen as intrusive'. (p27)

That teachers can utilize their classroom autonomy and isolation to resist a headteacher's educational aspirations, whilst at the same time complying with his organizational requirements, is evident from Hartley's (1985) study of a Scottish primary school with 372 children on roll. Commenting on the distance between head and teachers, Hartley observes:

'It was the very isolation of the teacher in her classroom that prevented [the headteacher] from closely ensuring that his policy was being realized. Teachers are adept at publicly assenting to the official wisdom and privately proceeding in their own classrooms in quite divergent ways'. (p52)

To some extent there could be an implication of opposed forces in these portrayals of primary headteacher and teacher perspectives with the picture of day-by-day strife springing to mind. This would be a largely incorrect way to see it. A much more realistic view would be that of head and classteacher, within the tradition and styles of primary schools, working out a *modus vivendi* in which each is complementary. A side effect, of course, of how that complementarity is constructed, can be that classroom privacy is further strengthened and the possibilities of professional discussion diminished.

Up to this point in our discussion on how the relationships of primary teachers and headteachers may influence perceptions of the shared or private nature of their professional task, we have made no reference to the other element to be found in larger primary schools, the postholder. It is to a consideration of the influence of the postholder upon the working relationships of teachers that we now direct discussion.

The Postholder in the Primary School

In the immediate post-war period, a further feature, that of the postholder, entered the organization and tradition of average sized primary schools. First introduced in 1948 as a gradation in the assistant teacher level, it is now a well established part of primary school organization. At first, the award of posts of responsibility as they are termed was made for relatively trivial reasons. (One of the authors gained one in 1959 for 'football, PE and gymshoes'.) The impact of postholders on the general work of primary schools, up to the time of the Plowden Report, was slight and, because their role rarely involved major curricular responsibility, they impinged little upon the zones of autonomy of either head or classteacher. Plowden, in recommending some limited degree of specialization, saw the postholders as capable of carrying a measure of leadership responsibility in this area. What the Committee saw of their contemporary use in schools, it found disappointing:

> 'The intention is that they should be awarded for specific duties, in practice, the duties for which they are awarded are sometimes trivial'. (para 936)

In the post-Plowden era, allocation of responsibility to postholders has undergone change. Emphasis upon the subject expertise and curriculum development roles of postholders has, since the Great Debate of 1976 and through various official documents (for example, the DES surveys of 1978 and 1982), shown considerable increase. That this reorientation of postholders' tasks is problematic and lacking anticipated impact is evident from the *HMI Primary Survey* (1978):

> 'It is disappointing to find that the great majority of teachers with posts of special responsibility have little influence at present on the work of other teachers'. (para 8.45)

That finding is depressing, particularly if one sees the postholder's role as one which could act to overcome the teacher's isolation in the classroom and one which could stimulate professional discussion within the school. Yet, there is little evidence of the postholder's success in breaking down the barriers we have already considered. Why should this be? Relatively little exists to help us to answer this question, although the University of Birmingham's Primary School Research and Development Group study (1983) offers a sight of how teachers view external help. Based principally on how teachers see it, rather than upon what teachers actually do, it nonetheless indicates generally that the primary teachers whom it studied saw themselves as less than fully competent in such areas as environmental studies, art and craft, but not particularly inclined to seek assistance. They did not appear to be bothered about music or religious education, and regarded their competence in the language and mathematics area of curriculum as satisfactory. In respect of these two latter areas, there were indications that intrusive advice would be resisted as an implicit comment upon their competence. It is, however, important to note that, with regard to the existence of specialist help teachers were not against the idea of seeking advice. Although they were resistant generally to the idea of postholders chairing meetings of colleagues for curriculum development purposes, it would seem that they were prepared to consult postholders informally. The ambivalence of the teachers with regard to the use of the teacher expert is captured in this comment by the researchers:

'One way teachers had of seeing the teacher expert was as an agent of change, alert to innovations in primary education and determined to make a contribution to the professional development of his colleagues. Another, as a quietly concerned colleague, ready to help if asked. In the main, it was the last way of seeing the teacher expert that was most generally supported. The former found more support among teachers with posts of responsibility and among teachers who belong to a teaching association. But this support, though evident was not strong'. (p98)

The Birmingham study would square with our experience of seminar work with teachers taking MA and in-service BEd courses in the curriculum area. Many of them identify two barriers to their efforts to act consultatively and to lead curriculum development. On the one hand, though they may be more expert than the head in their specialism, many encounter headteacherly constraints on their activity. On the other hand, they report difficulty in influencing classroom practice, not least because often they are perceived as extensions of the headteacher's will. Not only do they identify lack of time as a problem, but also the boundary maintenance strategies which teachers use to ward off intrusion into their classrooms. Some of the postholders we teach, with rare access to their unconscious mind, can identify conflict within themselves, simultaneously warding off attempts by others to influence their personal practice, whilst seeking themselves, to penetrate the practice of others.

Our purpose, in considering the interplay of organization and tradition, and its influence upon professional interrelationships in conventionally sized primary schools has not been to criticize the manner of their functioning nor the work of their teachers. Rather, we have sought to indicate that, so far as providing conditions of professional openness, which is the first antidote to teacher isolation, they may not be without their problems. This, of course, is not to say that, for different reasons, the small rural school may also contain isolating features. What must be pointed out however is that when the rhetoric of rural primary teacher isolation is stereotypically employed, there is implicit in it a stereotypical view of the urban primary school as an isolation-defeating institution. Further, what the rhetoric fails to do, is to consider the small rural school in its own right, considering not merely those elements of its tradition and organization which may make for isolation, but also those which encourage professional discourse. Here, we turn to consider the tradition and organization of the small school 'in its own right'.

The Traditions and Organization of the Small Rural School

A village school of two or three teachers, even when the part-time staff of secretary, caretaker, welfare and dinner assistants is taken into account, is a very small educational unit and, at one and the same time it is both a simple and a complex organization. So far as the teaching staff are concerned, it is simple to the extent that, because of its size, it possesses no posts of responsibility and so the distinction between levels of authority is straightforwardly between those of headteacher and assistant teacher. It is made complex by the two components which comprise the rural headteacher's role. Small as his school may be, he is endowed with the power and authority which tradition and the law confer upon all headteachers. However, for day-to-day purposes, and unlike the headteachers of larger primary schools, he is traditionally a practising teacher and, in that sense, he is no more than a professional equal with his colleagues. Hence, the legitimacy which he is accorded by his teachers rests not only upon his status as headteacher, but also upon his classroom performance. Pollard (1985), in no more than an aside, identifies this distinction between the power components of teachers' and headteachers' roles in large and small primary schools:

> '[Classteachers'] power derives from the fact that they work at what used to be called 'the chalk face'. They teach and have contact with children far more than any headteacher (excluding the heads of very small schools). Headteachers are thus in a position of being largely dependent on their classteachers for the quality of education provided in the school and this can give the teacher a significant degree of power ...' (p133)

Given the practitioner element in the role of the small school headteacher, it is possible to suggest that the power components of both the headteacher and class teacher roles are likely to differ from those in a larger school. Because the headteacher is as much at the chalk face as his teachers, he shares their working life and experiences the same problems. Further, because he is a classroom practitioner, his class teachers cannot claim sole rights to the delivery of classroom quality. In that endeavour, headteacher and class teacher are equal partners.

No research exists to illuminate the implications which this aspect of small school organization holds for the influence which headteacher and class teacher can wield over each other. Certainly, it would seem that the separate zones of influence affirmed by the primary teachers whom Taylor *et al* (1974) studied, and which stressed classroom autonomy, must be markedly different in the small rural school, where the headteacher is also a full-time practitioner. What may be crucial so far as the presence or absence of internal isolation is concerned in the small school, is which aspect of his role the headteacher chooses to stress. If it were to be the headteacher component *per se*, then it could well be the case that his teachers would choose to emphasize their traditional rights to classroom autonomy. Here, for example, if it were the case that the headteacher was junior trained, his infant's teacher might well choose to stress her right to exercise her professional infant expertise and to resist what she took to be unenlightened intrusion into her practice. In that sort of circumstance the consequences for individual teacher isolation in the small school could be considerable. If, on the other hand, the rural headteacher proves capable of providing leadership whilst at the same time stressing his identity as a practitioner, then the possibility exists that he and his staff could constitute a small but strong cooperative professional group where each practitioner has yielded a measure of classroom autonomy for the good of the school. Given that configuration of roles and relationships one would anticipate that internal isolation would be low.

It is also possible that another feature, that of the psychological bond between teacher and children, functions differently in the small school. Leese, we may recall, suggested that the bond between the teacher and her class could be such as to cause her to emphasize her classroom task and to resist wider commitment. It may be that the small size of the rural school influences a teacher's perceptions of her allegiance to the children in the school rather differently from those of her urban counterpart. Because of the sheer pupil numbers in the larger urban school, it is inevitable that teachers will experience some sense of anonymity with respect to a proportion of the school's pupils. By contrast, because of the small number of pupils in the small rural primary school there is a much greater likelihood that the teaching staff will know all the pupils well, not simply because there are fewer children to know, but also because at one time or another the teachers will have taught them all over a sustained length of time. Thus, while a rural teacher will undoubtedly give first priority to her own class, it is also likely that she will have a wider sense of relationship across the pupil range. Tessa, one of the teachers in the rural school study mentioned earlier, indeed suggests that the range of relationship reaches out beyond the immediate confines of the school:

> 'You have more continuity with the relationship because you see the families. Although children leave your class and others come, you can stay in touch with whole families. And families are interconnected as well in a small village, many of them. So actually we are talking in many instances about families who are well known to staff who have been at the school for some time and see through a whole generation.'

The implications of a more extended bond between teacher and children are considerable for, if teachers come to share it across the school, the effect could well be a widening of what they choose to define as their professional endeavour. A further consequence could be an eroding of the insulating barriers between teachers which spring from the conventional 'my class/the school' dichotomy.

A further factor, dependent upon how the rural headteacher sees his role, can also influence the extent to which his teachers see themselves merely as agents of his professional will, or as partners in a joint enterprise. Not infrequently, headteachers maintain authority over their staffs by the gatekeeping role which they take on, for example by insisting on the rule that parents must observe a strict protocol when visiting the school and also by choosing only to divulge such parental information as they think teachers should know. That kind of behaviour is strictly within the 'my school' headteacherly tradition. Rural headteachers, because of the practitioner component of their role, face a problem in this respect. If they are to meet their teaching commitment in full measure, they must devolve some of the head-teacher role on to their colleagues. To the extent that such devolution occurs, whether as a result of a pragmatic decision or from philo-sophic intent, the effect can be to give teachers a greater stake in the school. With respect to the matter of parental consulations, Neil, the headteacher mentioned earlier, makes his position clear:

> 'In schools I've worked in before (urban schools) most rela-tionships have tended to be formalized through the head-teacher and the secretary and meetings with parents have been formalized through that system. Here it is an expectation that

people will negotiate directly with the classteacher. I mean, a teaching head for a start doesn't have time to take on all that role. Now, I take it on in one or two specific cases where I think the parents like to feel it's important enough for the headteacher to be involved but I much prefer it not to be the case and I think the teachers do as well'.

Pat, his lower junior teacher, conveys her view of the difference between the more formalized arrangements of her previous urban school and the more participant arrangements of her present school:

'Even though the last school was not huge, there were many more official channels to be taken but here they (parents) can just walk into the classroom while they are waiting for the children. They can have a chat'.

Substantially to this point, our discussion has centred upon the way in which traditions, organizational structure and the interpretation of professional roles can act to influence teacher isolation. Schools are, however, more than the sum of those three features. They are places where people come together day by day, share experiences and create informal group cultures which may also influence the isolation of teachers. This we turn to now.

The Informal Culture of Schools

When a group of people meets regularly over long periods of time they generate their own particular informal culture. Because the people in the group share common experiences, they come to possess a shared view of them. A family, for example, establishes particular patterns of behaviour around when, how and what, it prefers to eat, and it generates norms with regard to how the young, the old and the sexes should relate. It comes to a mind about what it is appropriate to talk about and places taboos on some words and some topics of conversation. Little rituals spring up around birthdays and festivals and in-jokes are invented which are beyond the comprehension of outsiders. All of these features amount to the culture of the family, sustaining it as a group, keeping members in line and affirming its way of life as worthwhile.

School staffs too, create their own distinctive informal cultures as a result of their day-to-day work. They come to share views of what constitutes a good and a bad pupil, what counts as proper classroom control and how the catchment area is to be viewed. Taboos generate around potential topics of conversation — ('Oh, she's going to lecture us about X again') and little rituals are established such as the provision of cakes by staff members on their birthday, or a glass of sherry on the last day of term. The informal culture of a school staff is, of course, created out of the many activities and incidents of the school's life. However it is principally celebrated in the haven of the staffroom where, away from pupils and out of sight of other non-professional eyes, teachers can discourse freely. It is here that the possibility exists for the insulation, created by their formal roles and the school's organization, to be cast aside so that teachers can offset their classroom isolation by sharing common concerns. To some extent this occurs. Primary staffrooms are places where administrative detail is exchanged, awkward pupils and their exploits figure and information is exchanged on such things as pupils' backgrounds. This, however, is only part of the scene for predominately, personal out of school activities are retailed and in-jokes are prominent.

The general impression we possess of urban primary staffrooms is of a lighthearted atmosphere in which wry good humour about common problems creates a 'We're all in the same boat' comradeship. Wood's (1980) depiction of the teacher strategy of 'morale boosting', in which jokes about shared difficulties are to the fore, conveys the sense of staffroom life, as does Hartley's identification of a very similar strategy used by his Scottish primary teachers which amounted to 'the expression of humorous analyses of the school — the 'black comedy' theme'. That sense of staffroom culture is also evident in the comments made by the teachers in the study by Nias, referred to previously. Whilst they claimed a readiness to talk about professional matters, they also identified the problem of colleagues who 'never talk about anything but football and the price of detergent', or who 'won't ever get involved in discussion of educational ideas.' Staffrooms do not seem to be places where deep discussion of professional problems occurs.

Hoyle and Bell (1972) in considering the professional autonomy of teachers, comment on how their classroom privacy 'is supported by professional norms which emphasize the non-interference of colleagues in the activities of the teacher'. The wider aspects of such non-interference is indicated by Hartley's observation of how the primary school staff which he studied, handled differences in their professional views:

> '. . . a facade of harmony prevailed among the teachers and the
> headteacher. In the main, teachers took their ideology into

their respective classrooms. They were rarely explicitly stated in public. Teachers who dissented from [the headteacher's] ideology were able to preserve their autonomy in professional matters though not in administrative ones'. (p151)

It is that inclination to avoid a public sharing of beliefs and problems and to create an impression of professional concord which McPherson (1972), an American researcher, sees as the basis of what she terms 'the ideology of non-interference'. On the basis of her study of teacher-teacher interaction, particularly in relation to staffroom talk, she suggests that teachers create powerful norms which place limits upon the kind of professional conversation which is permissible. She regards the ideology of non-interference as serving a number of social functions, not least of which are those to do with keeping teachers in line with common views and diminishing the possibilities of friction and competition. Taboos within the ideology work against teachers recounting episodes of success which might implicitly betoken the inferiority of colleagues. Equally, sincere cries for help can be met with light hearted responses which hide the shared nature of problems. ('Oh him. I tried a whole year and got no-where at all.')

In McPherson's view, whilst the ideology of non-interference may fulfil a peace-keeping function, it also contributes to teacher isolation because it frustrates teacher cooperation on difficult problems. Just as the ideology of non-interference may act to put down a bumptious teacher, so it can seal off the problem which all face individually but which none wishes to acknowledge collectively. Further, the ideology of non-interference may help to create cultural interpretations of difficulties which locate the roots of general problems elsewhere. As King (1978) found, infant teachers generate firm home background theories which serve to explain difficult pupils ('They're all thick in Dock Street') thus protecting the teachers' views of their practice by placing the cause of the problem beyond their control.

For McPherson:

'Talk among teachers tended to be light, superficial and rarely serious. One teacher listened only sporadically and half-heartedly to another ... Many conversations hardly touched upon school matters. Those that did rarely focused on teaching methods, educational philosophy, or the content of class material'. (p73)

Webb, commenting on the influence of the ideology of non-interference has this to say:

'It increases the insularity of teachers, protects their classroom autonomy, lessens conflict and promotes teacher solidarity ... By refusing to reveal their insecurities about education, they maintain a front of self-reliance. By refusing to discuss fundamental questions about education, they guard themselves against criticism from colleagues'. (p256)

He concludes:

'... this superficiality does not give teachers the feedback they need in order to know how they are doing. It hinders the development of worthwhile aims, substitutes apparent camaraderies for real community and leaves teachers fundamentally alone and apprehensive'. (pp256–7)

A question to consider is the extent to which the ideology of non-interference is, so far as the internal functioning of schools is concerned, more of an urban than a rural phenomenon. This is a difficult question to face because of the lack of information on the informal culture and relationships found in small rural schools. Here, we can offer only a limited illumination from the small scale study on which we have already drawn.

Relationships and Informal Culture in the Small Rural School

A striking feature of all the three schools in that study was the way in which the teaching, administrative and domestic personnel resembled a face-to-face primary group. Although the headteacher and teachers were at the top end of such overall hierarchy as existed, what was much more apparent was the informal nature of relationships between all the personnel. A second feature of some importance was the fact that the non-teaching staff were all from the communities which the schools served. This circumstance was due in part to the low levels of pay which made it uneconomic for them to seek such work at any greater distance. The combination of informal relationships between the teaching staff and these members of the community created a forum of easy exchange from which the teachers gained a great deal of knowledge about the community and their pupils' families. Mary, headteacher of one of the three-teacher schools explained it like this:

'You get overlapping relationships in villages ... I suppose with a smaller staff you are closer. In the town schools, I hardly knew the dinner ladies except just to say good morning to and to pass the time of day. Here you feel you really know them to talk to. They are a good liaison between the school and the community'.

Another factor, apparent in all three schools was the marked absence of confrontation between teacher and pupils, or between pupils. When this observation was presented to the teachers for comment, they were quick to assert that they did sometimes experience control problems, almost as if one could not be a proper teacher without them. Pat, as she compared her previous service in larger schools with her current school, attributed the present positive relationships not to her own skill, but to the cooperative nature of the children:

'There isn't any conflict is there? I remember in my previous schools you'd always have to watch that particular boy get up from his chair when he went to change his maths card to make sure that he didn't do something on the way, or that he is likely to upset people at the back or disappear for ten minutes. Here, they are very helpful to one another . . . they very rarely come to me when they can't find something. They'll go to another child who obviously knows where it is because he's been using it and he'll say, "Come on, I'll show you"'.

In Tessa's view, it was the fact that the teachers in a small school could know all the children, which worked against the development of control problems. For her: 'Control isn't a pre-occupation at all'.

What seemed to be evident, because of the links which the staffs of all three schools possessed with their localities, was that the teachers felt no sense of isolation from the community. The communities were not largely anonymous catchment areas about which one gleaned only fragments of information. Equally teachers were untroubled about the control aspect of their relationship with pupils. In these two respects, Skinner would seem to be correct when she observes of rural teachers that they '. . . may not suffer from the stresses and problems of inner city school . . .' Also, it would seem that the absence of pressures endemic to larger schools created conditions in which the teachers could engage in professional exchange. Pat, again reflecting on her previous experience in a larger school recognizes a personally imposed condition which isolated her and, in a further comment, identifies the possibility her present school offers:

'Before, I used to isolate myself because — I don't know — perhaps I felt the pressure more. I had a good number of books to mark and I didn't used to move out of my classroom until twenty-past one and we'd all meet in the staffroom for a quick cup of coffee and a quick chat. You never seemed to see anyone — the whole thing seemed to be so rigidly controlled'.

And,

'I think you are much more isolated in larger schools. I thought it was going to be one of my problems when I came here. I thought it would be difficult to cope with the people who are always around, always moving through my classroom. I thought I would be screaming and tearing my hair out. And yet the whole thing seemed perfectly natural. It's lovely to sit around at lunchtime and talk to people about what you are doing and to exchange ideas and to discuss difficulties you've come across. It's so natural'.

Tessa too, identifies how the absence of the directive pressures of the larger school makes possible a more open staff dialogue in the small school:

'There's more direction in larger schools. You can be more informed in curriculum in a small school. We talk together all the time about what we are doing — we don't have formal meetings but we talk about our teaching in the lunch hour, just the three of us'.

Neil, reacting to the suggestion of the rural school creating isolation, also asserts a greater possibility of professional openness:

'It's untrue because professional isolation at an individual level in the classroom unit in a large school can be immense and classroom autonomy can be defended with a great deal of hostility. In our situation, there's a certain amount of classroom autonomy but we know far more of what is going on in each other's classrooms in a three-teacher school because we talk about a large number of matters just on a day-to-day basis — on informal matters, curriculum and individual children'.

Evidence from field notes across the three schools, which were gathered prior to interviewing the teachers, indicate that the teachers' claims of easy professional dialogue were not merely observer-pleasing assertions. Lunchtime talk, untroubled by organizational politics or morale boosting, was directed at teaching concerns. Field-notes on lunchtime activity record such things as a discussion on computer use in which the school secretary (a computer buff) made a major contribution, a reviewing of recorded television programmes and consideration of their use, a pooling of ideas for the planning of an environmental studies topic and a discussion of children's progress, together with the compilation of materials which would aid them. Planning for the integration of a child with special needs was carried forward. Discussion was notably free of negative perceptions of children or of their home circumstances.

Manifestly in this small scale study, there were few signs that the ideology of non-interference was present in these three schools. A number of factors may have contributed to this. Certainly all three heads gave evidence of full commitment to the teaching component of their role and the teachers regarded their responsibilities as wider than those of their own classroom. Moreover they were easy about the presence of each other in their classrooms and relationships with pupils, parents and community posed few threats to their professional sense of well-being. It would be difficult, on the evidence of this study, to suggest that any of the three schools was characterized by internal teacher isolation. More apparent was a cooperative readiness to share, and to take on board, each other's curriculum problems.

That said, it is important to note the problems which the teachers identified in the setting of their small schools. They recognized how the small school, with the amount of peripatetic help reduced from former levels, created a considerable curriculum challenge. The overarching task which concerned them was that of developing and maintaining a curriculum comparable in breadth and quality to that of schools three and four times their size. Confident in their professional and pupil relationships, the teachers saw the task of curriculum generation as their foremost concern. In one sense, both the size of the task and a feeling of responsibility to the small colleague group appeared to be a motivating factor in attending in-service courses. Pat seemed to represent this orientation:

> 'Funnily enough, I find that I have become involved with more [in-service] things since I've been here, because I feel more need. There are so few of you to carry the burden that you feel you must keep in touch. Something I haven't felt before'.

It must be remembered that rural teachers, because their classes contain two or more age ranges must, over much of their curriculum, plan a longer cycle of activities than that required by a class teacher in a larger school, where responsibility is limited to a single age span. For example, if one's class contains a three-year age span, then necessarily, one needs a wider selection of literature, poetry and music, in order to avoid repetition. Equally, if an environmental study of the local church is made, it cannot be easily repeated until one's class consists entirely of new members. The rural teachers whom we are considering all had a clear view of the time scale within which they worked. In the strongly sequential curriculum elements, for example, mathematics and the teaching of reading, they had evolved, in collaboration with their colleagues, planned frameworks of books and equipment to ensure progress and continuity. In other parts of the curriculum too, they possessed schemes which took account of the extended age range of their class.

The part of their task which the teachers saw as more demanding than that of the teacher with a single age class, related to the range of small scale day-to-day activities which are the tiny vehicles of cirriculum transmission. For example, whereas, at that traditional point of the primary school year, the Christmas season, the urban teacher can make use of last year's craft activities, the rural teacher must avoid doing so. Just as these rural teachers used their urban experience as a reference point from which they gauged the advantages of their present setting, so they used it to identify a practitioner problem. This centred around what is often called 'tips for teachers' — small ideas which provide the fuel for day-to-day activities. When the teachers talked of their problems by reference to their previous urban experience, the sense of how such ideas were acquired in that context was not so much that they were gained from discussion as from what was to be observed 'on the walls'. In the following comments, that sense of 'seeing' rather than 'talking' is evident, and indeed, Mary appears to intimate that the acquisition of ideas almost amounts to a breach of classroom privacy:

'You don't get the ideas rubbing off as you could by walking past twelve or fourteen classrooms. You know — you have a peep'. (Mary)

'If you are in a large school you can wander round and see what's on the walls of people's classrooms and think — that's a good idea'. (Margaret)

'I suppose in a large school you see lots more ideas around. It's a problem with regard to ideas. It does help if you can talk about ideas. If you are going to do a project and another teacher has done it before, they can suggest ideas. We do here. Joan was doing a space project last term and I was able to suggest ideas, but there are only two of us'. (Elizabeth)

The sensation, which these comments convey of the problem represented in the search for small scale ideas with which to nourish the overall curriculum, seems both to represent the kernel of such isolation as these teachers experience, and to offer a beginning point for overcoming it.

Teacher Isolation: A Reflection

The phenomenon of teacher isolation is influenced by a variety of factors. The individualistic nature of teaching, the doubts which a teacher possesses of her professional self-worth, or the commitment which she gives to her class may all, singly or in combination, cause her to turn inwards upon her own practice. What might cause her to turn outwards? How the school is organized, how the headteacher defines his role and how the professional expertise of the staff is tapped, as we have seen, are problematic and at the mercy of tradition, interpretations of classroom autonomy and the extent to which the informal culture of the school incorporates the ideology of non-interference. Because of such complexities, it is not possible to spotlight the urban primary school as an institution possessing mechanisms which automatically prevent teacher isolation. If the relationships any given urban school contains do not foster genuine professional dialogue, then a form of reclusiveness is possible. In circumstances of that kind, the only advantage which the urban teachers might possess over the rural teacher is an amplified array of 'ideas' to 'pick up' or 'see'.

For the rural school too, reclusiveness is a possibility. In the three schools we have discussed, the absence of problems to do with the community context and with pupil control seemed to free the teachers from those familiar anxieties and allowed them to focus their attention upon the core of the teacher's professional life: the curriculum and its transmission. There is little doubt that three other rural schools could be found in which the absence of threat from the external environment and from the pupils could engender a cosy and unquestioning tranquility and foster restricted professionalism. The three schools we have considered were ones in which the teachers were aware of their colleagues' work, shared a purpose wider than their individual classroom and possessed informal cultures in which professional matters could be discussed. That the teachers were not internally isolated was due, beyond all other factors, to the nature of their relationships. A single incompatible teacher, or a head practising to be headteacher of a large primary school, could have severed the delicate threads of co-operation which held the staff of each school together. The first and crucial antidote to the internal isolation of the small rural primary school is the presence of ordinary human relationships which mesh with an interpretation of the headteacher's role admitting the participation of the teachers in forming and pursuing the purposes of the school.

In this chapter, we have sought to probe the assumptions which underly the rural stereotype in respect of teacher isolation. In doing so, we have attempted to show that urban policy makers, rather like the urban visitors to the Cumbrian inn, may be in error in believing not only that isolation is inevitably a feature of rural life, but also that large-scale urban institutions automatically prevent it. It is also apparent that, in our view, given the presence of positive relationships, rural teachers may be less isolated from their immediate colleagues than are many teachers in urban schools. However, overcoming teacher isolation in its wider aspect is not just a matter of satisfactory relations within schools; it pertains also to the kinds of stimulation and refreshment which can only be obtained by professional contact beyond the school itself. So far as that wider contact is concerned, it is a fact of life for rural teachers that, as Skinner suggests, access to centres of in-service education is more difficult for them than it is for their urban peers. A further problem too, for the rural teacher may be that the in-service education provided at such centres may be structured and premised upon the needs of urban, rather than rural, schools. (As one rural teacher remarked to us, 'In-service education! They all seem to assume that you're teaching in a big city middle school.')

We will be considering the provision of in-service education for rural teachers more extensively in chapter 9, and we do not propose to dwell upon it here, other than make one observation. A trick of the Victorian moral value system was to decry the general ignorance and squalor of the lower orders, whilst at the same time avoiding acknowledgement of responsibility for the social order which created the conditions in which they flourished. A similarly questionable moral trick occurs when a policy maker, who has given little thought to the appropriateness of the in-service education for which he has responsibility, casts the professional isolation of the rural teacher fatalistically, as a condition induced by rural circumstance. The plausibility of that trick depends upon the extent to which it is possible to overlay the rural stereotype with the urban stereotype and get away with it.

Chapter 6

The Curriculum of the Small Rural Primary School

In the last decade, the curriculum that is presented to pupils has been brought to the very centre of public debate about the quality of schooling. This interest in what is actually taught in schools has been fuelled by an unprecedented flow of documents from the DES and the Inspectorate and the proper importance attached to the curriculum is indicated by the Inspectorate's definition in *Curriculum from 5 to 16:*

> 'A school's curriculum consists of all those activities designed or encouraged within its organizational framework to promote the intellectual, personal, social and physical development of its pupils'. (HMI, 1985a, para 11)

Clearly the curriculum can be seen as the essence of whatever benefits pupils derive from their experience of schooling. It follows, therefore, that the charge that, in a small rural primary school, this is liable to be narrow and restricted, is the most serious one that can be levelled against such schools.

The indictment is, as we saw in chapter 2, relatively recent, and part of the explanation for it lies in the fact that public and professional expectations for what a primary curriculum ought to contain have expanded immeasurably over the years. The list of subjects to be covered as far back as the 1905 *Handbook of Suggestions* may look substantially the same as that which appears in current documents from the DES, but there the similiarity ends[1]. The terms used are the same but they conceal a remarkable extension in what a pupil is expected to encounter, to know and to be able to do. Bolton (1985) puts it neatly:

> '. . . the best practice in primary and secondary schools reveals a depth of study, learning and degree of competency in chil-

dren that would not have been thought possible thirty years ago'. (p205)

That is true, but because the normal pattern of primary school organization is that of the general class teacher, it must follow that meeting the demands of a very much wider curriculum is a burden which has fallen upon all teachers across those thirty years.

Although some specialist teaching does take place and some teachers do swap their class for limited periods, most children between the ages of 5 and 11 receive most of their instruction for most of the time at the hands of their classteacher. This is so, regardless of the size of the school. The expectation that teachers should provide a broader curriculum has affected the climate in which primary school teachers work, regardless of the size of the school. So, if small schools are singled out for particular concern, we might reasonably ask if there is any clear-cut evidence which indicates that the curriculum they offer is narrower than that in large schools.

Evidence on the Quality of the Curriculum

Since January 1983 reports following formal inspections of schools by HMI have been available for public scrutiny. These published reports, although they cannot be presumed to represent a carefully selected cross-section of schools, are nonetheless an obvious source of data since the inspections have included schools of all sizes. We have examined all those published to date that are based upon inspections of schools with less than 100 pupils on roll and compared them with a sample of reports on larger schools. In all of them there are references to the curricular issues which have figured so prominently in the recent debate — the scope of the curriculum, evidence of planning for continuity within the school, the kinds of learning demands that are made upon pupils — but we found it impossible to detect any association between school size and the judgment made by HMI on the quality of the school's educational programme. On the basis of the criteria used by the Inspectorate, excellent schools and mediocre ones seem to come in all sizes. You can encounter warm praise such as the followings statements, not necessarily in order, one from a report on a two-teacher school and another from a report on a school with over 500 pupils:

> 'The children are attentive and enthusiastic in their work: they are offered a broad and generally well balanced curriculum and

they achieve sound standards of performance overall with particularly pleasing standards in numeracy and literacy'.

and,

'Studies cut across subject area with information being factually recorded and also used in a number of ways that included imaginative writing, drama, drawing from direct observation of artefacts and model making. Pupils of all age groups were able to discuss their work in an intelligent and interested way and made good use of books of information'.

You will also find more critical comments such as the following, again not necessarily in order and again from reports on a two-teacher school and a very much larger one:

'A considerable amount of the work is narrowly conceived with work cards, text books and television programmes used in a way which provides insufficient challenge. There is a need to consider ways in which children's experience can be made a focus of work through a more stimulating environment and more regular use of the immediate locality'.

and,

'It [the school] is less successful in making appropriate demands on the children in terms of the increasing range and complexity of ideas and experiences which could be provided through the curriculum. It needs to create more opportunities for the children to express their own ideas, whether in movement, drama, art and craft, science, English or other areas'.

Open any report on an individual school, selected at random, and you are unlikely, so far as its comments upon curriculum quality are concerned, to have much idea of its size.

This conclusion is supported by the periodic reviews produced by HMI which summarize the major themes to have emerged from their individual inspections.[2] Those issued to date contain no indication that the size of primary schools is in any way significantly related to the quality of their curricula.

The Aston University (1981) research team was concerned to appraise the breadth of the curricula in the rural schools in its sample. As with HMI inspections, we cannot assume the sample to be nationally representative, but nevertheless, it found little evidence to substantiate the view that the curricula were restricted:

'The fears often expressed about the limited curriculum of small schools received very little support from the visits, except in the case of science, which is a weakness in primary education by no means restricted to small schools. Music, one of the two subjects generally considered difficult to provide for, had good provision in all the schools and was quite outstanding in one ... Physical education, the other subject area most often regarded as difficult to provide for, was not seriously restricted, except in one school'. (p34)

In addition to commenting on individual schools, HMI also report on the work of individual local authorities. These entail full inspections of a few schools and a briefer survey of a larger number of schools considered to be representative of the authority's provision. Looking at these, we again see diverse perceptions. The report on Norfolk (HMI, 1984c) firmly rehearsed the view that the curriculum in a small rural school is likely to be restricted although, on the basis of the Inspectors' observation, there was considerable variation:

'Over a third of the [primary] schools in the survey had fewer than sixty pupils on roll. It is difficult for such small schools with only two or three staff and limited resources, to provide curricular of breadth and intellectual stimulation but to their great credit some were managing to do so'. (para 39)

Comparing the quality of the curriculum in small and large primary schools, HMI concluded:

'... there was good work in some very small schools and poor work in larger ones. Nevertheless, within the variation that exists in the primary sector, the majority did not offer the breadth of curriculum present in the larger primary and middle schools and which all children and their parents can reasonably expect'. (para 113)

However, when we turn to another Inspectorate report on an equally rural part of Britain, Inverness-shire, (Scottish Education Department, 1974), the primary schools emerge in a quite different light:

'Pupils are lively, responsive, knowledgeable and industrious and join, regardless of age, in art and craft activities, outdoor expeditions, and discussing and writing about subjects of common interest, all without detriment to progress in basic skills. There is no doubt that the atmosphere of intimacy among staff, pupils and parents which exists in the one to four-teacher schools is a contributing factor in the success of those which have adopted these desirable approaches to primary education'. (p22)

It is possible that these different conclusions stem from differing procedures used by the two sets of Inspectors or that they indicate real differences between the two authorities. The one major project[3] that has investigated the breadth of the curriculum in small schools has yet to publish its results, but the Director of the project has indicated to us that substantial variations were found between the nine local authorities from which the sample of schools was drawn. Within any one authority there were substantial differences to be found in the breadth of curriculum in large schools just as there were in small schools. Overall, there were few differences of any significance between the large schools and the small schools.[4]

An alternative source of data might be sought from measures of pupil achievement in different sized schools, on the assumption that this would be a reflection of the quality of curricula and teaching programmes. Such data are not easy to come by, but, as we have seen in chapter 4, what limited material there is does not lend much credence to the view that achievement is associated with size of school. The paucity of comparative data was encountered in the OECD/CERI survey of rural educational provision in developed countries. Reliable information was found to be generally limited and absent altogether from some of the participating countries. Thus, Sher (1981) comments:

'There are bits and pieces of evidence that students in rural schools do as well as or even slightly better than urban students on basic literacy and mathematical tests. Other reports give the impression that rural student attainment is below average across the board, particularly in the less well-developed OECD nations'. (p50)[5]

No definitive conclusion could be drawn.

One judgment that did emerge forcefully from the survey, however, was that the quality of small rural schools was enormously variable. Because of the small size of their staff, they become highly sensitive to the personal and professional qualities of their teachers, more so than larger schools. Some of the best and some of the worst primary education in developed countries is probably to be found in small schools in their rural areas. This, as we have seen, is rather the view that the Gittins Report took; it is implicit in the various reports of HMI and it chimes with the commonsense view of many parents who repeatedly say, 'It all depends on the teacher'.

On the basis of the evidence that is publicly available to date, it is only possible to conclude that the general case against small rural schools is unproven. What, therefore is the cause of the concern? To answer that satisfactorily, we need to consider in more detail the perceived deficiencies in primary education in general and the kind of remedial action that has been proposed by the central authorities.

Deficiencies in the Primary Curriculum

An appropriate place to begin is with *Primary Education in England* (HMI, 1978), the report of HMI's survey of 1127 classes in 542 English primary schools which were selected as a representative national sample. The anxieties which the Inspectorate express stem from their observations of the work in those classes, which was often judged to have been over-narrow in its scope, with too much concentration on the teaching of basic skills in isolation from the remainder of the curriculum. Teachers, in considerable numbers, were depicted as having difficulties in selecting and properly utilizing subject content in both science and the humanities. In many areas it was felt that there was a need for written guidelines which would point out clearly demarcated sequences of learning and thereby avoid the fragmentation and repetition that were reported as being common features of the curriculum in many schools. Frequently pupils, especially those regarded as being most able, were considered to have been presented with work that was insufficiently demanding. These features of schooling were seen as being general — not the exclusive property of small schools — and the concerns about them reappeared in later Inspectorate reports on first schools and middle schools (HMI, 1982, 1983). Bolton (1985) summarizes the problem thus:

> 'The key question relating to these curricular issues raised by *Primary Education in England* is that of how to make the best uses of the curricular strengths of all the teachers. Essentially this question is about the balance between class teaching and the use of specialists in some form or other'. (p212)

The question, in other words, is not simply about having a certain minimum number of teachers in each school because that in itself offers no guarantees about the quality of its curriculum. As Bolton identifies it, the question is about how a mechanism can be found that will harness the skills and knowledge of the whole staff to improve the curriculum throughout the entire school. It is a search directed towards a future strategy that will enable real curriculum development to occur.

A Strategy for Curriculum Development

The policy, which successive publications from the central authorities have refined, envisages the establishment of a national curriculum framework to bring about fundamental changes in education as it is provided and received in the state system. Plainly stated in *Better Schools,* it is to accomplish a 'substantial and sustained improvement [because] the standards now generally attained by our pupils are neither as good as they can be, nor as good as they need to be if young people are to be equipped for the world of the twenty-first century'. Explicit in the framework is the view that the aims of compulsory education between the ages of 5 and 16 should be common to all pupils, should be related both to their needs and to national priorities and should command general agreement. The curriculum designed to reflect these aspirations should be broad, balanced, relevant and differentiated and should be capable of translation into objectives for each of its areas which will also achieve broad assent.

At local authority level, these objectives are expected to be formulated into sets of written guidelines which identify the knowledge, concepts and skills that are to be acquired by the pupils, in an orderly and predictable progression, in the authority's schools. This, it is anticipated, will help to ensure coherence in curriculum delivery and continuity within and between schools. It is also hoped that it will go some way towards eliminating the unacceptably wide variation that HMI report finding between one school and another.

Within each school, two mechanisms are seen as being critical for the successful implementation of this national framework: curriculum development is perceived as involving all members of staff, a 'joint enterprise of the staff as a whole' as it is expressed by the Inspectorate (HMI, 1985a and 1985b); secondly, teachers designated as having a special responsibility for specific areas of the curriculum are required to become more effective. Together, these two aspects of school organization constitute what is meant by 'making the best uses of the curricular strengths of all the teachers'.

The national framework has many of the utopian characteristics which Sockett (1976) associates with 'grand design' programmes of curriculum reform and in this respect, it is reminiscent of Hadow's glimpse of an educational utopia to be brought about through streaming by ability. Like all such designs, it seeks a thorough reappraisal; it begins with such fundamental questions as to what the aims of contemporary schooling might be and how they can be harnessed to national priorities in a technological age. In staunchly rational fashion, it identifies the ends sought and articulates the means judged to be best suited to their attainment. As Sockett puts it:

> 'Part of the utopian suggestions entail detailed specification of objectives derived from general aims'. (p36)

What is more, the programme is imperative in its demand for serious attention. In fact, the single-minded determination, and at times, barely disguised impatience, with which it has been driven forward by the central authorities has surprised many teachers.

But any national plan, if it is not to become immediately redundant, requires some measure of control of the variables on which it is premised, in part, this means the teachers, because it is they in their classrooms who, in the end, shape whatever success a programme of curriculum development will enjoy. Although the proposals contained within the framework do not entail anything so uniform as a centrally determined syllabus, they do, by their nature, imply some curtailment of the classroom autonomy which individual teachers have traditionally experienced and which has been one of the distinguishing features of British primary education. The closely interrelated strategies of guidance by subject specialists and whole-staff planning across the entire curriculum and age range imply some restriction in that tradition of teachers operating individualistically within the privacy of their own classrooms. It is here that we see the alleged structural weakness of small rural schools when measured against the requirements of the national framework. In particular, they lack an adequate cast of supporting members — the school is not large enough to contain a necessary range of specialists. It is, therefore, to the role of the curriculum specialist in primary schools, briefly touched upon in the previous chapter we will first turn.

The Curriculum Specialist

In none of the recent curriculum documents that have been issued by the central authorities has there been a clear indication as to how much specialist teaching ought to take place in primary schools beyond the injunction in *Better Schools* that it should be systematically introduced to older pupils, and the Senior Chief Inspector's widely publicized view that it should not occur with children below the age of 9.[6] In a number of recent reports, the Inspectorate claim evidence that specialist postholders have been able to exert a beneficial influence throughout their school. Where this occurred, instances were reported of collaborative planning, better standards of pupils' work and a more accurate matching of teacher expectations and pupil ability, Yet overall, the picture which emerges from these observations by HMI is a pessimistic one. Only in a minority of cases was the specialist seen as being effective in these ways and in making a significant impact on the school's curriculum.

> 'In the remaining schools [i.e. 75 per cent] there was little evidence that the influence of teachers with curricular responsibilities spread beyond the work in their own classes'. (HMI, 1978, para 4.5)

> 'Too often, however, the role of the teacher with responsibility in this important part of the curriculum [mathematics] was limited to the production of guidelines or checklists or even, as with the equally important area of language, solely to the provision and organization of teaching material'. (HMI, 1982, para 3.21)

It has to be remembered that the role is a comparatively recent innovation in primary schools. Campbell (1985) shows how it is only in the last two decades, beginning with the first tentative hints in the Plowden Report, that 'some of the major educational documents have transmitted a gradually clarifying image of the responsibility and significance of the curriculum postholder'. That the current influence of postholders is limited to a minority of schools, and even there does not always amount to a great deal ought, therefore, to cause no surprise. Campbell himself takes a somewhat more optimistic view, arguing cautiously that recent studies such as the Birmingham University investigation (referred to in chapter 5) indicates a shift in teachers' ideas about curriculum planning.

That may indeed be the case, but what Campbell's work undoubtedly demonstrates are the problems that are inherent in the demands being made on postholders to instigate and sustain curriculum development, and the fact that these have been consistently understated in the official literature. The job demands a range of complex inter-personal skills without which the most knowledgeable specialist is likely to be ineffectual beyond his own classroom. Campbell emphasizes their importance:

> '[These skills] in addition to demanding considerable charm and character, also required sensitivity and tact, and a number of headteachers made the point that such *personal qualities* in the postholders were prerequisites for the successful implementation of the development. Even an apparently simple task such as giving advice to a colleague informally in the staffroom had to be done without seeming to patronize'. (p58)

It is always possible that reorganizing a school, previously run according to the principle of generalist class teachers working independently, so as to strengthen the authority of curriculum specialists will merely bring about more impersonal forms of social relationships, rather than the professional cooperation which the Inspectorate intends. Enhancing the competence of the whole staff through the work of curriculum specialists would seem to depend on creating a sense of trust among teachers. It is not a mechanical process based simply on an agreement to whole-school curriculum planning, essential though that is; it demands the kinds of personal and professional relationships which Campbell describes, very aptly, as *collegial*. Without that, it is difficult to see how any postholder can influence the school's curriculum, except at relatively trivial levels. In fact, the effect could be counter-productive as MacLennan (1985) argues in the case of primary school French:

> 'Having set up expectations of specialist competence, the danger is that non-specialists are seen both by themselves and by others as inferior and only marginally competent'. (p2)

These interpersonal complexities in the job are exacerbated by the fact that postholders are usually class teachers with virtually a full-time teaching commitment. Not only does this impose conflicting responsibilities upon them in which the demands of class teaching are likely to be the more immediately pressing, it makes it difficult for them to operate in the context in which they might be thought to be most effective — alongside the other teachers in their classrooms. As Campbell indicates, for the postholder this 'raised questions of priority as well as feasibility'.

We have dwelt upon the matter of the subject specialist in the primary school at some length for a very obvious reason. It is precisely on the grounds that a small rural school is structurally incapable of containing a specialist staff who encompass the full range of the formal curriculum, that it is alleged to be prone to suffer an inadequate and restricted curriculum. That may certainly be a disadvantage, yet it is quite clear that the strategy of implementing curriculum change through the use of subject specialists offers no simple panacea to the general problems of the primary curriculum as they have been identified in reports from central authorities. Linking the award of posts of responsibility to specific areas of the curriculum is one thing; producing significant curricular improvements throughout the schools as a result of it is another matter altogether. Even Campbell's optimism is tempered with a realistic caution and the knowledge born of past experience of curriculum development, which shows that maintaining improvement is often more difficult than establishing the initial impetus. Normally, the proponents of a utopian programme of educational improvement are able to point to evidence that the strategy is effective in the context in which it has been devised and from which it will be exported. Here we have the unusual situation that even those who have championed the strategy have expressed their disappointment at its achievements to date. So, to convict small schools on the charge of curriculum narrowness, because they are structurally inadequate to match a prescription which itself does not yet show evidence of realizing substantial improvement to curricular practice is, to say the least, somewhat premature.

When we turn to the second element in the proposed strategy to improve the quality of the curriculum whole-staff planning, we see how interrelated the two elements are. If curriculum postholders are to be effective beyond the confines of their own classroom and effective in more than trivial aspects of curricular provision, it is clear that they must work in a collegiate atmosphere in which all the staff share some responsibility for the design of the school's curriculum. But with this recognition, we can begin to see small schools in a different light. As we indicated in the previous chapter, the social characteristics of small rural schools (sometimes aided by their architectural peculiarities) lend themselves more easily to the professional openness and exchange of ideas and curricular experiences which collegiality demands. The teachers' practices are often more visible to each other than in larger schools; the headteacher is a practitioner; all of the pupils are likely to be well known by all of the teachers and the smaller scale of the enterprise simply makes it less feasible for teachers to adopt individualistic roles in their own private classroom.

None of this guarantees that cooperative curriculum consultation will take place, still less that the curriculum will be enhanced, any more than the presence of a range of subject specialist postholders in a large school ensures that a broader and better taught curriculum will be made available to all the pupils. The point is simply that joint planning of the curriculum ought to be more easily engineered in a small school and this constitutes a potential strength which is directly comparable to the advantage of having a wide range of specialists which the large school enjoys. It is a point that the official literature has not acknowledged in its assumption that rural schools are endemically weaker in the curriculum they offer.

As we have shown earlier, official judgments on rural schools have tended to emphasize their disadvantages (however they have been perceived at a particular time) rather than any potential advantages they might possess. The alternative to this persistent line of thinking is suggested by Darnell (1981). After quoting a report from the Department of Education of Western Australia which speaks of the State's commitment to 'reduce as far as possible any educational disadvantages that might be derived from living far away from the urban and larger town centres', he goes on to argue that this represents a false approach:

> 'The key to recognizing that we have been coming from the wrong direction is found in the phrase "*reduce* as far as possible any education *disadvantages* ...". Because of our notions of stereotypical rural residents, we often assume the urban model to be the preferred model to which all people aspire. What would we do differently as educationists if this phrase is changed to read "*amplify* as far as possible any educational *advantage* that might be derived from living far away from the urban and larger town centres"?' (p34)

The first thing we would want to do would be to specify what advantages in relation to curriculum there might be.

Curriculum Advantages in Rural Primary Schools

Knowing the Pupils

Foremost among the advantages that can reasonably be claimed for the rural school, because of its location and characteristic size is what is frequently referred to as its 'family atmosphere'. As we saw in the two case studies of closure in chapter 1, this is conceded by those who would, on other grounds, judge a school to be educationally defective. What the metaphor of family atmosphere comprises is the view that the relationships which exist between teachers and pupils are more intimate, more personal and less governed by formal rules regulating behaviour than are typical of larger urban schools. The image of the school as a 'family' is, as King (1978) has pointed out, a dominant one throughout our educational system; even headteachers of large secondary schools endeavour to mobilize the motif. In a small rural primary school it is almost certainly closer to reality. A teacher in a three-teacher rural school drew this comparision with her previous city school experience:

> 'Here it is a much more tightly-knit community — there's so much more of a family atmosphere altogether. Everybody knows everybody else'.

The remark is one of the most commonly heard in relation to the small rural schools. Similarly, the Schools Council (1975) report on rural schools commented:

> 'By far the most significant advantage of the small school from the point of view of the child was the close relationship between pupil and teacher ... Teachers were, for the most part, able to diagnose particular problems and relate them to the child's home and school situation. This awareness, so frequently lacking with the best will in the world in the larger school, is one of the small school's greatest assets'. (p5)

It is this opportunity to know the child more intimately, to know his interests and particular abilities as well as his problems, and to know them in a context far broader than an individual classroom, that commends such schools to many parents. It is this that they have in mind when they speak of 'individual attention' or their child's 'sense of security'. Some of the pupils in Finch's (1986) study were making the same point:

> 'It's good because Mr T has more time for you. He can listen to each one of us in turn'. (Boy, 10–11, Northby)

> 'You get more time and less interruptions. You can just go up there and she sees us. In my last school we had to be called out in groups'. (Girl, Infant, Cailey)

> 'I went to one school with several hundred children. We never got a chance to talk. You just had to do your work, have lunch, do the rest of your work, and go home'. (Boy, 10–11, Northby)

A corollary to this is that ensuring curriculum continuity is a quite different activity, and potentially an easier one, than in the larger school where it has to depend to a greater extent on written records being transferred between teachers at the end of the year. It should also avoid the September syndrome which Bennett *et al* (1984) describe where the pupil's work is dominated at the beginning of the school year by revision tasks as each teacher sets about ascertaining both what her incoming students have achieved in the previous year and what levels of work seem appropriate for them.

The image of a family atmosphere also includes relationships among the pupils. We have argued in chapter 4 that peer groups in small rural schools are less determined by age and gender than in the larger school, where the age graded class becomes the most important regulating factor. This extended peer group of the small rural school provides more numerous opportunities to encourage social and co-operative skills across age ranges. Older pupils assume positions of responsibility more naturally and younger pupils can learn from the interactions between teachers and older pupils which are more visible than in age-graded organizations. In addition, peer relationships tend to be less prone to hostility. This was the observation of a head-teacher, again making the contrast with previous urban experience:

'They live together; they play together. Their grievances are therefore quickly healed. They have to be in this kind of village where everybody knows everybody. It's the same with boy/girl differences; they are more natural. There's no sniggering'.

Another teacher, with experience of rural schools both in this country and in America, seemed to be making the same point when he remarked to us:

'The students in rural schools don't seem to feel the need to prove anything to each other; they can be more themselves'.

It is as if the characteristic of traditional small-scale communities of people dealing with each other, not so much as occupants of particular roles, but as people personally well known to each other infuses the school also.

The comparative ease with which small schools in a rural catchment area are able to form close links with the parents is also one of their major and potentially advantageous characteristics. The Schools Council report commented on this:

'Nearly all teachers spoke of the easy and friendly relationships which a small school staff were able to establish with parents. Most heads thought a parent-teacher association unnecessary [only eight out of the sixty-five schools in the sample had one] because parents could come and go at any time and this 'family' nature of the school was generally welcomed'. (p4)

This facilitates the movement of information into and out of the school and makes it that much easier to strengthen the continuation of the child's experience across the boundary between his life at school and at home. It also partly accounts for the high measure of support that small rural schools are able to engender in the parents. So Taylor, Chief Education Officer for Somerset remarks:

'A head of one school speaks for many in saying, "Parents feel it is *their* school, teachers are familiar figures"'.

The frequency with which campaign literature up and down the country is dotted with references to 'our school' rather than 'their school' (the latter in the sense of the school the children happen to attend), suggests that that Somerset headteacher does indeed speak for many. The sense of having a real stake in the school can often be demonstrated by the reinforcement that parents give to the work of the teachers. The head of a three-teacher school described to us the interest of the parents in what he called 'the social side of schooling':

'The children knowing right from wrong and valuing their surroundings, having respect for individuals and respect for the community. I think there's an awful lot of that kind of valuing and, if the school is promoting those values in a reasonable way, then I think they are very supportive of the school'.

They are supportive if they see the school promoting those values. We have argued before that the closeness of school-community links makes small rural schools extraordinarily accountable to their public. Probably more than any other type of school in the state system they reflect government aspirations for their policy that schools be sensitive to the legitimate aspirations of the parents of their pupils.

The support that parents frequently offer to rural schools which they value can be demonstrated even more pragmatically, by the considerable financial contribution they have made, in recent years especially, to help under-resourced small schools to purchase books and equipment to buttress the formal curriculum.

But by community, we mean more than just the parents. Other adults living locally can also be supportive in the same moral and financial ways. Taylor again:

'We have in the area many retired people who come to open evenings; are loud in their praise of the work of the children and contribute generously to fund-raising activities'.

Reciprocally, many small schools in the countryside view their community as more than the parents of their pupils. It is a strength of such schools that through the external links they are able to forge and the events they are able to arrange, they make a contribution to the cultural life of their surroundings which is quite disproportionate to their size. This is not only a significant social asset; it is potentially of direct benefit to the pupils, as Addison (1985) indicates:

'When children are educated in a community where people all know each other and where many of the people have roots going back several years, they are more likely to be better understood in that there are more adults than just their immediate family and their teachers who are interested in their growth and development'.

Curriculum Flexibility

A teacher in a three-teacher school, recruited from a much larger suburban school commented to us:

'When you come here, they [pupils] may be doing those same things, science or geography, but it would be almost alien to them to arrange school days in that way — in set time slots. I mean you may be better to go for a long block of time, going for a topic over two or three weeks'.

He was making the comparison with his previous school wherein 'it had become normal practice for teachers to submit their timetables to the year group organizer or for the whole year to be doing the same thing at the same time because of resources'. The considerable flexibility that enables the teacher to organize and to pace the curriculum in a variety of ways is seen by many teachers in small schools as a strength. An obvious advantage is that it permits the teacher to capitalize on the pupils' engagement with the task in hand. As one put it:

'You do organize your curriculum in a different way. It means that you can keep the children's interest for so much longer because if they are involved in what they're doing and it's coming on naturally, they are much more likely to remain interested than if you say, "Time you went to pottery now, the pottery teacher is waiting for you".'

An additional spin-off is that teachers too can focus on one or two aspects of the curriculum at any one time, rather than having to deal with all elements in the course of the day. It also facilitates a curriculum which is less marked by subject division. Plowden's remark that 'pupils do not see the world in separate subjects' is one that continues to be echoed by many primary school teachers. The organizational informality in small rural schools and the curriculum flexibility that this permits does give more scope to their teachers to design a more integrated curriculum. The teacher quoted earlier, who felt his pupils would find a timetable alien, went on to suggest that such a curriculum was rendered more feasible because of the response of the pupils:

'I think there is far more opportunity for the integration of ideas and subjects because they [the pupils] seem to view the world in this way. They appreciate the inter-relatedness of things'.

This is an intriguing idea, that rural children have a different perception of the curriculum and of its relationship with time than urban children. Apart from isolated pieces of research, which appear to show that children raised in remote rural communities display more of a task orientation towards school work as opposed to a more characteristically urban sense of achievement as measured by work done in a set time, we know of no evidence to support this view.[7] Yet it is not implausible. The teacher just quoted, particularly identified children from traditional rural families with this view of knowledge, rather than those whose parents commute to white collar urban occupations, and for these rural children especially, the various elements of the social world they inhabit are more organically related than is the case with children brought up in an urban environment.[8]

Curriculum Differentiation and Participation

An inevitable feature of small primary schools is that classes contain children whose ages span more than one year and this can be seen as a problem for teachers. The Inspectorate, in the 1978 primary survey, reported that teachers in such mixed age classes were definitely less successful in matching the level of difficulty of the work they set to their pupils' capabilities. But 'mixed age class' is not a unitary concept; it covers a multitude of organizational forms, as Bennett and his colleagues (1983) have demonstrated. At one extreme is the situation typically found in a rural school with (say) three teachers where there will be two or three age groups of perhaps equal numbers in each class; at the other extreme the class may consist almost entirely of one age group with only a handful of older or younger pupils which is the situation more often found in those urban schools which experienced sharply falling rolls. Between these two, there are many other variations. HMI's highly generalized conclusion, based as it was upon observations of all manner of mixed age classes, is therefore difficult to interpret.

A more systematic follow-up study by Bennett *et al* (1987), using explicit criteria of matching, albeit on a small sample, found no significant difference between teachers of single age or mixed age classes in their ability to set work of appropriate levels of difficulty. This work was conducted largely in urban areas. The position in small rural schools is different in two respects. Firstly, the pupils stay with the class teacher for more than one year, which we argued in the previous chapter causes them to have to search for material which will not duplicate the pupils' experience. Secondly, this is the normal situation in small rural schools, and part of a tradition, rather than something which has recently been imposed upon the teachers by the pressure of falling rolls. We might therefore anticipate that rural teachers perceive the mixed age presence more favourably.[9] Many of the teachers we have met in rural schools do see the age mix, together with the children's extended time with the same class teacher, as a positive incentive to devise a more individually differentiated curriculum in which pupils will spend more of their time working independently. For such teachers, this represents a real advantage, as the head of a three-teacher school explained:

'You've got to build a completely different way of working. They've got to be more independent. To do that, you've got to take on a different approach. I am convinced there is a whole philosophy that is part of a rural village school and it affects the curriculum and it affects the way in which children work and it affects relationships within the school and outside it. At the heart of it is a notion of children being able to work independently, able to work autonomously'.

In part, the perceived advantage of having to arrange more individualized curricula and then permitting children to work more independently in a mixed age class may be dependent on having a relatively small class. The smaller number of pupils compensates for their greater age range. That was the case with the teacher quoted above, and is true of many (but by no means all) rural schools. Another teacher of a class which contained a three-year spread took just this view. There were, she said, 'only twenty-two in the class':

'With a greater number of children I think you teach much more formally and you plan very carefully what you are going to do. You allow for a certain leeway in the follow-up, but particularly in something like science which is very practical, I think perhaps you give up on experimental work earlier than you might do because it is all very difficult. Whereas in this type of school — and I think it's a lot to do with the attitudes of the children — you can let them carry on and you can see that they are getting something from it. There's only twenty two in the class; it's much easier to get around them all and make sure that they are all busy and learning and achieving'.

In the extreme case of the one-teacher school, the need to entrust a greater degree of independence to the pupils extends beyond the formal curriculum, for the entire running of the school hinges upon it. A Scottish teacher, well known to us, who has been working in this circumstance for fifteen years, indicates her thinking as follows:

'I organize my children so that the only thing I have to do is teach'.

A weekly rota is established so that each child is assigned a specific job: tidying the room, checking the playground, collecting and distributing milk, ensuring the television is correctly tuned five minutes before the programme is due and so on, More demanding jobs are allocated on an annual basis to older pupils who are trained by the teacher or by their predecessors; the dinner money, distributing notes to parents, answering the telephone to ensure that the teacher is rarely interrupted while teaching — 'unless it is somebody she knows is important, she is trained to explain that Mrs. S. is busy just now and to ask them to ring back at lunch time'.

> 'So, having organized all that, the actual functioning of the school carries on while I teach'.

There is, of course, nothing in that which could not be done in a larger school and many teachers in larger schools do arrange for their pupils to assume such responsibilities. The one obvious difference is that in the very small school it becomes possible for all the pupils to be *organically* involved. There is no need to invent tasks; all can be given a real task and experience directly and regularly the responsibility it entails. To adapt an analogy we have used before, the larger scale institution is like a play in which there are not enough roles for the number of actors present, while in the small-scale institution, there are often more parts than there are players.

The consequence is a higher degree of participation and this can occur in aspects of the formal curriculum as well. The use of microcomputers is a case in point. We know of many schools in which, often because of local financial support, there is a computer in each of the two or three classrooms which makes possible more regular hands-on experience for the pupils and for the technology to be more readily incorporated into a range of curricular areas. One teacher in such a situation remarked:

> 'I think it's going to be more easy for us because we work in smaller groups and in an individual way which can bring in computers as part of our everyday system far more than in a large school ... especially if there it is strictly used in maths lessons or a specialist room is set aside'.

Music and team games, paradoxically the two areas of the curriculum that are most frequently cited as likely to be deficient in a small school are, similarly, activities in which a higher proportion of pupils can actually take part because of the total numbers involved. There can be a role for each player. Likewise, French is considered to be a subject which small primary schools are ill-equipped to teach because they usually lack a teacher with specialist skills. Yet, only a few years ago, when French was being strongly advocated for inclusion in the primary curriculum, a study for the National Foundation for Education Research found that pupils in small schools consistently maintained higher levels of achievement than did pupils in larger urban schools. Burstall (1974) reported the finding as being an unexpected one because the classroom conditions were assumed to be inimical to the teaching of the subject with pupils differing widely in age and ability. She concluded:

> 'The possibility remains that the high level of achievement in the small schools stems partly from the heterogeneous nature of their classes. If a given class contains pupils who vary greatly in age and ability, the individual pupil is not in direct competition with others of his own age-group; the concept of a 'standard' of achievement, which a pupil of a given age 'ought' to be able to reach is difficult for either pupil or teacher to acquire. The classroom situation in the small school tends to encourage cooperative behaviour and to lack the negative motivational characteristics of the competitive classroom in which success for a few can only be achieved at the expense of failure for many'. (p31)

As we saw in chapter 4, there is evidence from work on both sides of the Atlantic that small rural schools do have some success in engendering a greater sense of independence in their pupils. The observation made by the Aston University (1981) team is typical of these research findings:

> 'One question which frequently arises when small rural schools are being discussed is how well the pupils were prepared for the secondary education in larger, more distant and sometimes urban-based schools. We had several well-founded reports that secondary schools found them not only as well prepared academically as pupils from other schools but that they generally had a better attitude to work. Having been accustomed to working for much of their time on their own, they could be given more responsibility for the organization of their school work. This question obviously deserves further study'. (p35)

One such focus of further study would be to enquire how it is that some small rural schools can achieve this with their pupils while others do not, because the characteristics we have listed here are, for the most part, no more than *potential* advantages. There are, to be sure, village schools that seal themselves off from their catchment community; there are teachers who act as if their class was a homogeneous single age band, despite the inappropriateness of such a teaching style in such a setting. In short, there is no automatic translation of these inherent advantages into a reality that pupils experience and can benefit from. That much is undeniable, but exactly the same is true of large schools which possess the potential advantage of a wide range of staff expertise. As we have seen and, as is thoroughly acknowledged, that too does not automatically transform the curriculum into a broader and richer experience for the pupils. It is for that very reason that we have the whole thrust of contemporary educational policy in relation to primary schooling. That is to set up a mechanism whereby the potential advantage of having a large staff can indeed be realized. What we are suggesting here is that a similar approach might be adopted towards small rural schools. A strategy which began by assessing their characteristic educational qualities and sought to enhance them, rather than one which subjected them to the utopianism of a blueprint drawn up from an examination of schools operating on an entirely different scale and in a quite different social location would probably stand a better chance of improving the quality of the curriculum they offered.

But then, what do we mean by a curriculum of quality? Even if it is accepted that small schools serving rural areas do have some intrinsic advantages which can be turned to good effect as revealed by the attitude and motivation of their pupils, could it not be said that this is not strictly relevant to an argument about the curriculum? It may be desirable that children should develop a sense of independence and self-confidence but this is an issue quite different from the considerations that are normally applied to a school's curriculum — its breadth, balance, relevance and so on.

It is not difficult to find hints of this in many of the school closure debates. In the two cases we considered in chapter 1, for example, education officers were willing to concede that the village schools in question did offer real advantages such as their 'family atmosphere' and the security that this might convey to young children, but this had to be weighed against the curricular advantages of the larger, alternative school. At the same time, parents protesting against the proposed closures, were citing individual attention and the personal attributes it was thought the small school could bring out in their children as being more important than the breadth of curriculum provided. From both sides, a distinction is implied between the curriculum on the one hand and the entire web of social experiences encountered by the pupil on the other hand. We need a clearer understanding of the term 'curriculum'.

What is the Curriculum?

The conventional view is that it is the list of subjects taught by the teachers to the pupils, yet the Inspectorate's definition cited at the beginning of this chapter explicitly broadens that notion to incorporate all the activities designed 'to promote the intellectual, personal, social and physical development' of the pupils:

> 'It includes not only the formal programme of lesson, but also the 'informal' programme of so-called extra-curricular activities as well as all those features which produce the school's 'ethos', such as the quality of relationships, the concern for equality of opportunity, the values exemplified in the way the school sets about its task and the way in which it is organized and managed'. (HMI, 1985a, para 11)

Here we have a view of the curriculum that is virtually co-terminus with schooling and which thoroughly dissolves the distinction noted above between the curriculum on the one hand, and children's experience of being a pupil on the other. On this account, the curriculum is the totality of the planned experience that children have of their school. HMI repeatedly assert that it is more than merely a list of subjects and indeed, that the more schooling is designed to promote attitudes and capabilities which transcend subject knowledge, the broader the definition has to be.[10]

It is not difficult then to see why the definition adopted by the Inspectorate is so extensive, because so too are the aims that have been heralded for contemporary education. They are catalogued in a series of papers from the DES (and reprinted in *Better Schools*) as follows:

1. to help pupils to develop lively, enquiring minds, the ability to question and argue rationally and to apply themselves to tasks, and physical skills;
2. to help pupils to acquire understanding, knowledge and skills relevant to adult life in a fast-changing world;
3. to help pupils to use language and number effectively;
4. to help pupils to develop personal moral values, respect for religious values, and tolerance of other races, religions, and ways of life;
5. to help pupils to understand the world in which they live, and the interdependence of individuals, groups and nations;
6. to help pupils to appreciate human achievements and aspirations.

This list is repeated (with one variation) in *Curriculum from 5 to 16* as also is the somewhat more elegant expression of the goals of education set down in the *Warnock Report* (HMSO, 1978):

> 'They are, first, to enlarge a child's knowledge, experiences and imaginative understanding and thus his awareness of moral values and capacity for enjoyment; and secondly, to enable him to enter the world after formal education is over as an active participant in society and a responsible contributor to it, capable of achieving as much independence as possible'.

When we survey these aspirations it becomes obvious why 'the curriculum' has been defined so broadly; the difficulty becomes that of knowing how to specify an actual curriculum that could be seen to be a means towards realizing them. In other words, how is a particular school's curriculum to be described if it is intended not only to make its pupils more literate, but also more tolerant of others, not only to extend their knowledge and understanding, but also to make them active, responsible participants in social affairs? Dearden (1981) refer- ring to the DES list does not overstate the case when he says:

> 'But this set of aims was never put to work in any way that was visibly generative of the curricular recomendations that followed'. (p108)

The recommendations that have followed in the various curricu- lum publications from the central authorities have been outlines of the kinds of experiences that pupils might have, largely within the subject areas which have been the traditional school diet, and sets of cognitive objectives for those subjects — what pupils might be expected to know and be able to do at specified ages. The Inspectorate is at pains to point out that subjects need not be taught discretely, in isolation from each other, but even allowing for that, it remains a narrow interpretation of their own definition of a school's curriculum.

To say that is not to denigrate the value of an acquaintance with the broad areas of systematic, intellectual understandings known to man. It is simply to point out that the aspirations for schooling contained in those stated aims carry us beyond that and invite a fresh look at the demands that are made on individuals if they are to become more competent in their social, occupational and personal lives. The aims are not only for what pupils should know, but also *for what kinds of people we want them to be*. We want them to understand their world; we also want them to acquire the will to operate within it, with confidence and perseverance, with respect to others and with a feeling for the communities from which they draw their identity. These are personal qualities for which neither the liberal education championed by the Inspectorate, nor the utilitarianism which flavours some of the DES approaches can be said to be an adequate preparation. Or, to take one of the many possible examples from *The Curriculum from 5 to 16:*

> 'As well as becoming more knowledgeable, pupils need to become wiser and to develop an ability to draw on what they have learnt to help them live their lives more competently and with a sense of fulfilment'. (para 119)

A school's curriculum which aspires towards the development of wisdom needs to be as generous as the Inspectorate's initial definition — the totality of the child's experience of schooling. As an earlier 'curriculum theorist', Thomas Paine, noted: 'Wisdom is not the purchase of a day'.

The problem of how, properly to conceptualize the primary curriculum is not a new one. The Plowden Committee had just as much difficulty. It asserted its commitment to child-centredness, its belief in the value of self-motivation and its conviction that 'children's learning does not fit into subject categories'. Having stated that, it proceeded to analyze the curriculum in terms of separate subject entities. The fact is that articulating the processes whereby a child's total experience of his primary school (the curriculum as he receives it) might engender the personal qualities that are aimed for, is immeasurably more difficult than stipulating objectives. It is an altogether more uncertain business and the temptation is to slide away into a description of the curriculum as areas of content to be covered. The gap is not bridged, except perhaps rhetorically, by adding riders such as 'balanced' or 'relevant' which are open to the widest possible interpretation.

We will return to this problem later in the chapter, but if for the moment, we retain hold of the Inspectorate's broad definition of the curriculum, we might then ask what it would mean to say that the actual curriculum in a small rural school was narrow. To be exact, the question we put to the head of a two-teacher school was, 'How would you defend yourself against those who would claim that your curriculum was restricted'?

'I would tell them to come and look for themselves', he replied. We went the following week.

An Afternoon at Ringby School

For the first hour of the afternoon the school's thirty pupils were divided into five groups of six pupils, each ranging in age from 4½ to nearly 11. Five groups doing five different craft activities for half-a-term and then rotating. It is known as 'the circus'.

The needleworkers consist of two top junior girls, a boy and a girl from the middle juniors and two infant boys; the group is taken by two mothers. Everybody is busy and the atmosphere is relaxed and there is a lot of conversation going on. It is the talk you might hear in any practical session, much of it based on local knowledge that is shared by all. One of the mothers comments to the other that there was some anxiety that morning because the mother who takes the cookery group was having to 'phone around to locate the mother she alternates with to ask her to look after her own child as he 'was down with the "bug"'. An older girl joins in — the "bug" was going the rounds of her family as well. An infant boy is making a puppet flannel for his younger brother and the conversation swings round to this youngster at home who will be joining the school next year. Everybody knows him and the family and has something to contribute to the exchange; nobody looks up from the sewing. Then the other infant is stuck. 'What's the matter, my love?' asks a mother. 'It [an egg warmer in the shape of a chicken] in't got no beak.' She sorts out his grammar and his chicken's beak. The other mother asks across the room, 'We've got a match tomorrow. Is it still on?' She is referring to the netball match with another school. The junior girl explains that it depends on the weather and asks if the mother will be coming. She will be; two teachers' cars, four parents' cars and the whole school can be moved, as they were last week to the museum and last term to visit a nearby potter. As a result of that visit, the school has built a brick kiln with a supply of bricks from one of the fathers.

The older girls are making lace dressing table mats for their mothers. The helper is apologetic about this — 'They're a bit old-fashioned but I had the materials at home.' She also has a friend who runs a dress stop and she is often able to bring in off-cuts. Previously, she explains, the older girls had both made gym skirts for when they move on to the secondary school next year. The mothers are not supervised; the head, Robin, later comments:

'I give the mums the responsibility and then leave them. I do make some inputs. I got some books and some handouts from the County Adviser and left them in the room. One of the mums took them home. I also give her the catalogue so she can make suggestions when it is time for ordering for next year. If you give them responsibility, they rise to it'.

Robin himself is next door with the woodworkers where a variety of articles are being constructed; there is no shortage of raw materials. 'I let the parents know when we are getting low, and it all comes in', he tells us. He also points to the tool rack which contains many such donations. In this session he moves round the room from pupil to pupil, sitting with each in turn, talking with each in turn, helping where needed, asking questions about the different constructions. Throughout it, he carries on a disjointed conversation with an older boy about skyscrapers and the history of New York. A junior girl is sawing her piece of wood clamped in a new vice. 'This is too hard,' she complains. 'You give up too easily', says Robin, without fuss. An infant boy gallantly takes over for a brief spell, but it is too hard for him and the girl perseveres.

This is Robin's room in which he normally takes the junior class with its four-year age spread. The pupils' work that is on the walls and on the side tables is vibrant. There is a shining climbing frame that swings out from one wall, obviously new:

'They weren't very sure about having a climbing frame inside the school at first, but I talked about it at a parents' evening and I got the Adviser in to talk about it. In the end, he contributed half and they contributed half, and then they raised four hundred pounds towards a crash mat. You have to be as open as you can with the parents and bring them into everything. Explain what you're doing and why'.

It is clear that his skills are not limited to the classroom.

Down the corridor another mother is running the cookery group. She had been a little late in arriving this afternoon and the older children had supervised getting out the equipment. All is now well, it seems. One boy wanders in from the cookery to Robin's room — his coconut pyramids are ready for the oven. He talks to a friend about the wooden crane he is making and then busies himself with the computer until it is time for his pyramids to go into the oven.

Across the playground, Lynda and the part-time welfare assistant are taking two groups in the infants' mobile classroom. Three separate modelling activities are in progress: finger printing, computer drawing and a delicate system of overlaying design that demands fine motor skills; several older pupils are also cooperating on a joint venture of a snowman model. The walls of this room, like those in the main school building, reflect vividly the range of work that has been going on recently; balloon model heads compete for space with Chinese New Year dragons, shopping bar charts, 'Looking Forward to Spring' and 'All Aboard Our Colour Train'. Towards the end of the lesson, as individuals finish, Lynda seems to have an inexhaustible fund of ideas that she invites them to explore from an over-flowing junk box. She is sitting down now, for the first time and for a few minutes we try to take notes of each interaction between her and individual pupils. We give up, not being able to write fast enough. Later, Lynda agrees:

> 'Yes, I have never enjoyed teaching so much, or gone home so tired'.

With five minutes to playtime, clearing up begins and with much help from the older juniors the classroom is back to normal. As the children move out of the mobile, an infant girl asks if she can have the dragon's head. Lynda takes from the cupboard a four feet long, exotically decorated model of a Chinese dragon's head and then the body which is two bedsheets sewn together and similarly painted. The girl puts on the head and a dozen or more pupils form the body beneath the sheet and led by the head infant girl, they conga their way round the playground.

Two of the oldest girls approach us to ask if we take sugar in our coffee. That is their job apparently, at lunch-time and break.

The 'phone rings and we overhear Robin: 'I've got two fourth years, three third years and two lower juniors.' A pause, then: 'OK, so I can put in another lower junior or a top infant.'

So, the teams are more or less equal; the football match will take place it seems, weather permitting. It has been raining in the last few days and the field is still wet. The adventure play area, built on the school field by the parents, remains deserted this playtime.

After play, the 'circus' is over until next week. Robin's class is doing geography. The evidence is on the wall — a large painted chart of the course of a river and on a table top — a construction of a hydro-electric station — to indicate the topic the whole class has been engaged in. But this lesson Robin calls a skills session and the pupils are in three groups corresponding roughly to their varying ages. He reminds them all that they know where they are up to in the work book and to get on until he has the chance to see them. It is the same quiet, conversational tone that he used before with his six wood-workers. Each group comes around his desk in turn.

From next door there is the sound of the piano. Lynda has come over from the mobile with her infants. Later in the week she will also take the junior class for music. Even if Robin was as capable musically, he would want to spend some time with the infant class. 'I need to know them and I want them to get to know me well, so that they are not anxious at all when they come up to the junior class.'

After school we cannot have long with Robin because he has an in-service commitment and it means a fifteen mile drive to get there, but he shows us the school's curriculum document. This is a substantial file which presents a weekly and yearly breakdown of the timetable together with sets of guidelines for each subject area. Whilst we read it, he goes over to talk with Lynda in the mobile. He returns ten minutes later and says, 'That's what we call a staff meeting around here. We have plenty of them.'

How much can you learn of a school's curriculum in one afternoon? If nothing else, you learn to appreciate the importance of that injunction, 'Tell them to come and look for themselves'. If the curriculum amounts to all the planned experiences that the school provides for the pupils, there can be no substitute for the direct experience. The descriptions in the school brochure and the typed pages of curriculum guidelines tell the visitor something about the school and its staff and its curriculum, but they tell nothing of the action they are designed to inform. They are part of the rational justification that any staff can reasonably be expected to make for what they do, but only a part. Gibson (1985) makes just this point with his recommendation that parents and other interested individuals be invited to see for themselves the curriculum in action:

'. . . for seeing, discussing, joining in does much to resolve the all-too-often misleading disjunctions between language and reality, theory and practice, rhetoric and action'. (p13)

It was precisely that disjunction between language and reality that struck us after we had left Ringby school. We had witnessed the responsible enthusiasm of the pupils and seen the vitality of their work, and then, at the end of the afternoon, there was the formalism of the curriculum structure as written down in the guidelines. Perhaps we were partially responsible for that, with our initial question to Robin about a restricted curriculum, but the problem of reconciling the two remained.

A Framework of Principles

The thrust of current government policy is towards improving the cognitive structure of the curriculum. The strategy, built around a national curriculum framework is designed to accomplish that, and clearly formulated guidelines specifying subject content, objectives and the proportion of time to be devoted to each area, such as Robin showed us, are central to that strategy. They are seen as the route to curriculum continuity, breadth and so on. But engaging the pupil in that curriculum and, most especially, encouraging them even at the earliest stage of their primary schooling to accept some responsibility for their own education calls for something additional. However well constructed the curriculum might be in the teachers' guidelines, it is not something that can be imposed with much profit on those whose enthusiasm it does not arouse. The phrase often used to handle the connection between what is written down and what is received by the pupils is 'curriculum delivery'. It is an unfortunate expression, implying as it does an ends/means distinction between (a) the curriculum; and (b) the effective manner in which it is transmitted. Moreover, it is quite at odds with the notion that what a pupil actually experiences constitutes the curriculum. For him the manner of delivery — and not only of the formal, academic material, but of the values exemplified in the way the school sets about all its tasks — is what he encounters. It is not separate from the curriculum, merely the means of its delivery, but an essential and integral part of it.

It is just this impossibility of drawing a neat distinction between the ends that a teacher has in mind and the means that are employed in the transactions within the classroom that has given rise to the kind of definition of the curriculum which, following the Inspectorate, we have been using in this chapter. Sockett (1976) provides a lucid account of what, at first glance, might seem like an unnecessarily obscure notion. He cites the instance of a teacher, Geoff, who has a demonstrable end in view for a particular lesson — teaching his pupils some aspect of contemporary history. As he proceeds with this task, it becomes evident from his actions, from the way he divides his attention among the pupils, from the way he speaks and probes with his questions and from whom he sits next to, as he progresses around the room, that he has other ends simultaneously in mind, such as:

> '... being fair to the groups, getting kids to ask questions, building up the weaker children's confidence, developing inter-pupil discussion and conversation and so on ... What is now apparent is the immense diversity of ends'. (p64)

Ends such as these are different from the specific objectives he may have set for the lesson — the pupils' increased historical understanding that results from his teaching. These ends are an intrinsic feature of Geoff's teaching, and a permanent feature, not something that is accomplished within a single lesson. With the end 'being fair', he moves from group to group and, in so doing, he *is* being fair, and (perhaps) teaching them to be fair. So, we have not only a multiplicity of ends, but ends doubling as means. The reason is that Geoff, like any teacher, is guided by certain *principles,* more often held in the head than written down, which inform both what he proposes to teach and how he proposes to conduct himself with his pupils.

Difficult though these ideas may be, they point a way through the problems we noted earlier of describing an actual school's curriculum. If the curriculum is thought of as the totality of the planned experiences the child has in school, and if we are seeking continuity and coherence across those experiences, it would seem appropriate for a staff to begin to define their own informing principles. Here, we refer to those principles, governing the transactions with pupils, about which a school staff aims to be consistent across the whole curriculum. Such an endeavour would be quite different from delineating subject material to be covered or objectives to be sought.

Articulating principles of procedure may be no easy matter, but nevertheless a number of local authorities have adopted this approach in response to the DES Circular (6/81) which required each LEA to review its policy for the school curriculum. A notable example can be found in Northamptonshire (1984). This document. *A Framework of Principles,* emphasizes the same encompassing view of the curriculum as does the Inspectorate and asserts that:

'. . . before a school can begin to define aims and objectives and identify the experiences, concepts, skills and bodies of knowledge within the curriculum there must be a consensus about the principles that are fundamental to such curricular activity'. (p10)

The structure of principles for the primary curriculum is given by an identification of what are suggested as the needs of each child, and the axiom that:

'Each need is likely to be met fully only through the total curriculum; that is to say the curriculum that is concerned with interrelated experiences rather than discrete and isolated subjects or skills'. (p22)

The substantial lists of subsidiary principles subsequently outlined in the Northamptonshire document are intended to stand as criteria against which the staff of individual schools can review their current practices. They invite staff to examine the principles that are actually enmeshed in all the actions that make up the curriculum of their school. Furthermore, since the view taken of the curriculum is that it includes all the experiences that the child may have in the course of the day, it is not only the teachers, but parents, non-teaching staff and voluntary helpers who need to be brought into discussions of informing principles and the practical implications they hold for specific planning of curricular experiences.

A strategy for curriculum development in schools such as exemplified by *A Framework of Principles* differs in important respects from the government's insistence upon a national curriculum framework of agreed objectives as indicated in *Better Schools*. In the first place, it shows a realistic attempt to come to terms with what it means to define a curriculum as including all the experiences that a school plans for its pupils. As such, it offers the possibility of putting to work the ambitious aims we have for schooling and of deriving from them curricular recommendations that do reflect those aspirations for the kinds of personal qualities we want children to develop. Secondly, it is a more obvious encouragement to the professional development of the teachers who are to enact any curriculum change. That said, the problems attached to generating an agreement among a school's staff on informing principles and then implementing them are not to be underestimated. The Northamptonshire document makes it clear that this is liable to involve 'considerable staff discussion'. Otherwise:

> 'It may be only too easy for schools to look at the principles superficially and fail to come to terms with the practical implications'. (p52)

That could happen in any school, but when we consider the process by which a principle might come to be considered, absorbed and put into practice with consistency over the whole curriculum of a school, we can begin to see once more the potential advantage that rural schools possess because they are small scale. The necessary process of staff discussion is simply that much easier to engineer when the number of teachers involved is few; the likelihood of arriving at some unanimity is that much greater when there are fewer; the opportunity for a teacher to assent to a policy in the formality of a staff meeting and then to act differently within the privacy of the classroom is that much less than in the larger school; the prospects for engaging parents and other involved adults in a consideration of principles are that much more feasible when the school has closer and personalized links with its community. In short, we are back with the issue of whole-staff planning and, as we indicated earlier, small rural schools do have some intrinsic advantages in this respect, but this time there is perhaps a difference.

Establishing a common understanding on fundamental principles that are to apply across the whole curriculum is probably not the same kind of exercise as reaching an agreement on guidelines for the formal curriculum structure, or on objectives for some aspect of it. Principles are informing ideas that gradually become refined in the process of their employment in classroom action. Hence the importance of staff discussion; it enables the separate experiences of teachers to be shared. But in a rural primary school staffed with very few teachers working in a context which permits their actions to be readily witnessed, it becomes possible (assuming the teachers to be compatible) for the informing principles to be endorsed by a tacit concordat. The knowledge they share of each other's working ideals substitutes for words. Effectiveness rests upon an empathy resulting from a shared reflection upon experience.

In Ringby, even after one afternoon, you sense that kind of unspoken understanding between the two teachers (and the parents) on the principles that inform the curriculum — the whole working of the school. Most visibly, there is the openness to the community; this is shown in the encouragement that is given to parents to participate in a variety of ways and by the frankness with which the headteacher explains his hopes and his concerns in all his transactions with parents. You see too the belief that maturity is achieved by giving real responsibilities to people — pupils and voluntary helpers; you detect that same principle also in the relationship of professional equality between the school's two teachers. In the dealings that all the adults have with the pupils you can sense a respect being shown for their world: the formal curriculum does not dominate the interests and knowledge they bring with them to school but endeavours to utilize it; the dinner lady is absorbed in the skipping game that three girls are playing in the playground; the weak boundaries between age groups and gender that exist outside school are reflected within it. And there is the obvious belief that for all who go to school at Ringby, the experience should be enjoyable. Nothing of the underlying principles which support all that are visible in the written down version of the curriculum and yet, they are what inform the curriculum as it is experienced day-to-day by the children.

We know that not all two-teacher schools provide the same quality of educational experience as Ringby does, but a recent study conducted by the United States National Institute of Education offered as its first conclusion a view that applies equally to this country:

> '"Good" schools and "bad" schools (however defined) come in all sizes. Educational improvement and economic efficiency are the real challenges, and schools of every size could benefit from efforts in this direction. However, there is simply no basis for the belief that making a school bigger will automatically make it better'. (Sher, 1981, p54)

What we have here been arguing is that a strategy to enhance the curricula in the schools which serve rural populations should begin by identifying the strengths their existing schools currently have, and as Darnell puts it, seek to amplify those. A programme which invites the teachers, the pupils and the adults of each school's catchment community to consider the principles by which the school functions, to judge their appropriateness and their practical expression in what the school provides for the pupils offers a more encouraging way forward, not least because it is based upon a sharing of responsibility. Even the best schools might profit from making explicit their informing principles rather than relying upon tacit understandings. This may seem to lack the urgency that lies behind the utopianism of a national curriculum plan and, therefore, may not appeal to everybody. As Sockett (1976) put it, through a metaphor that is singularly apt in the case of small rural schools:

> 'For those who approach the schools with bulldozers rather than trowels, of course, the radical solution is the only one'. (p104)

Yet, a principles-based strategy recognizes the reality that a school's curriculum can only develop from where it currently is, with the strengths that it currently possesses. It has the further virtue that, in so far as it avoids the righteousness of the 'one best system' approach, it might encourage those who were involved in small rural primary schools to examine what it would mean to have a curriculum that was 'relevant' to their pupils and the communities they served.

We will return to these issues of educational improvement

in rural schools in the final section of the book. Before then we will consider the second challenge that Sher mentions, economic efficiency.

Notes

1 See Schools Council (1983), *Primary Practice,* working paper no 75.
2 HMI (1984a, 1984b and 1985b).
3 *Provision in Small Schools* (PRISM), based at the University of Leicester. The small schools sample was taken largely, but not exclusively from rural areas.
4 Professor M. Galton, personal communication.
5 Strictly speaking these judgments do not relate to size of school except inferentially in that rural pupils are far more likely in all OECD countries to be attending small schools.
6 In a speech to the National Association for Primary Education, 12 May 1984.
7 See, for instance, Smith, C. (1948).
8 The idea is also reminiscent of Thompson's (1967) argument that task orientation is the natural work rhythm of traditional rural communities, and has not entirely lost its meaning in rural parts of Britain today.
9 Bennett reports that the schools in his urban sample, to alleviate what they saw as the problems of a mixed age group and to continue with their normal style of teaching, often arranged the classes so that they contained the minimum age spread — sometimes with a narrower actual spread in pupils' ages than could be found in 'single age' classes.
10 *Curriculum from 5 to 16* uses the term 'areas of experience' rather than 'subjects' in line with previous descriptions such as Hirst's (1965) 'forms of knowledge' and Dearden's (1968) 'forms of understanding' whereas *Better Schools* sticks to the more conventional 'subjects'. In reality, the terminology appears to be used somewhat interchangeably.

Section III
The Economic Issues

Chapter 7

The Economics of Rural Schooling:
Direct Costs and Benefits

The provision of primary education in a rural area through a dispersed network of small schools is expensive. Any school, however few pupils there are enrolled, incurs certain fixed costs — the building to be maintained, heated and cleaned. It is also likely that when the pupil roll is small the pupil-teacher ratio will be correspondingly low, and the cost of teachers' salaries in relation to the number of pupils therefore high. When all of the costs of running a small school are spread across only a few pupils, the unit cost (that is, the average cost per pupil) is likely to be distinctly higher than in a larger school. If, however, some of the smallest schools in a particular rural area were to be closed, and their pupils transferred to larger schools in adjacent villages or nearby towns, the local authority would stand to reduce its overall expenditure. In such a move there would probably be some additional expense through having to provide transport for more children over greater distances, but despite this, overall savings could still be made. A more concentrated system of fewer, larger schools, operating at lower unit costs, opens up the possibility of securing economies of scale which are denied by a more dispersed pattern of primary school provision.

That, at its briefest, is the economic argument that has been advanced to support the rationalization of rural school systems wherever this has occurred in Britain and in many other developed nations. It is an essential element of what Sher (1977) calls the 'conventional wisdom' which has produced the massive programme of consolidation of schools in rural America. In England, this economic rationale is almost invariably cited by councillors or LEA officers when the closure of a school is being proposed. It is rarely given as much prominence as the educational arguments, at least in the public meetings in school or village halls; sometimes it is expressed in rather coy phrases such as 'We also cannot ignore the financial considerations'[1], but it remains a part of the complete case for closure. In fact, of course, the financial considerations cannot be ignored. These form the entirely legitimate concern of an authority, for it would be regarded as irresponsible if it did not consider the costs of the services that it provided.

Yet, many who have campaigned (successfully or otherwise) for the retention of a village school have become sceptical of the LEA's motives for proposing closure. Although the case has been put primarily on educational grounds, opponents of closure have often suspected this of being a disingenuous cloak to hide what is perceived as being the real reason — the urge to reduce public expenditure. It may be that local councillors have traditionally given greater weight than LEA officers to the economic considerations; Newby (1978) for instance has documented the former's concern in Suffolk with curtailing rate increases by holding down expenditure over a variety of public services. But officers have to work within the economic parameters that are set for them, and changing management structures within local government has brought budgetary control down into individual departments. Frequently senior accountants have been attached to public service departments as part of the policy of devolving control from the treasury department. What is not at issue is that, in recent years, county councils have been under considerable governmental constraint to seek opportunities for reducing public expenditure and the DES has made it unambiguously clear that it believes substantial savings are to be had from closing small schools. Mordey and Judge (1984) put it accurately:

> '. . . the assumption that large savings can be achieved by closures is written into central government's plans for local authority finance, and the cost of defying central government advice will continue to mount'. (p10)

The view that significant savings might be won by closing small schools was firmly articulated in the DES Circular 5/77, (DES, 1977c). These savings could include those in 'non-teaching staff, caretaking and cleaning, heating and lighting, maintenance and sometimes, on equipment and materials'. It argued further that 'important educational advantages may follow from the more efficient and economic deployment of teaching staff'. Two sets of criteria labelled 'educational' and 'economic' were delineated and the first three elements of the latter which LEAs were required to examine were:

    (i)   Unit teaching costs per child.
    (ii)   Unit non-teaching costs, other than premises, per child.
    (iii)   Unit premises costs per child.

The implication was that demonstrably higher unit costs of small schools (compared with those of other schools within a given authority) indicated a *prima facie* case for closure and local authorities were encouraged to adopt a 'resolute approach to closure'.

The Cost of Small Schools

How justified is the assumption that significant savings are there to be achieved through a policy of school rationalization? Are small schools in fact costly? There have been a few published studies of comparative unit cost for schools of different size and many LEAs have conducted costing investigations for their own planning purposes. Coatesworth (1976) reports the results of one such enquiry undertaken in Norfolk:

> 'In 1974–75 the running costs of a sample of primary schools of different size were calculated on a cost per pupil basis. It was found that the average cost per pupil is reasonably uniform for schools with more than seventy pupils on roll, but below that number the increase in cost rises sharply as the number on roll decreases. Schools with less than twenty pupils on roll require three times as much money per head as the average school'. (p276)

A number of similar LEA studies is reviewed in the Aston University research project and they too point to the rapidly escalating cost per pupil of increasingly small schools (Aston University, 1980). In Suffolk, for example, unit costs in a sample of ten schools with less than thirty pupils on roll were anything between 18 per cent and 95 per cent higher than the county average; in Warwickshire the cost per pupil in schools with less than fifty pupils on roll was, on average, 60 per cent above the county average for primary schools; in Salop estimated unit costs were 50 per cent above the country average in the case of schools with 30 pupils on roll, almost double for schools with twenty-five pupils and, as in Norfolk, nearly three times higher for a twenty pupil school. Mordey and Judge (1984) cite evidence from a costing exercise undertaken by the North Yorkshire Education Department which shows very similar results, as do those of Welsh authorities summarized in the Gittins Report.

A small number of published studies of local government planning have included an examination of the relationship between school size and unit costs. Gilder (1979) conducted his work with thirty-six primary schools in West Suffolk; Curry and West (1981) looked at unit costs of all the primary schools in two district council areas of Gloucestshire; Cummings (1971) investigated the costs of a range of schools in Scotland with pupil rolls varying from ten to 650. The research technique was broadly the same; the major items of recurrent expenditure were calculated for each school over one year and divided by the number of pupils on roll.[2] The results of all of these studies point unambiguously to the existence of economies of scale in rural primary schools. This is in line with the investigations conducted by individual LEAs and also with work done elsewhere. In America, Canada and Australia, similar studies have reached similar conclusions.[3] Hind (1977) for instance, comparing unit costs of schools varying in size from nine to 928 pupils on roll in New South Wales, confirmed that there were economies as schools increased in size up to 100 pupils; thereafter, gains were slight and diseconomies appeared at the threshold at which schools had non-teaching principals.

Among the British studies there is some variation in the estimates of the size of school below which unit costs begin to rise disproportionately. The Aston group suggested it might be as low as sixty; Coatesworth implies seventy; Cummings claimed that economies were exhausted once pupil numbers were over eighty, whereas Gilder maintained that there were still slight economies to be gained up to a pupil roll of 200. Curry and West found evidence of diseconomies of scale setting in above 200 due to higher administrative costs (such as a non-teaching headteacher) and argued that the most economic figure was between 100 and 200 pupils; the North Yorkshire data used by Mordey and Judge also hints at slight diseconomies in the largest schools. Several of the studies that have been undertaken have been reported in sufficient detail to indicate a substantial range in unit costs for schools of similar size and that this range tends to be wider in the case of smaller schools.

Too much significance should not be attached to these precise differences in the conclusions reached. The precise relationship between size and costs is bound to reflect variation in LEA staffing and capitation policies. An authority which insists upon there being a minimum of two full-time teachers in every school will produce a different relationship from that of an authority which employs a full-time and a part-time teacher in its smallest schools. The really significant point is that economies of scale are present in primary schooling and these economies are quickly extinguished as pupil numbers rise.

By far the most exhaustive investigation of school costs (as incurred by the local authority) in relation to school size is one conducted for the Commission for Local Authority Accounts in Scotland (1984). This calculated the total revenue costs for eighty-five schools in the Borders Region, ranging from schools with as few as eight pupils on roll to one with 457 pupils. The scatter diagram, shown in figure 5 is derived from these data. It relates unit costs to the size of the school.

The broad pattern is apparent at a glance; sharply escalating costs of very small schools below twenty-five pupils on roll; rapid evaporation of economies once school rolls move above 100. What is also immediately visible from the diagram is its very considerable scatter; unit costs can vary greatly for schools of similar size, most especially in the case of very small schools. Thus, a school with less than twenty pupils can incur annual unit costs double that of another school with the same number of pupils on roll. But also schools with more than 200 pupils can find their costs varying by as much as 65 per cent. The net result is that there are several instances in which unit costs in small schools are lower than those in schools very much larger. In other words the relationship between size and cost, although striking in the case of very small schools, is not invariant, and disappears altogether once pupil numbers exceed 100.

The reasons for this variation are not hard to discern. Education is labour intensive, teachers' salaries acounting for something over 60 per cent of the annual current expenditure on the maintenance of a school. The structure of existing salary scales is such that there can be a significant difference in the cost of employing a teacher; a teacher with several years of experience, at the top of the salary scale, costs nearly £3000 per year more than a newly appointed teacher.[4] So, a two-teacher school with a recently appointed headteacher and a young assistant teacher will produce a variation in staffing costs alone of £5500 compared with a similar school staffed by an experienced headteacher and an assistant nearing retirement. Spread across only thirty pupils that translates into a difference of £150 in unit cost terms.[5]

Another factor which accounts for variation is the discontinuity in the total salary costs around the size of pupil roll where a school qualifies for additional staffing. A two-teacher school with just under fifty pupils may have a pupil/teacher ratio close to the authority's norm, whereas a school very slightly larger may qualify for three teachers, in which case it will have a much lower pupil/teacher ratio

Figure 5: Scatter Diagram of Total Average Revenue Costs
Per Pupil: Border Region

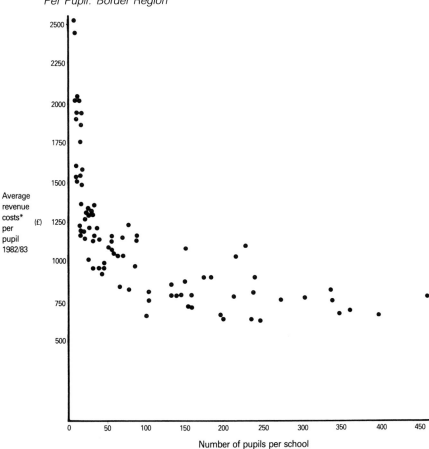

*Costs included: salaries of permanent, temporary and visiting teachers; salaries of secretarial and ancillary staff; repair and maintenance; caretaking and cleaning; heating, lighting, water and rates; insurance; telephones; school meals; transport. (from Commission for Local Authority Accounts in Scotland, 1984)

and consequently higher unit costs. A recent costing survey by Nor-folk County Education Department shows that average unit costs in a sample of schools with forty to fifty pupils are substantially lower than those in either smaller two-teacher schools or three-teacher schools with up to sixty pupils on roll.

Unit costs are sensitive to variations in pupil/teacher ratios and small schools are expensive largely to the extent that they operate with comparatively low ratios, but in addition to variations in salary costs, there are substantial differences in the costs of transporting children to and from school in rural areas. These costs are randomly distributed between schools; they relate to the nature and size of the catchment area and the dispersal of its population rather than to school size. There are also variations associated with the maintenance and running of the premises. These costs are governed partly by the number on roll and the size of the buildings, and the fact that some methods of construction require more frequent maintenance than others. There are also historically arbitrary factors such as the existence, or otherwise, of playing fields which bring about random variations in premises-related costs.

For all these reasons we can expect to encounter considerable variations in the recurrent expenditure necessary for maintaining schools of similar size, whatever their size. The fact remains, how-ever, that on the basis of unit costs (and discounting the limitations of that instrument) small schools are usually more expensive to operate than larger schools, and very small schools of thirty pupils and less are almost invariably so. That, in itself, does not demonstrate the pro-position that there are substantial savings to be made through a policy of consolidation. What has to be considered are the costs of any proposed rationalization compared with existing costs. Almost any plan for reorganization is likely to incur some additional expenditure, on extra transport or new buildings for instance, and it is only if total costs including these additional transport costs are lower than existing costs, that net savings become possible.

In some circumstances, perhaps because of local peculiarities in transport networks or patterns of population distribution, it appears that additional transport costs have outweighed the potential savings that the closure of a comparatively expensive small school would have brought. Rogers (1979) quotes the reply of the Chief Education Officer of Somerset to the *Where* survey:

'The mere fact that the cost of maintaining one school instead of two would be less has not at any time been a major influencing factor; indeed had the Authority some years back closed schools with this aim and this aim alone in mind, they could well now be incurring expenditure over and above what would have been necessary because of the escalating costs of transport'. (p39)

The Aston University (1980) team make a similar point:

'... a number of authorities have shown that, in the case of some recent proposed closures, any savings from amalgamation would be more than offset by the cost of providing transport'. (p44)

This however, is certainly not every authority's experience. It may well be that transport systems are better managed now than in the period covered by the *Where* survey and, at the present time, transport costs are not escalating to the extent that they were in the 1970s.

The other major factor which may render a proposed reorganization uneconomic is the necessity for additional capital expenditure on enlarging those schools which are retained. Where there is an overall decline in primary school numbers, it is probable that there will be spare capacity in these schools into which additional pupils from closed schools could be accommodated, without any extra building costs. If pupil numbers rise in rural areas and as plans for rural school provision begin to take into account the need to bring schools up to the requirements of the revised School Premises Regulations[6], the marginal capital costs of rationalization may become a more significant influence in determining whether potential economies can be realized.

It would appear then that the opportunities for bringing about savings through a programme of concentrating the network of rural primary schools, and thereby eliminating the high unit costs of some small schools, is dependent upon local circumstances: the existence of spare capacity in other schools; existing and proposed transport arrangements; the possibilities for redeploying or retiring teaching staff. This was the conclusion reached by Hind (1981):

'In a way, to talk about the economics of rural education is a trap, if in so doing we are led to believe that we can find some widely applicable formulae that indicate the optimum way of providing services in rural areas generally'. (p137)

Similarly, the Aston University team, reviewing instances of school closures in England, decided, 'There are no simple rules to apply to particular cases'. They reported that some LEAs had estimated that in the most favourable circumstances it had been possible to save almost the entire cost of a very small school, but that usually the saving had been appreciably more modest. In the case study schools they examined, it amounted to the equivalent of one teacher's salary on average. Although it has to be remembered that such savings are cumulative, this evidence does not offer much encouragement to the belief that rationalization will yield substantial savings when set against the total education budget of an authority.

Perhaps occasionally, savings, in the sense of actual reductions in the revenue costs to the local authority, have been made when small schools have been closed. The economic case for rationalization of resources is, however, usually put differently. It is not that money is saved, so the argument runs, rather that the resources released through the closure of a comparatively high cost village school can be put to greater educational benefit elsewhere. This is the point made in *Better Schools* when it is stated that, given limited resources, expensive small schools can only be maintained at a cost to other schools, or to the provision of other valued educational facilities elsewhere within the authority. In other words, the overall quality of the education provided by the authority could be improved, within existing expenditure, through the elimination of the exorbitant demands made by a dispersed network of small schools. The concept that is being used here is referred to by economists as 'opportunity costs'. The opportunity costs of maintaining a small school with high units cost is the opportunity foreseaken to provide better facilities for its children and for those in other schools in the authority's system.

To illustrate this, and the economic factors which have to be taken into account when plans are being drawn up for the provision of primary schooling in a rural area, we propose to use a case study. The purpose of this is not to try to draw from it some simple generalizable rule, but rather to highlight the calculations that need to be made, to show the possibilities and difficulties in securing savings in public expenditure, and the opportunities that exist if potential savings can be realized.

An Illustrative Study: How Many Schools?[7]

The area comprises sixteen parishes around a village of just over 500 inhabitants in which the largest primary school (school 1) and a

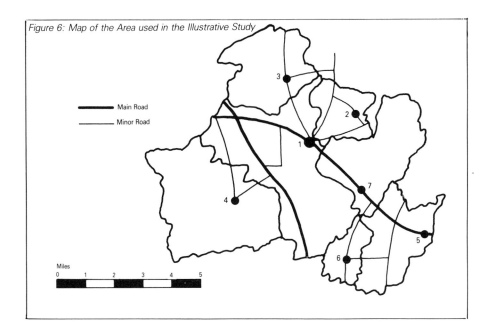

Figure 6: Map of the Area used in the Illustrative Study

Main Road

Minor Road

Miles

secondary school are located. The total population of the area was almost 4000 at the 1981 Census, having increased by slightly over 10 per cent during the previous decade. The area is served by seven primary (age 5 to 11) schools and in 1985, the total number of pupils in these schools was 349. It was anticipated by the authority that this figure would remain more or less constant during the coming decade. The map set out in figure 6 shows the location of the schools and their respective catchment areas.

School 1, the largest of the seven, has 109 pupils currently on roll and four teachers; it is expected to grow to 120 pupils by the mid-1990s. Five of the remaining schools operate with two teachers, pupil numbers varying from thirty-two to forty-two. School 7, in the parish which had experienced the highest percentage growth in population during the 1970s, has three teachers and a pupil roll of fifty-three, but this is expected to drop rapidly in the next few years. Five of the schools are county schools; school 4 is voluntary controlled and school 5 is voluntary aided. Some details of the schools are given in table 2.

Table 2: Details of the Seven Schools in the Illustrative Study

	Current roll (1985)	Anticipated roll (1996)	Current staff	Year school built in	School transport (no. of pupils)	Unit cost (£)
School						
1	109	120	4	1932	58	654
2	37	28	2	1879	22	709
3	42	42	2	1873	8	657
4 (VC)	32	34	2	1859	1	766
5 (VA)	38	45	2	1844	—	696
6	38	38	2	1868	—	763
7	53	35	3	1878	—	702
Total	349	342	17		89	Average £694

It can be seen that the largest school (school 1) is fractionally the least expensive to maintain and the smallest school (school 4) (by a similarly small margin) has the highest unit cost, but in fact the costs are remarkably uniform. This reflects their similarity in pupil roll, period and style of construction and physical premises (with the exception of the larger, more recently built school 1); the expenditure on premises-related costs such as energy, repair and maintenance is low in each of these Victorian schools, in part because the buildings themselves are small. With the exception of schools 1 and 2, both of which have a somewhat dispersed catchment area, these are very much village schools, their pupils living only a short distance away. Consequently, only a comparatively small proportion of the total of primary children in the area require free school transport (26 per cent) and the current unit cost of transport of £141 is well below the county average of £215. As might be expected, there are no outstanding debt charges on any of these schools.

In recent years there has been a substantial in-service programme in this area, much of it at the instigation of the teachers and supported by some of the authority's advisory staff. There is a supportive network among the teachers in the different schools and a considerable degree of inter-school cooperation in various curricular ventures, an important element of this being the involvement of teachers from the secondary school. Generally speaking, the schools enjoy a good reputation locally.

From the authority's point of view, a major problem with the provision of primary schooling in this area centres on the quality of the school buildings. With the exception of school 1, all are mid-Victorian in construction and fall a good way short of the latest minimum specification contained in the 1981 regulations. Four of these schools still have outside lavatories; only one has a hall; only two have adequately sized playgrounds; they are small and cramped. School 1 also fails to meet the minimum standards, but that could be rectified at very little expense; for the other six schools it is a more serious business. LEAs are required by the DES to bring schools up to the standards of the new regulations by 1991. In this particular area, what are the options?

Three possibilities will be examined and costed according to the authority's estimates of capital and recurrent expenditure. In each case, costs will be calculated on the assumption that the schools will be brought into line with 1981 specifications. In one sense, this may be an unrealistic assumption; the Chief Education Officer has argued that if the government's present restrictions on capital spending and close control of revenue expenditure continue, it will take at least thirty-five years to bring all the schools in the county up to those building standards. On the other hand, any rational planning for the provision of primary schooling in this or any other area would need to take into account those regulations, and in that sense it is a realistic assumption. The three options to be considered are outlined below.

Option A: The Area School

The first option is to create one school to serve the whole area. The rationale here is provided by the White Paper *Better Schools* which claims that 'in order to secure the necessary range and mix of teacher experience, for older primary children, it is desirable that 5–11 schools should have at least one form of entry'. That means, in practice, schools of at least 200 pupils. Given the estimated school population of 342 pupils by the mid-1990s in this area, only one school would be required if this principle were to be fully implemented and the only feasible school would be school 1. The proposal therefore is that this school be substantially extended to become the area school. The others would be declared surplus to requirements.

Option B: The Status Quo

The second option is to retain all seven schools in service and to re-model them to meet the new Schools Premises Regulations. Behind this proposal is the assumption that it would most meet the wishes of the parents and village residents of a scattered population with no major centre nearby. Furthermore, the existing schools have established, within the constraints of staffing resources, a strong co-operative network among themselves which has shown itself capable of supporting the curricula they offer. There is an immediate problem however; school 3, already over-crowded and built on a cramped site with no possibilities for expansion, could not be brought up to the required building standards. The only alternative within this option would be to dispose of the premises and rebuild school 3 on a new site.

Option C: Five Schools

The third option is a compromise. It attempts to retain as many schools in the area as possible, commensurate with another principle given in *Better Schools* that 'the numbers of pupils in a primary school should not in general fall below the level at which a complement of three teachers is justified'. Three teachers and about sixty pupils on roll is how this principle will be interpreted, although the White Paper does indicate that 'geographical and social factors need to be given their full weight' and therefore, exceptionally, a smaller school might be entertained. As we saw in chapter 3, the recent County Guidelines for Norfolk were exactly in line with this principle, spelling out a minimum size of sixty pupils as being the norm for primary schools in rural areas but allowing smaller schools to be retained if they could be 'strongly justified'.

In order to retain as many schools as possible, school 1 should not be increased beyond its natural anticipated expansion to 120 places. The expected population of school age children in the north of the area would warrant only one school; given the problem of the inadequate premises of school 3, the proposed solution would entail closing this school and transferring its pupils to an enlarged and re-modelled school 2. In the south-east, projected pupil numbers could support two schools; the current quality of the buildings of the three existing schools in that part of the area and the opportunities they afford for remodelling indicate that the most feasible plan would be to close school 7 and redistribute its pupils (the number of which is expected to decline sharply) between the other two. Schools 5 and 6 would be suitably modernized to accommodate about sixty pupils each. School 4 would be remodelled in accordance with the 1981 Regulations and would remain a two-teacher school because of the 'geographical and social factors'. The school serves an important social function in the sparsely populated south-western parishes which have few other social amenities and its continued presence would obviate the necessity of a lengthy and complex bus route to transport the children to school 1.

The Cost of the Three Options

Capital costs are calculated according to the LEA's estimates (at 1985 prices) of the expenditure that would be required to bring existing schools up to the standard necessary to meet the 1981 Premises Regulations, and, where new building is required, according to the LEA's estimates of the cost per pupil of providing such accommodation. It is assumed that any school declared surplus to need will be sold on the open market and the revenue set against the capital expense of remodelling the other schools.

Recurrent costs for each of the three options are calculated (again at 1985 prices) for the following five major items of operating expense: teachers' salaries; transport costs; maintenance of the premises (including heating, lighting and cleaning); welfare assistants' and clerical staff salaries; capitation and supplies.

The details of these calculations, including the particular assumptions that have had to be made in arriving at them, are given in the appendix (p278). They are summarized in table 3 below.

The first point to note is the substantially higher cost of establishing the area school option. Even when the revenue gained from the sale of existing schools made redundant by the proposal is set against the capital necessary, it remains more expensive than either of the other options which rely on remodelling the current schools. The reason for this is that creating an area school out of school 1 means building what is not far short of a new school. More than two-thirds of the pupils in the area would be accommodated in wholly new premises and the cost per pupil of new school accommodation is at least two-and-a-half times higher than typical remodelling costs. Whereas the cost of refurbishing existing schools to bring them up to the standard required to permit a roll of sixty pupils is of the order of

Table 3: Calculation of the Costs of the Three Options

	Option A	Option B	Option C
Number of schools	1	7	5
Total number of (full-time) teachers	13.5	17	15
Average pupil/teacher ratio	25.9:1	20.5:1	23.3:1
Number of pupils living more than two			
miles from school	290	89	176
Net Capital Costs to LEA (£000)	*520*	*316*	*217*
Recurrent Costs (£000)			
(i) Teachers' Salaries	140.4	177.4	156.0
(ii) Transport	37.7	12.5	23.8
(iii) Premises	29.6	48.4	38.9
(iv) Welfare/clerical salaries	5.4	10.2	9.0
(v) Capitation and supplies	11.3	12.6	11.6
Total Recurrent Costs	*224.4*	*261.1*	*239.3*

£50,000–£60,000, the LEA calculates the expense of new building on a figure of £2500 per pupil place.

This observation is in line with Gilder's (1979) study of primary school provision in West Suffolk. One of the aims of his investigation was 'to draw attention to the importance of past capital investment in rural services' and his conclusion was that the cheapest solution in public cost terms was one which was 'based on the fullest use of existing rural capital assets'. A similar conclusion was reached by Nash (1977) in an examination of the economic effects of replacing five small schools with a new area school. He was able to demonstrate that by retaining three of the schools and remodelling them in accordance with prevailing regulations, capital expenditure could be reduced to two-thirds that of the area school option.

In our illustrative study, options B and C are cheaper because they do make use of the past capital investment which the existing schools represent, but that is not to say that they are necessarily more cost effective than the more expensive option A. The issue (which neither Gildern or Nash address) is the comparative quality of what is provided when capital is invested in new school building as against renovating and modernizing Victorian schools. The investment that is estimated in either of options B and C would bring about the basic structural alterations that would be necessary to bring the schools up to the minimum requirements of the 1981 Schools Premises Regulations. It would produce the requisite size of teaching space for the number of pupils envisaged, but no more; lavatories could be brought inside; some accommodation would be provided for teaching and ancillary staff; the playground would be extended by the extent required. Yet the facilities would remain inferior to those of new accommodation which would be found in the area school of option A. There would not, for example, be any separate large activity areas; any large hall space would need to double up as classrooms with consequent limitations on the use of gymnastic equipment. There would not be the range of small group quiet areas or library facilities. To provide accommodation of a variety and quality in seven or even five schools which matched that which could be built in the single, large area school would entail substantially more new building in each of the schools at prohibitive cost.

When we turn to the recurrent costs of each of the proposed patterns of provision for the area, the presence of internal economies of scale becomes apparent. Comparing the area school proposal (option A) with the existing pattern of seven schools (option B), staff requirements are reduced from seventeen to thirteen-and-a-half full-time equivalent teachers; premises-related costs are reduced by nearly 40 per cent and non-teacher salaries are cut by a half. The negative impact of increased transport costs to the authority is also made visible. They are tripled as over 80 per cent of the pupils would live more than two miles from the area school and thereby qualify for free transport to and from school. Even allowing for this, however, it is clear that savings on recurrent public expenditure are possible.

It has to be remembered that direct costs are borne not only by the public authority. Parents and their children also incur direct costs. Rationalization of schools in rural areas almost invariably results, as in this illustrative study, in more pupils having to travel greater distances to get to school, and once there they are obliged to have school lunches (or take prepared packed lunches). How much financial outlay this involves for parents is impossible to quantify. The Aston University study suggested that it was not substantial; a more recent survey by CARE (1986) in Cumbria implies that additional personal direct financial costs are experienced chiefly by those parents who use their cars to reduce the length of journey time their children would otherwise encounter. Clearly some expense will be incurred if parents are ever to visit the more distant school. More obviously their children are obliged to spend a greater time in travel. In the case study, option A would cause about 290 pupils to be bussed, up to eight miles in some cases, even by the most direct route, which rural school buses rarely take. As parents frequently complain,[8] it makes for a much longer school day for children. Apart from the time involved — two hundred hours per year, which adds up to an entire year's schooling in the career of a primary child — children travelling on school buses are subject to incovenience and often to considerable physical discomfort. Massey (1978) reports that they 'must routinely submit to conditions that no adult would accept'. Bullying by older pupils on unsupervised buses are among the conditions that parents resentfully report.

These represent part of the direct costs of rationalization borne by local inhabitants. They do not figure in an LEA's financial estimates of its own costs, and it is extremely difficult to see how any form of cost-benefit analysis could place a monetary value upon them so that they could be brought into any calculation of overall costs. They are direct costs nonetheless, real enough to those who have to pay them.

How Many Schools?

From the authority's point of view, it is clear from the outset that the option of retaining and remodelling all seven schools has little to recommend itself. It would necessitate substantially higher capital investment than option C, and would incur significantly greater re-current expenditure than either of the two alternatives. Even compared with retaining five schools its extra operating costs would be more than £20,000 per year. That represents the opportunity to maintain a support system for the five schools in option C consisting of, for instance, an advisory teacher to encourage curriculum development and cooperation in the schools plus supply teacher cover to release the permanent teachers for in-service activity, or alternatively, it would pay for a minibus to be used exclusively in the five schools.

The choice between the area school proposal (option A) and that of retaining five of the village schools (option C) is rather less straight-forward. Recurrent costs are less with option A, by £15,000, and that represents the opportunity to finance three one-term secondments to enable teachers in the area school to undertake in-service courses, or to provide the school with its own minibus to supplement the teaching. But against those savings, we have to set the capital costs which are very much higher for this proposal. We need, therefore, some means of taking into account both the immediate capital expenditure, and the long term operating costs of both proposals.

Cash flow discounting is the technique usually employed to deal with this kind of problem. This is an attempt to predict the stream of cash flows (in this case, costs to the authority) over a set number of future years, discounted to present day values. Put more simply, net present cost is the sum that would need to be set aside now to finance the proposal over a given number of years. The technique is not without its difficulties; it involves making assumptions about future interest rates and future rates of inflation. The latter would not be serious if it were uniform for all elements of future costs but that may well not be so; differential inflation between teacher salary costs and school transport costs, for example, would affect this present calculation. For all its problems, it is the most appropriate accounting technique for deciding between the two options.

The net present costs of the different proposals have been calculated over a period of twenty years; beyond that time scale it is virtually impossible to make predictions about the number of school age pupils there will be in the area. Using the discounting rate of 10 per cent, recommended by the Treasury for public authority investments, the net present cost of option A is £2,426,000, and for option C it is £2,250,000.[9] In other words option C is favoured, although the difference is only 7 per cent, and that is probably within the margin of error of the base line figures on which the calculations are made.

Does that mean that the authority should decide to adopt option C and retain five of the existing seven schools? It might if its chief concern was with financial costs. That is a perfectly legitimate concern for the authority, but it is only part of the calculation that has to be made before deciding which alternative proposal is the more cost effective. Mackay (1983) points out that 'cost effectiveness':

> '... is an emotive title, implying "value of money" by gaining the maximum return from a given level of expenditure, but often becoming, in practice, the provision of a given level of service for a minimum level of expenditure'. (p177)

To decide whether a particular proposal offers the maximum return on expenditure requires a judgment about the nature of the return as well as a calculation of its financial costs.

The costs of providing a particular product or service can be calculated, and expressed in unit cost terms, but that concept is drawn from the economic theory of the firm which presupposes a unitary product, for example a light-bulb or a sparking-plug. Education is not a unitary product, except in the very minimal sense that seven years of schooling constitutes a primary education. There are, as we have seen throughout, substantial disagreements about what constitutes a good education; the one thing that people can always agree on is that individual schools differ markedly in the quality of the education they provide. Therefore, an elaboration of unit costs, or of net present costs, gives an indication of the alternative ways in which resources can be deployed, but says nothing about the relationship between that expenditure and the value of the services thereby produced. Unless we know something about both parts of the equation, we are not in a position to comment on cost effectiveness.

So, although option A is more costly, it might be judged to be more cost effective if we set high value on the superior educational facilities it would bring about. LEA officers do seem to place considerable importance on the quality of the premises. Talking to them, one is made aware of the fact that better accommodation represents for them one of the hallmarks of successful reorganization. Invariably this is cited as a major facet of the educational advantage that would accrue to the children who would be transferred following the closure of a small school in antiquated premises. This appears to contrast with the views of parents, for what evidence we have suggests that, where they value the teaching staff, parents place a relatively low priority on the physical quality of the premises. In fact, Forsyth (1983) claims from her Scottish sample that they were sometimes inclined to view inferior facilities almost as the acceptable cost that had to be paid for the retention of a village school. A concrete example of this claim was furnished at a recent meeting connected with possible school closures. The local councillor observed that the alternative school, possessing better facilities, was just a little over two miles from the village. A mother responded with the remark. 'It can be two miles or twelve miles. I'm not interested. It isn't in this community.'

Similarly, option A facilitates the educational advantages that are claimed for a more concentrated, larger scale provision such as the opportunities for teacher specialization and a larger peer group of similar aged children. For the officer who advocates this option, these factors may well represent the opportunity for maximising the return on public expenditure. The alternative proposals contained in option C preserve the educational advantages that are claimed for smaller scale village schools, a better pupil/teacher ratio and the security afforded to young children being educated closer to their home and so on. In addition, the net present cost of this option is lower, and together, these factors could be argued to indicate it is the more cost effective plan.

Unless there is some agreement on the value attached to different forms of educational provision, the economic analysis can only take us so far in answer to the question as to which of a set of proposals is the most cost effective; it can only demonstrate the demands that each proposal is likely to make on future resources and hence, indicate the opportunities foresaken by whatever decision is made. To be sure of maximizing value for money, we need to know not only the opportunity costs, but also which educational opportunities we most value. In the illustrative case we have been considering, the calculations of capital and recurrent costs, discounted to net present values, suggest that on grounds of cost alone, there is very little to choose between the area school proposal (option A) or retaining five smaller schools (option C), although the latter is marginally favoured. If the authority's officers had a clear view as to whether they saw direct educational benefits stemming more readily from a single, large and substantially new school, or from a dispersed network of smaller, local schools, the decision would be a relatively easy one to make. But, as we emphasized earlier, the local circumstances are paramount. If they were different — if for example, the existing small schools currently had high unit costs, or if the largest school was on a site which restricted its possibility for expansion — the costs of the respective proposals might then be significantly divergent. Then, the decision might be much more difficult.

Simkins (1980) makes it abundantly clear that two essential questions have to be asked when the notion of opportunity costs is being employed: whose costs are being considered and how are they being identified and measured? In this chapter we have been identifying and endeavouring to measure the direct costs which are incurred largely by the local authority. In the following chapter, we will examine the indirect costs and benefits which accrue both privately and to the public authorities.

Notes

1 Chapter One, second case study.
2 There is some variation in whether or not minor items of expenditure were included.
3 Hind (1981) provides a useful summary of this research.
4 Calculated on 1986 salary scales.
5 Calculated on 1986 salary scales.
6 The government stipulates minimum standards for the size and facilities of school premises and for their site area. The most recent revision of these, contained in the Education (School Premises) Regulations (HMSO, 1981) are required to be brought into effect by 1991.
7 The initial data for this study was provided by officers of Norfolk County Council for an education workshop on the problems of primary schooling in rural areas of the county. This was a remarkably innovative venture in consultation attended by some 200 people together with elected members

of the Education Committee. Additional information was subsequently furnished by Mr. J. Bradford, Principal Assistant Education Officer. The authors would like to acknowledge their debt to him for this and for his valuable comments on the analysis. Any faults that remain in the analysis are, of course, the responsibility of the authors.

8 See CARE (1986).

9 The comparable figure for option B is £2,537,000.

Chapter 8

The Economics of Rural Schooling:
Indirect Costs and Benefits

When a local authority proposes the closure of an individual school, or a more extensive reorganization of primary schooling in a rural area involving perhaps the closure of several schools, it is likely to submit, as part of its proposal, an estimate of the financial implications of the new arrangement. In the case of an individual school closure, this invariably means the projected savings that can be made. The estimates that are being made in such instances are of the direct cost that the public authority will have to meet. Occasionally, action groups that are opposed to the authority's plans have been able seriously to challenge those figures, but more frequently the response is to challenge the assumptions upon which the authority has based its figures and to demand what is often referred to as a 'wider form of social accounting'. What the demand amounts to is a call for opportunity costs to be looked at from the point of view of the local population and that the examination should pay serious attention to the indirect costs and benefits that relate to the proposed reorganization.

Indirect Benefits to the Local Economy

There are indirect benefits to a local community through the presence of a school and there are losses that accrue through its closure which do not appear on an LEA's balance sheet of direct costs and benefits. An obvious example is that the school makes an impact on the local economy. Work done by Mackay (1983) in Scotland suggests that on average almost a fifth of the gross current expenditure on a rural school makes a contribution to the community surrounding the school. This may not be a very substantial amount, because many teachers no longer live locally and therefore spend little of their income locally, and second because the centralization of schools' support services diverts much potential benefit to larger centres. For example, building and maintenance is organized through a centralized department which may not lay off work to local small firms and the 'local purchase account' represents a small proportion of each school's capitation allowance. Nevertheless, what is retained locally from the total expenditure on the school is of some importance. This is especially so because in many rural areas the school often represents the only feasible source of employment for caretaking, secretarial, meals and welfare staff. In the illustrative case we were considering in the previous chapter, the existing pattern of seven schools probably provides part-time occupation for about twenty-five women. The closure of these village schools resulting from the adoption of the area school proposal would result in most of them becoming wholly unemployed.[1] The inability of women to find employment because opportunities do not exist very close to home is a form of hidden unemployment which particularly affects rural areas. As the Association of District Councils (1986) report indicates, 'in rural areas female activity rates tend to be significantly below the national average' (p10).

A more general claim for the indirect benefit of a local school is that its presence helps to ensure the demographic balance and economic viability of a village. Numerous Case for Retention campaign documents which we have examined contain statements such as:

> 'It is extremely important to the long-term survival of the village that the school should be retained'.

and:

> 'Closure — another nail in the coffin of rural life'.

The closure of the school, it is suggested, will lead to a decline in population as couples with children move away and others are deterred from migrating into the village. At least, there will be a change in the demographic structure so that the village is transformed, to become populated chiefly by the old and the retired and (according to its location) those seeking holiday homes. The SAVE Group's document[2], put it with deliberate irony:

> 'The absence of a school will eventually make the village a pleasant place — to retire to'.

This link between the village school and the long-term viability of rural villages is argued not only in the campaign literature about school closures. Various reports on the future of rural areas have, in recent years, made the same point. Thus, *The Decline of Rural Services,* a report of the Standing Conference of Rural Community Councils (1978), suggested:

'It is the link between the retention of the village school, with the attendant opportunities for natural growth of the community, and hopes of maintaining a balanced age and social structure in the village, that makes this facility one of the most crucial under consideration in this report'. (p17)

Similarly, CARE's (1978) paper *The Case for the Small Rural School,* quoted the Cumbria Structure Plan as claiming:

'[The loss of a village school] from closure can deter people from remaining in or moving into rural areas, thereby accelerating the process of population decline'. (p11)

The argument has a commonsense ring about it. It seems reasonable to suppose that parents, given any choice at all, would prefer to live in villages in which there was a suitable school rather than in one in which there was not. That being so, we could expect school closure to result in a gradual population decline which would further undermine the economic viability of other services. The village shop, it is often said, is frequently an early victim of a school's closure, itself forced to shut down because people's shopping habits change if they are no longer delivering or collecting their children from the local school. If that were generally the case, the adoption of the area school (option A) proposal in the illustrative case study would probably entail the additional cost (to the area) of the loss of at least some of the twelve village shops and post offices in the outlying villages. Despite the plausibility of the argument and its very widespread acceptance, the evidence for it is not compelling.

The Aston University (1981) study appears to provide some support. Although hampered by a lack of between-census data, it does indicate an association between the presence of a school and the recent demographic history of the village. Over the period 1971 to 1977, those case study parishes in which schools had closed experienced a population decline of 2.7 per cent compared with an increase of 6 per cent in those in which the school had remained open. The same contrast was evident in the wider area of parishes adjacent to the case study settlements; here, there was an average decrease of 0.5 per cent where the school had closed against a 2.9 per cent population rise where the school had been retained. In parishes where there had never been a school, the population decrease, 3.7 per cent, was even greater. Calculated over the longer time span of 1961 to 1977, the contrasts were more marked and there was also evidence of slight shifts towards an older age structure in villages without a school. Similarly in rural areas of Sweden, although the school system is rather different, Rydberg was able to show a connection between accelerated rural depopulation and school closures.[3] Yet there is in all this something of the chicken and egg problem. To show an association is one thing; to demonstrate causality is another. The problems of isolating the specific fact of school closure from other attendant variables such as housing policy, changing occupational opportunities and curtailment in public transport are formidable.

The data obtained from interviews with village residents conducted by the Aston team did not lend much support to the proposition that the presence or absence of a local school was a causal factor in population movements. Similarly, Forsythe's (1983) study, which also asked rural residents about their past migration and invited them to speculate about future moves, also indicated that school related concerns did not figure largely in people's calculations; occupation and housing availability were uppermost. These, however, were scarcely adequate tests of the proposition. A satisfactory inquiry would, as Forsythe states, 'involve a series of long-term studies monitoring specific communities before and after school closure'. To date, that work has simply not been carried out.[4] It cannot be surprising that issues such as the availability of jobs and housing are the major determinants of individual mobility decisions. The important question is the extent to which the provision of primary schooling links with the wider planning of the rural economy, including the development of occupational opportunities and housing facilities. One possibility is put by Mackay (1983):

> '. . . if the number of pupils depends upon the level of population and thus on the level of economic activity in the area, but the ability to attract economic activity is related to the educational provision, then redevelopment of population is as effective a means, and perhaps more socially desirable than the concentration of population which successive closures bring about'. (p177)

The limited evidence we have suggests that school closures are more often the consequence of reduced economic activity leading to population decline rather than the cause, but what can certainly be said is that successive governments have, for many years, acknowledged the need for a fair distribution of economic activity throughout the country. The provision of public services (such as education) is recognized as being one measure to bring about an equitable regional distribution of economic activity and employment. In some countries, this is very explicit national policy. North Norway, for instance, has problems similar to those encountered in rural Britain and there Solstad (1981) indicates:

'To counteract the "imbalance" in national patterns of economic development, Norway has implemented a series of political, economic and social policies designed to strengthen the peripheral areas of the country ... Obviously achieving this goal implies that existing occupational opportunities must be safeguarded and that new economic opportunities must be created. National policy has addressed these issues both by restricting economic activity in the already developed areas and concomitantly stimulating investment and other forms of economic activity in the "poorly developed" regions. In addition, there has been a very active effort to enhance the infrastructure of rural regions, in both physical and human terms. Among other initiatives, this has included major investments in education at every level'. (p303)

In Britain we can notice the contrary situation of national government initiatives to stimulate the rural economy through the Development Commission in precisely those areas where local authorities are closing rural primary schools.

Indirect Benefits to the Local Community

The imagery of life and death contained in phrases such as 'the school is the heart of the village', which, as we noted earlier, is repeated in numerous Case for Retention documents, does not only refer to the economic future of the village whose school is threatened. It also depicts the school as being central to the existing social life of the village. In addition to its direct benefit of providing a primary education for the young, the presence of the school is seen, locally, as having the indirect benefit of enriching and in some fundamental sense, supporting the pattern of social relationships of young and old alike. It is possible to distinguish two separate strands to this argument. In the first place, the school is seen as serving an integrative function, bringing about and reinforcing social contacts between parents and across the generations; secondly, it is depicted as being symbolic of the quality of life in a rural community.

The Social Function

There is convincing evidence that small rural schools do succeed in bringing residents together for regular face-to-face contact in what is felt to be a commonly shared and significant interest. Forsythe's case studies document the effect of the programme of formal events that rural schools stage in encouraging social interaction between residents and in 'motivating people to work together for what they see as the common good and thus creating bonds between the people themselves'. The case accounts echo verbatim remarks such as:

> 'We all go to the Christmas party. Everyone bakes for it, and the same for the school whist-drive. Everyone hands in prizes and helps with the decorations. I feel I'm putting these [decorations] up for *our* school'. (p156)

There are frequent references in Forsythe's material to 'our', 'we' and 'us', just as there are in many campaign documents produced by individual action groups, as for instance in this submission from a village in Durham:

> 'The school is the centre for our community, for the harvest festivals, Christmas carol services, jumble sales, local history lectures, film shows, photographic exhibitions, outings in summer and winter and both WI and 'Over Sixties' participate in fund raising events'.

Not all of these kinds of events take place in the school itself. In fact, in many rural areas in Britain, recently constructed village halls have superseded the school as the one public building that provides adequate accommodation. Of the sixteen parishes served by the seven schools in the illustrative case study in the previous chapter, eleven had a hall suitable for village meetings. The point is, however, that even where such events take place away from the school premises, it is the presence of the school that is frequently the reason for their taking place. They are, Forsythe maintains, well-attended, enjoyed, and locally significant in facilitating social interaction. This is especially so in dispersed settlements where difficult terrain, winter weather conditions and the loss of other institutions and services can combine to make for social isolation.

It might be argued that in lowland rural areas, where physical communications are easier and where there is likely to be a greater preponderance of ex-urban residents, the social importance of the school would be diminished. This indeed is claimed in the Aston University report, based upon a sample of schools in varied West Midland districts. The level of involvement in school-related activities among villagers, apart from parents who have a direct interest, was repeatedly described as being 'relatively low'. Yet it is difficult to see how this conclusion was derived from the data presented in the report. For example, in villages with schools, 45 per cent of non-parents had visited the school at least once in the previous year, 73 per cent had visited it at some time in the past and 52 per cent perceived it as being an important meeting place for villagers. The corresponding figures for parents of children in the schools were naturally much higher, but if those proportions among non-parents represent 'relatively low levels' of involvement, we need to ask what the basis of comparison is. There is no equivalent data for urban or suburban schools but it is hard to imagine such schools generating that level of support for their activities. The only comparative data that the Aston report does provide is from villages without a school and there, the proportion of non-parental contact with their nearest school was very much lower.

The formal event which brings a number of people into face-to-face contact is one aspect of the integrative function a school may serve. In addition, there are numerous informal contacts between residents which are occasioned by the presence of a school in a rural community through its day-to-day working. Parents accompany young children to school and collect them in the afternoon; the school gate and the school cloakroom provide a daily rendezvous. For mothers potentially isolated during the day and for newcomers, these are not insignificant events. Forsythe's case studies provides many illustrations of this:

> 'The school is the centre of activity in the glen. When you see mothers you always talk about what's happening at the school. Without the school, there wouldn't be the same communication. It gets you out more, you're more involved. I would hate to see the school closed'. (p166)

and:

> 'If there was no school in the glen, the mothers wouldn't know one another'. (p166)

Our own interviews with mothers in villages where the school has been closed reveal the same sense of the value of those indirect benefits which have now been lost:

> 'We never see each other now because I take John to [the new school] by car and therefore I go through the village by car. I drive through the village and drive back again'.

and:

> 'Last week I was on holiday and I walked through the village with Brian and that was the first time I had walked through the village since I don't know when'.

This attenuation in social contact is not only between village residents but also between parents and the teachers of their children. When a local school is closed and its pupils transferred to another school in an adjacent village or larger nearby town, the informal contact which previously parents had known with the teachers is invariably reduced. The Aston University research shows how conscientiously many headteachers of receiving schools had approached the task of making the new parents feel welcome, but despite that, social contact tended to become limited to formal events and the very occasional visit:

> 'Whilst most parents felt that reorganization had had little effect on their attendance at the occasional *formal* event staged by the 'host' school, it had produced a marked reduction in the opportunities for informal contact with teachers at the school gate'. (p56)

Our own observation in areas of Norfolk which are poorly served by public transport and where many parents do not have private transport confirm this impression, and that, despite the extraordinary lengths to which some headteachers do go to make themselves available to talk to parents.[5] Forsythe reiterates the same point; with the closure of a village school, parents have less contact with the 'new' school, meet the teachers far less often and feel they know less about their children's education. Furthermore, she suggests, the passage of time does not lessen the social distance any more than it reduces the physical distance:

> 'Even many years after reorganization, the alternative school remains to both parents and non–parents a more remote institution'. (p134)

A second indirect benefit that is said to derive from the presence of a village school is captured in *The Times* editorial ('Village Schools Revalued') which followed the publication of *The Decline of Rural Services*:

'It is not the rural bus, post office, shop or pub, important as all these can be in safeguarding a village's identity. It is, above all, the school which is felt to embody the idea of the village as something alive and enduring'. (11 September 1978)

The local school is depicted as symbolically representing its rural community and as being the focus for a set of subjective experiences which we can call 'a sense of community'. Newby (1980) refers to this as 'communion' — 'a sense of belonging, of sharing a social identity in a spirit of friendliness and common emotional experience' (p154). It is probably the locally perceived loss of this symbol that largely accounts for the recurrent death imagery in so many of the Case for Retention documents.

This view of the rural community is not one that is universally shared. Newby himself warns:

'All too often English villages are projected as ideal communities, where life is more wholesome, more reassuring and more indefinably valid than in, say, a suburban housing estate'. (p23)

In relation to the school closure issue, Warner (1973) dismisses the argument as 'merely emotional' and the Aston University report cautions policy makers of the 'need to make a distinction between "feelings of loss" and changed patterns of social/community behaviour'. Quite why feelings of loss should be regarded as less real than changed patterns of observable behaviour and hence of less salience to educational planners is not made clear. Certainly the emotional attachment to the school has been real enough to provide the fuel with which many defence campaigns have been driven. What perhaps needs to be asked is why it is that in recent years village schools have been invested with such a symbolic function that reorganization proposals from county halls have been translated locally as threats to the identity of the village itself.

From the 1960s, the long running trend of rural to urban migration has halted and been reversed. The census results of 1981 showed that in almost all rural districts in England and in many in rural Wales, population had increased during the previous decade. The drift out of agricultural work brought about by capital-intensive farming has continued, but at a reduced rate, and has been more than offset by an increasing flow of ex-urban dwellers moving into rural districts (mainly into the small towns and larger villages). Growing affluence and the spread of private car ownership were the initial factors that made this movement possible. The resulting change in the social and occupational composition of villages is, claimed Newby, the most important social process to have occurred in rural areas in recent years:

> 'The result is that today the bulk of the population of most of our rural villages are able to live in the countryside and work in nearby towns and cities'. (p22)

That process has been more advanced in lowland England than in the upland districts where there has been a slower exodus of farm workers and where the road network has extended the commuter belt less deeply into traditional rural areas, but few areas have remained totally unaffected by the transition. Since 1980, two further factors have become apparent: small firms have moved out of urban centres into rural areas and escalating urban unemployment has made migration an unattractive option for traditional rural dwellers. These points are well illustrated in a recent survey in two rural districts of Northumberland:

> 'The particular characteristics of rural communities — their flexibility, informality and personalised relationships — are proving to be strengths under present circumstances ... In comparison with 1972 [the date of a previous survey] this survey has shown a marked decrease in the out-migration of school leavers, some changes in the number and variety of jobs available in the local areas and an unexpectedly low rate of outright unemployment'. (Community Council of Northumberland, 1985, p17)

There are, of course, numerous and varied personal motives that lie behind this reversal of a long-established pattern of migration. For some, it is the utilitarian consideration of lower house prices, and possession of a car not only enables such people to live in the country and work in the town but also allows them to retain the town as the focus of most of their social activity. For many others, however, the decision reflects a dissatisfaction with contemporary urban culture and a desire to enter (or perhaps remain in) what is thought to be a more genuine, less impersonal, smaller scale community which a village is felt to represent — the 'village in the mind' as Pahl (1965) puts it. For migrants such as these, feelings of belonging and wanting to share a village identity are important. So too is the idea of a village school because it reflects precisely those characteristics of community and personal social relationships that they are seeking and which prompted their migration from the towns.

Set against this, the symbolism of the small rural primary school starts to become apparent. Through a period of rapid transformation of rural populations and the social structure of rural settlements, often to the accompaniment of conflict between newcomers and locals, the school represents, for many, a marker of continuity. It is an institution which is relatively impervious to social cleavages in a village and which encourages a harmonious interaction between different socio-economic groups and between newcomers and locals alike. As Forsythe describes, 'It is a valuable institution because it may be the only one which everyone can value'. The point is perhaps demonstrated by the fact that the signatories to Case for Retention documents are usually drawn from all segments of the local population and the accompanying petitions often reveal a virtual unanimity.

Both Forsythe's survey in Scotland and the Aston University's parallel study in lowland England testify to the value that is widely attributed to the local school as agent and symbol of village identity. Similarly, in a sample of Norfolk parishes (some with and some without schools) Connor (1977) was able to establish a strong positive relationship between the presence of a school and the 'sense of community' felt by residents in the parish. Even where parents harbour some reservations about the educational quality of the school, it can be the case that the school's presence is still valued for its benefit to the village. A parent we interviewed had been the secretary of a vigorous and unsuccessful action group; she commented:

> 'My son has gone to the new school now — he's happy; he's doing well there and perhaps he's doing things he may not have been able to do here. I'm sorry that it's shut but I'm not too upset now because of the way he has settled down. But it's just as important to the village as it is for the children. That's what it comes down to in the end. It's just as important for the village. I would do it all again'.

That last remark, in its homely and personal way, makes clear what much of the research has shown about the connection between the small rural schools and the populations they serve. A distinction needs to be made between the direct benefits which derive from the LEA's provision of schools — the education that children receive — and the indirect benefits that accrue to the local area from a school's existence — their contribution to the local economy and to the vitality of social life in its catchment area. For parents who hold their village school in some esteem, closure means the loss of their opportunity to secure a particular kind of educational experience for their children. It also means, and not only for parents, the disappearance of a set of indirect, but often strongly felt, benefits whose costs are not quantifiable in the same way that the costs of direct benefits are.

In one sense, the local commitment that might exist to a local school is peculiarly narrow. The opportunity cost to the local authority for maintaining that school, which may be represented as, for instance, foregoing the opportunity to employ an extra adviser for the whole county or the chance to reduce the pupil/teacher ratio elsewhere is not seen as a cost by the local community. In fact, it is not a cost that is borne locally. But in another sense, the value that is attributed locally to a village school, incorporating as it does, a range of indirect benefits, is more diffuse than that used in the local authority's calculations. An individual officer may have considerable sympathy for the local view but his responsibility is more limited. The rural school is one outpost in a county-wide system of primary education; the quality of life in rural areas is the business of other departments. This division of labour in local government is likely to make rather less sense to a rural population with a wholistic view of the relationship between the school and the welfare of the community. The demand that wider, indirect benefits of the school should be acknowledged and figure in the balance sheet is at the root of their call for 'a more sophisticated form of accounting'.

Costs and Cost Effectiveness

In 1978, Taylor, Chief Education Officer for Somerset, warned against what he termed the 'superficial attraction in rationalization of resources', arguing that the savings that could be made were relatively small and had to be set against a cost of, amongst other things, 'immeasurable, but very substantial loss of public goodwill'. He doubted if 'even the most blinkered cost accountant would regard such a policy as a vital contribution to the containment of a total budget of £60m'. There are several points there which are pertinent to our discussion in this, and in the previous chapter, on the economics of rural primary education.

In the first place, it is clear that small schools usually incur higher unit costs (for the LEA) and that therefore, rationalization has an obvious attraction. The resource savings that can be made may not always be large, especially when they are offset by the inevitable increase in transport costs (private and public); they certainly will not look substantial when put against the total recurrent costs to the authority in its provision of primary education. However, at a time of restraint on public expenditure, they are not necessarily trivial. When savings are translated as opportunity costs they can start to look more worthwhile, as we saw in the illustrative study in chapter 7. Saving the salary equivalent of one-and-a-half teachers may look superficial when the revenue costs for the area amount to a quarter of a million pounds, but it represents the opportunity to provide in-service support or additional material resources which may bring significant direct educational benefits.

But in the second place, there are costs to be set against the resource savings which rationalization makes possible. The very process of rationalizing the provision of rural schooling can create a substantial loss of public goodwill. Archbold and Nisbet (1977) report 'a widespread feeling of powerlessness, or political alienation' among parents when a local school is threatened with closure. The follow-up study at Aberdeen University reached a similar conclusion, although there was considerable variation in parents' views occasioned largely by their recent experience of the politics of closure:

> 'Thus it seems that school closure not only heightens people's feelings that they are powerless *vis a vis* the authorities, but also contributes to a widespread feeling of dissatisfaction about that situation'. (Forsythe, 1983, p114)

In the second of the case studies presented in chapter 1, there are sharp indications of alienation from the processes of local political decision making. People who entered the campaign believing that the democratic process would at least be fair and reasonable, emerged at the end not simply defeated, but convinced that it had been a sham, the decision already taken before a word had been uttered in public debate. We had a number of other glimpses of this when interviewing people who had previously taken an active role in a school defence group which always took us by surprise. People began the interview, recalling in a matter-of-fact manner the events of several years before, and an hour later, were close to tears. The telling had rekindled the emotions of the time, and these were chiefly feelings of anger and frustration at the perceived impotence of local inhabitants to influence the decisions of a remote county hall. In a democracy, that has to be considered an indirect cost which bears upon how people perceive the quality and condition of their social life and their capacity to shape it.

Quite apart from these consequences that the political process of rationalization can bring about, it is clear that the maintenance of a village school confers indirect benefits which disappear when the school is closed. They are not, as Taylor's remark indicates, quantifiable, but the formal and informal activities which spring from a school's presence and the way it helps parents and non-parents to define and share some common identity are almost invariably valued locally. Schools in compact urban areas are rarely required to serve this function which may partly explain why the argument about indirect benefits carries comparatively little weight in educational debates. Ironically, however, when urban schools are designated 'community schools' and are called upon to undertake a broader responsibility, not only do they still draw upon the original rural prototype, the Cambridgeshire village college, they are highly prized for such successes as they achieve.[6] In remoter areas where distance and sparsity of population hinder opportunities for social contact, small primary schools may be the major institution that encourages interactions among a significant proportion of the local inhabitants. For that reason, their continued presence is valued, sometimes irrespective of their strictly educational quality.

It follows from this, rather as Taylor seems to be suggesting, that a dispersed pattern of schools could be viewed as a legitimate feature of a county council's policy of development in its rural districts because of the variety of indirect benefits it could produce. It would, however, cost more. How much more is open to debate and would in any case be dependent on the scale of dispersion, but without doubt, it would involve higher annual revenue costs to the local authority than would be incurred if primary education were to be provided through a more concentrated pattern of fewer, larger schools. The question therefore becomes: would it be cost-effective?

This has to be asked in relation to any kind of public service provision. A case study undertaken in Norfolk[7] to examine the cost effectiveness (over a range of public utility, community and social services) of alternative patterns of new housing development reached the conclusion that any form of dispersal results in higher costs than does a concentrated pattern. This might, nonetheless be countenanced. As Shaw (1976) in his paper *Can We Afford Villages?* put it:

'The capital and revenue price of dispersal is high, but the two factors mentioned above [school closures and stimulating community groups' activity], coupled with the additional choice of new village housing sites implied by dispersal policies are powerful arguments in favour of accepting the cost ... Clearly village development is not a bargain, but may not be an expensive luxury either'. (p137)

We encountered the question of cost effectiveness at the end of the previous chapter when considering the direct costs and benefits of different strategies of educational provision. There it was argued that making a judgment about an educational proposal depended not only upon being able to calculate its costs but also upon assigning some value to its direct benefits to the pupils. Simkins (1980) expresses it well:

'The point is that costs per pupil in themselves tell us very little about the relation between resources expended and results achieved. Cheap education is not necessarily economic education ... Data on costs per pupil will always be inadequate by themselves for decision-making therefore, and will need to be supplemented by information concerning the quality of education provided as a result of the resources expended'. (p89)

The difficulty with education is that it is not a uniform product about which there is little disagreement; on the contrary, what comprises a 'good education' is a value-laden issue. As we have seen throughout, the evidence that does exist on educational quality in relation to rural schools is extraordinarily inconclusive and open to different interpretations. If we now insert the whole issue of indirect benefits into the calculation, the matter becomes more complicated still. Simkins again:

'Thus even if it can be shown — and often it can — that school closures produce resource savings, any final decisions still depend on the value attached to educational and social outcomes judged to be associated with different patterns of provision ... The final decision will continue, therefore, to depend on judgments which may give varying weight to estimated educational, social and, indeed political outcomes'. (p90)

The outcomes that Simkins is referring to are the (direct) education benefits to the pupils and the (indirect) social consequences that stem from, or are believed to stem from, any particular pattern of provision. We do not know with any certainty what these are. Furthermore, even when there is no dispute about the material facts, there is still much scope for disagreement about how much importance to attribute to them. In short, the economic debate about the cost effectiveness of alternative ways of providing primary education in rural areas is as much about educational and social values as it is about comparative unit costs.

Having said that, the fact remains that decisions still have to be taken about patterns of school provision. It is possible, as Shaw indicates, that:

'. . . restraint on public expenditure may well force the adoption of the cheapest [public] planning strategies . . .' (p137)

That, however, should not be automatically equated with the 'most efficient and economic deployment of teaching staff', as *Better Schools* puts it. Cheap education is not necessarily economic education. But we have known this since the beginning of mass education in this country. Over a century ago, Robert Lowe justified the Revised Code to Parliament saying:

'If it is not cheap, it shall be efficient; if it is not efficient, it shall be cheap'.

Notes

1 To an extent this would be offset by the increased demand for bus drivers although that would probably have greatest impact in the key village in the area.
2 Chapter 1, first case study.
3 See Dahloff and Andrae (1973).
4 The one, seemingly robust, piece of evidence that primary school closures precipitate village population decline is said by many school retention documents to be offered by Lee (1961). In fact, Lee was concerned with the effects upon population change of eliminating all-age schools and the establishment of separate secondary schools in rural areas. Villages in which the primary school had been closed were eliminated from his sample.
5 For instance, we know of one headteacher in a particularly isolated area of Norfolk, poorly served by public transport, who regularly holds consultations with individual parents in her car, which she drives round to outlying districts. She has also constructed an elaborate network of telephone numbers and parental contacts so that she could, in any emergency, convey a message to any parent.

6 A further irony of course is that as more urban schools are being transformed into 'community schools' in an attempt to combat some of the social
problems found in urban areas, rural areas are being required to accept an
increasingly urban model of school provision.

7 Norfolk County Planning Department (1976) *The Walsham Area Study*.

Section IV
The Future of the Small Rural School

Chapter 9

Beyond Mere Survival: Supporting the Rural School Teacher

Anyone who has lived in a rural area since the end of World War II has been witness to a decline in local institutions. 'Rationalization' and 'reorganization', those key planning concepts have, between them, seen off the branch railway lines, have reduced the presence of vicar and policeman alike, and have placed the village post-office and the village school within the category of endangered species. Decline, from the grassroots vantage point appears inexorable. Yet Sher (1981), in his overview of rural education in those nations belonging to the Organization for Economic Cooperation and Development, (OECD), ultimately strikes a cautiously optimistic note. Giving what he terms the 'bad news' first, he observes that up to the mid-1970s:

> 'Just as country roads have been routinely left off national maps so too country schools have been routinely left off national education agendas'. (p1)

He also notes the consequences for rural schools of being 'left off the map'. The deflection of physical resources to urban areas has resulted in school buildings falling into disrepair. Educationally too, attention has been devoted to the curriculum needs of urban children, whilst rural schools have frequently been seen as the test-beds for bright young educators destined for the heights of urban office, or alternatively, as the Siberias for those teachers falling foul of administrators. Moreover, of the period up to the mid 1970s, Sher observes:

> 'Politically, too, rural education fell into a measure of disrepute. Policymakers dealt with country schools largely in negative terms (when they gave them any consideration at all) instead of recognizing or building upon their capacity for excellence. In addition, the discovery that rural schools could be ignored,

closed, or treated less than equitably without serious political repercussions made the temptation to treat them in this way enormous. The result, even if unintentional, was that national bureaucracies behaved as if quality education should not be wasted on children in sparsely populated areas and as if second-rate schooling was good enough for their rural consti- tuents'. (pp1–2)

Acknowledging that his discussion takes no account of the initia- tive underlying the many local examples of excellence in rural educa- tion to be found in OECD countries, Sher asserts unrepentantly of his overview, 'pointing out the failure of national educational policies and practices to fully satisfy the needs of rural children and rural communi- ties *is* accurate' (p2).

Having offered the 'bad news' of the time up to the middle of the seventies, Sher offers the subsequent 'good news'. He claims that since the mid-1970s there have been signs of a change in attitude towards rural education and that, whilst such change is by no means of high priority, political debate about rural affairs is now much more evident than a decade ago. This modest shift of interest, observable across OECD countries, Sher attributes to a variety of factors including 'demographic and economic changes; trends towards decentralization, dissatisfaction with traditional policies; renewed respect for rural models; and, perhaps, most important, pressures for equal educational opportunity' (p5).

If one considers the Scandinavian context, then Sher's choice of the mid-1970s as a point when a sea change occurred possesses some validity. The beginning of the 1970s, as Findlay (1973) points out, saw the first official questioning of the Norwegian policy of small school closure, and subsequently, government encouragement for the reten- tion, and even, the building of small schools in sparsely populated areas — an inconceivable policy ten years before. At about the same time, Sweden initiated a feasibility study of the adoption of multigrade classes in upper secondary schools as an alternative to closure (Dahloff and Andrea, 1973). With respect to curriculum, the Lofoten Project was established to explore ways of generating curricula more re- levant to the rural context, (Hoegmo and Solstad 1977). In the same year, the Norwegian voice within the Nordic Council of Ministers, with pre-school and community links in mind, asserted:

'Stressing the community culture in the shaping of pre-school activities strengthens the popular feeling of village and district identity, a change which is in line with other social and political trends in Norway'. (p33)

Outside the Scandinavian orbit, Fthenakis and Bauer, (1977), speaking of the Isolatenprojekt in Upper Bavaria observed:

'The knowledge of the world, of life and experience of country children must be at the basis of our work. This is of special importance if we consider the danger of alienating these children from their social context and environment'. (p14)

A British cynic could observe that one requires an extremely sensitive litmus to indicate change in the official attitude towards the small rural school and its future in the United Kingdom. That observation would undoubtedly be true, yet change is detectable. One aspect of that change, across the period Sher has in mind, is evident in the differences of view to be found in the comments of Forsythe, (1969) the then Chief Inspector for the Highland Region of Scotland, and those of his successor, (Johnston, 1981).

Forsythe, charting the changes in rural life, the increased accessibility of towns for work and leisure and the consequences of these for the village school, regarded the demise of many of its kind as inevitably part of 'a process of reorganization and rationalization ... so that it may better match the conditions and needs of the times'. Twelve years, and many school closures later, a change of perspective is detectable in the observations of Johnston:

'The really important debate about the future of the smaller school in rural and sparsely populated areas should be about the conditions for its effective life. By such an examination we shall best clarify the issues in any fights for survival that may still ensue. More important, we shall reduce the chances of mere stagnant survival which is perhaps the more dangerous insidious prospect ...

Ultimately the success of small schools depends upon the preparedness of sufficient teachers to work in them, and have more than a fleeting affinity with them and their environments; upon the quality of these teachers, which depends upon their pre-service training and support they get while they are in post; and upon the quality of partnership established between the public whose children go to these schools and the teachers who serve in them'. (p31)

It is important not to draw from Johnston more than he has said.

His comments do not constitute an announcement that the era of small school closure is at an end. What is evident is a recognition, first of the need small schools have for teachers of quality, who are professionally and socially sensitive to their environments and second, for those teachers to be provided with support.

Whilst the central government has set its official face firmly against small schools with under 60 children on roll, between 1985 and 1986 it has funded, via its educational support grant system, no less than a dozen local education authority projects the aim of which is to 'improve the quality and range of curriculum provided in primary schools in rural areas'. If one sets aside the apparent contradictions in a government policy which, on the one hand, appears to be bent upon the eradication of small schools, and, on the other, offers funding for projects designed to enrich the education they provide, there remains one important and novel feature which should register on our litmus indicator. For the first time, a central policy has recognized specifically that teachers in small rural schools require systems of support and development which may be different in kind from those in urban areas.

The history of national recognition of the need for the professional support of teachers in small schools, prior to this time, fits snugly into the 'bad news' aspect of Sher's overview of national policies. Across the post-war years, advice on what teachers in small rural schools might do about their professional development has in no respect amounted to an overall policy. *Primary Education,* the Ministry of Education's 1959 replacement for the *Handbook of Suggestions* urged village school headteachers to 'seek exchange of ideas' and gave credit to those of them who journeyed to conferences because they 'courageously surmount these difficulties and revitalize their work by the stimulus of discussion with their fellows elsewhere'. By 1967, the Plowden Report was emphasizing the need for a much expanded provision of in-service education for all teachers. Yet, despite its anxiety over rural teacher isolation, it had little to say that was specific to that group. Beyond commendation of an example of inter-school cooperation, it advised the rural school staff to work as a group, affirmed the need for residental courses, and observed that 'country teachers also need to meet teachers from a wide range of schools'. Limited as that advice might be, it remains the greatest recognition that rural teachers have achieved in a national report. The James Report (1972) whose task it was to survey both the initial and in-service education needs of the nation's teachers, and to recommend an overarching policy, did no more, with respect to the rural school, than to employ it in order to exemplify the diversity of experience which novitiate teachers might experience as they entered teaching. It observed:

'The same pattern cannot be right for a three teacher school in a rural area and a large urban comprehensive school . . .'

That observation, directed as it was, to the needs of probationer teachers, also bears upon the question of the appropriateness of particular kinds of support and in-service education for small rural schools and their teachers. From chapter 5, we may recall that Skinner was concerned not simply that rural teachers missed the stimulus of a large school staff, but also that they were separated by considerable distances from urban centres of professional refreshment — universities, colleges and teachers' centres. Given that the major provision of in-service education is urban based, then Skinner's worry is valid.

Crossman (1985) studied the perceptions which twenty rural teachers had of their task and of the local in-service education available to them. The six schools in which the teachers worked were located at distances ranging from twenty to thirty-five miles from the teacher's centre which was the main in-service base. In the year prior to his study, all but two of the teachers (the two oldest) had attended courses. Fifteen teachers claimed to have attended seven or eight single course sessions: two claimed to have attended between twelve and fifteen single course sessions, whilst the remaining teacher, with log book to prove it, had attended fifty-three single session courses and twenty-four courses of two or more sessions. Crossman's sample is a small one and he provides no comparative urban sample, yet his indication that rural teachers are prepared to undertake in-service commitments, despite the distances involved, receives some support from the findings of the PRISM Project. Comparing teachers in large and small (and hence predominantly rural) schools, no significant difference was found in the amount of in-service training they had undertaken. Both groups were just as likely to have attended courses at teachers centres.[2]

Whilst a willingness to reach out for professional refreshment is evident in the teachers in Crossman's sample, they also measured the cost. Nineteen of the twenty teachers identified distance and travelling time as the major barriers between them and the take up of in-service provision. As one teacher observed:

'Distance is another factor. It's a long haul over to [the teachers centre] and especially from here at half-past three trying to get there for a 4.15 start or even a 4.30 start'. (p49)

Supporting the Rural School Teacher

The time of year, too, was a considerable factor influencing their decisions. One of Crossman's teachers commented:

'I know what I don't do. I don't put myself down for courses in winter, because you just don't know what the fog and ice and road conditions will be. Therefore you miss out'. (p49)

At a practical level of difficulty, over half the teachers referred to the failure of course organizers to take account of the distances rural teachers were required to travel, when planning the starting times of after-school courses. However, it is not just problems of access which may deter rural teachers from attending in-service courses, but also the extent to which such courses fit their particular needs. Whilst twelve of the teachers were generally approving of the in-service courses available, the remainder were less so, perhaps measuring the 'cost' of travel against the 'profit' from attendance. One teacher plainly had the 'cost/profit' view in mind when she observed:

'It has often seemed that the information you have got [at the course] could have been condensed into a handout you could have read in 10 minutes, rather than an hour and a half talk'. (p48)

Although no major criticism of formal, centre-based in-service provision was made by the teachers, eighteen of them asserted that they could identify their own needs more clearly than could outsiders. As one put it:

'We're the people who know what it is we need. It's alright to sit up there in the office and say, 'Ah the rural primary schools all need to do science', but they don't know what science we are already doing, they can't know what our needs really are'. (p54)[3]

Crossman, summarizing his impressions of the teachers' views of their in-service education needs, observes:

'This group of teachers ... see a role for themselves as INSET providers. They appear to be willing to put their expertise and experience at the disposal of the group, to help other teachers ... The INSET needs of the group are met in broad terms by the official county provision. However, matters of specific interest and concern to small rural schools do seem to be missing ... By adopting a strategy whereby the members of this group were identifying their own needs and were then actively involved in providing the solutions, a wider view of INSET could develop'. (p69)

The problems of distance and accessibility, of course, have been long-standing preoccupations of those responsible for providing support to teachers in rural schools. Moorhouse (1985) provides a moving account of her efforts as an Assistant Education Officer to provide in-service support to small rural schools in Oxfordshire in the relatively car-less decade from 1946. Whilst increased car ownership since then has somewhat lessened the problem of accessibility faced by rural teachers, nonetheless, as we can see from Crossman's small scale study, the factor of distance remains cogent. A further factor, perhaps more important than distance, may be that much of in-service education which is course-based requires the teacher to be reactive to a provision which does not exactly match her needs or those of her school. Put briefly, a liaison group sounds teacher opinion, courses are organized in the light of those soundings, a programme of courses is published and the teachers 'react' by 'taking' the courses.

That issue, of how one engages teachers proactively, rather than reactively, in professional development, has engaged the minds of many educators, rural and urban alike. The problem of how one simultaneously defeats the difficulties of access *and* encourages a proactive stance to professional problems has provided a challenge peculiar to the rural scene.

Efforts by local advisers and rural teachers to meet the challenge of creating active in-service development are no recent novelty. For example, the instancing by Plowden of a group of small schools cooperating in the interchange of staff, the exchange of ideas and the initiation of new methods, certainly locates an embryonic proactive rural teacher perspective in the mid-sixties. Its emergence too, probably owes more to the pragmatism born of circumstance than it does to elegant theorizing about professional development. Faced with the intractable problem of accessibility to urban sources of inservice education, small groups of rural schools, by themselves, or with the active encouragement of local advisers, have set about the exploration of ways to improve their teaching and curriculum. Almost always, prior to recent, more consciously structured developments such as those arising from educational support grants, the genesis of locally based activities has been idiosyncratic, often arising from a felt need, identified first by one or two people, which, when shared with people in similar contexts, has provided a springboard for action. Two accounts of the early formative developments of small groups which emerged in this grassroots' way are illustrative.

The Litcham Federation[4]

Litcham is a village in North-West Norfolk which, because it stands at the confluence of six roads, is the natural position to locate the secondary school. Apart from the primary school in Litcham itself, nine other small schools, scattered in a radius of six miles, represent the catchment of the secondary school. Fifteen miles from the nearest town and twenty-five miles from the nearest major centre of in-service provision, the Litcham area represents the conventional paradigm of small school isolation.

In 1978, the newly-appointed head of the secondary school, soon to be reorganized as a comprehensive 11–16 area high school, took up his post. One of his first priorities was to encourage his staff to consider the types and range of experience which children from the surrounding small school brought with them on transition. The conclusion drawn from this activity, in the words of the headteacher, was:

> 'If you just looked at the list of headings for the curriculum, then the children had been taught pretty much the same things across the schools. However, if you looked at the nature of the experiences which the youngsters had had, then there was very considerable variation'.[5]

The lesson drawn from this conclusion was not that diversity of experience within a common framework was to be deplored, but that both the secondary school and the primary schools were little aware of the separate contributions which they made to the education of the children in the catchment area. The felt need of the headteacher of the high school became that of exploring the nature of curriculum continuity between the primary and secondary stages. His problem, in seeking cooperation in such exploration, focused upon allaying the familiar 'take-over' suspicion which primary teachers experience when a secondary school takes an unusual step in their direction.

An initial suggestion to the primary headteachers, that it would be useful to meet and talk informally about what the new high school was planning to do and what the primary schools were currently doing, met with a positive response. The informal, and as it turned out, inaugural meeting of the group, which the secondary headteacher did not chair, to avoid 'laying some sort of path, or setting out a way ahead', was fruitful. The participants decided to focus upon a common specific aspect of their teaching, and mathematics was chosen. At the subsequent meeting, chairmanship neutrality was ensured by an outsider, a local adviser, filling the position. From this meeting emerged a purpose aimed at a product; it was decided to consider the kinds of mathematical work upper juniors should experience and the levels of achievement that should be expected. A schedule of regular meetings across the year was drawn up, and these yielded a list of thirty-seven mathematical objectives, which not only served their obvious purpose in the primary schools, but also provided the basis of a mathematics profile for pupils as they entered the high school.

As the (by now) Litcham Federation entered its second year, recognition of the worth of its activity by the local authority, yielded a small, but valuable, addition to staffing which freed teachers to visit, observe and consult across the primary schools and the high school. The timely publication of the Cockcroft Report on mathematics education provided an external stimulus for further consideration of the subject, and provoked a strategy subsequently employed in other activity. Small cells, each of two or three primary members and a member of the high school's mathematics staff, took on different sections of the Report and produced relevant teaching materials. These were first trialled by groups of children from the primary schools in a mathematics workshop held in the high school, and subsequently in the primary schools themselves. Importantly, the small cell system of working allowed work groups to meet in the primary schools, rather than the high school, and became a regular feature, alongside the larger meetings, of the Federation's style of working. Fortune too, smiled upon its activities when the headteacher of the high school won a minibus in a Heinz Foods educational competition, thus providing much needed transport for all the schools. The Federation, now in its eighth year, and with enhanced local authority support, continues to develop.

A Cornish Cooperative Teaching Venture

Ohlson, (1983) one of the headteachers in a cooperative venture between three small rural schools, identifies the spur to action as a disturbing assertion made in a meeting that: 'small schools could not compete with large ones'. The basis for the assertion, it would appear, was that inevitably, larger schools contained a greater array of specializms. In a subsequent discussion with a neighbouring headteacher, the idea was born that if a third headteacher in a nearby small school could be involved, the specialisms of music, environmental studies and science could be deployed across the three schools. The third headteacher, when approached, agreed to participate. Two of the headteachers also agreed that a further area of cooperation, in the field of mathematics and involving the other teachers in their schools, should be undertaken. Their first attempt at cooperative working took place in the summer term of 1980.

The pattern of working, for the purposes of specialist teaching, involved the three headteachers in a three-way exchange on two afternoons per week, with each headteacher taking full responsibility for planning, carrying out the teaching and marking the children's work in their chosen specializm. Ohlson observes that all three learned much about their own schools by working in the other two and by discussing levels of expectations, standards and pupil behaviour.

At the end of the first full year, a change was made, chiefly because all three headteachers felt that they were away from their individual schools for too long and because travelling time was uneconomic. To offset these problems, changes in the times and the style of working were effected, whereby exchanges were timetabled from 9.00 to 10.30 on two mornings each week. On those mornings, the headteachers travelled directly from home to one or other of the schools, taught their specialism and then returned to their own school during the mid-morning break, leaving follow-up activity to be completed. This, as Ohlson observes, made self-contained specialist work difficult to maintain, but produced weekly planning meetings which were professionally beneficial. Partly as a result of such discussion, and partly as the consequence of a stimulus from an in-service art course, a switch was made to topic work informed by the principle of direct learning experience and in which, each headteacher took responsibility for a particular component.

Disappointingly, the attempt to hold joint meetings of staff in two of the schools to develop their mathematics curriculum did not succeed. In Ohlsons's view, failure was due partly to the fact that the infants' teachers had not shared the experience of class exchange and because little interchange between infant and junior teachers in the two schools had occurred. Hence, the meetings were theoretical rather than grounded in professional familiarity and shared practice.

Despite changes in personnel and the style of cooperation, the venture continues, having gained along the way Schools Council recognition and support from Cornwall LEA.

It is, of course, not always the case that the source of action has its location within the small schools themselves. Often primary organizers and advisers, sometimes flying in the face of county policy, and sometimes, with its backing, have devised and implemented schemes aimed at supporting and developing the work of small schools. The Northamptonshire Rural Schools Project, commenced in 1974, when the 'large is beautiful' orthodoxy was particularly strong, is illustrative of a county policy aimed at small school support, as is the Nottinghamshire Small Schools Project.

The Northamptonshire Small Schools Project

In 1972, with the appointment of Northamptonshire's first primary school adviser, a survey was carried out of the resource provision, the range and quality of curriculum, and the extent to which certain small schools could still be regarded as viable. At the time, Northamptonshire possessed seventy-five schools with less than 100 pupils on roll. The survey completed, a report was submitted and on that basis, the Education Committee established the first phase of a project to support and enrich the curriculum of small rural primary schools at a cost, in 1974, of £50,000. Three groups of schools, in different areas of the country, were selected. One group comprised seven 4–9 schools, and the other two groups each contained nine 4–11 schools.

Resources formed the first priority. In terms of personnel, each group of schools was assigned the services of a scale 4 advisory teacher with a designated responsibility for project development. A peripatetic music teacher was appointed to each group of schools after consultation with school staffs and, following a survey of the schools' staffing establishments, extra teaching hours were allocated to those schools whose establishments were below the 'most favourable' for their category. Schools with less than 100 on roll were also given an additional five hours of secretarial/ancillary help to provide each of them with twenty hours per week. Physical resources included a minibus for each group, free of charge with respect to use and maintenance. The provision of equipment shared by schools and based on resource centres, included a head copier, 'jumbo' typewriter, film projectors, cine camera, duplicator and kiln. Further, a schedule of equipment such as might be put into a new small school was drawn up, and allocations made to schools in relation to deficiencies in the resources they already possessed. The only direct financial help given to schools was a per capita £1, for the purchase of practical equipment for mathematics. Maintenance of equipment and TV rental costs were taken by the authority.

Addison (1982) observes, that when the project was first discussed with schools, it received a mixed reception with regard to almost all aspects of provision. The advisory teachers represented a novel kind of appointment and, following as they did, close behind the appointment of a primary adviser, also a novelty, there were suspicions that a good deal of the headteachers' autonomy could be lost to the advisory teacher who could well become a kind of chief headteacher. Addison observes: 'there is no doubt that the holders of the posts needed to exercise the greatest tact and to work hard for credibility and acceptance in the early days'. The scale of resources too, provoked some unease. The provision of the minibus was seen by some as pointless, principally by teachers who at first could envisage its use only occurring out of school hours. Some teachers criticized what they took to be excessive provision, for example, microscopes, collecting equipment and binoculars. One head in fact complained to the Chairman of the Education Committee about the provision of binoculars for use in a primary school. Ancillary help had only been provided the previous year in Northamptonshire primary schools and the increase in such provision proved too much for schools which had not made use of their existing allocation. Addison comments: 'For such schools, it was difficult for them to imagine how two adults could work in one classroom, particularly when one of them was not a teacher'.

Despite these initial concerns and criticisms (felt by approximately 30 per cent of the schools involved) there were heads and teachers who identified the possibilities from the outset and responded positively. Addison observes that, eight years after the start of the project, almost all the schools in the original group are very supportive, use the resources well and are pleased to be part of the project. In assessing the factors which she regards as chiefly responsible for bringing about a change of attitude, she nominates resource provision, a range of INSET activities on which the schools can draw, greater concern within the county generally with regard to curriculum development, and some personnel change within the groups of schools, allowing an influx of people keen to participate. However, for Addison:

'... there is no doubt that the main reason for the changing attitudes is the way in which the Advisory Teachers in different ways established confident relationships and showed by example what could be achieved with children given some of the resources now at their disposal'. (p3)

Scoley (1983), Chief Inspector for Northamptonshire, assessed the main benefits of the project as follows:

'It can be observed generally that the curriculum is more lively and practical, that schools are more willing to involve a range of outside resources to support the curriculum, that much more use is made of the involvement for learning, that more children have an opportunity to work with children from other schools and that liaison with the other phases of education is much more effective'. (p7)

The Nottinghamshire Small Schools Project

Betty (1985) reports that in 1981, a group of local primary inspectors, concerned about the nature of support to be provided for small rural schools, visited a number of shire counties to see developments in small school support elsewhere. With that background, the local inspectorate met with rural headteachers to find out what their 'problems, difficulties, hopes and aspirations' were for their schools. An extension to the county in-service provision had made available to the inspectorate the resource of an additional 1000 'teacher days' for in-service work in schools, and the views of the headteachers were sought on how this enhanced provision might be used. On the basis of this consultation, a policy emerged in which the main thrust was to employ the 1000 teacher days to provide curriculum input via the employment of 'consultant-support' teachers and to enable headteachers to use a number of the days available to provide cover for teachers to attend in-service courses. Additionally, an increased allocation of part-time teaching help was made available, as was a small amount of time to enable teachers to visit other educational establishments.

For the purpose of the project, schools were grouped in federations of four or five. Consultant-support teachers were recruited on their known excellence in those areas of curriculum which the schools had identified as requiring enrichment and extension. The consultant teachers, drawn from both large and small primary schools, were seconded for periods ranging from half a term to two terms.

The consultant-support teachers worked broadly in two ways,

assisting schools to draw up programmes of work and also working alongside individual teachers, where they engaged in the joint planning, organization, teaching and analysis of an agreed area of curriculum. In one group of five schools, the consultant teacher was employed to assist the staff of the schools in drawing up an art and craft programme and to work alongside the teachers in its implementation. In another, science was identified as a curriculum priority and, following a planning meeting, each of the schools undertook the development of a specific science area. With the aid of the consultant teacher, the individual schools worked out a programme which was then implemented via co-teaching and shared with the other schools. Other areas of the curriculum which were developed in broadly the same way were mathematics, topic work, language development, craft design and technology and a programme for the rising fives.

The school-based work also yielded initiatives from the schools in terms of in-service courses and workshops which made use of official in-service agencies, consultant teachers and teachers from the schools themselves. Commenting upon one locally inspired in-service initiative, Betty observes:

> 'This was an excellent initiative which came from the schools themselves. They applied for course support through the local authority's in-service education procedures. The fact that the course was school-based and centred on the needs perceived by individual teachers gave the course far more relevance to classroom practice than might be the case where an outsider proposes a series of meetings, some of which could be useful but others less so'. (p20)

The Small Rural School: Images of Professional Development and Support

In all four preceding accounts, the locus for generating beneficial change has not been the formal provision of centre-based in-service programmes, rather it has been upon how teachers in their small schools can act upon what they define as the priorities demanding action. In the case of the Litcham Federation, the stimulus to action came not from within a formal in-service framework, but from a headteacher's professional interest in how continuity at the stage of secondary transition could be achieved. With Ohlson and his colleagues, the action sprang from a desire to strengthen the curriculum of their schools through their own planning and activity. Both the Northamptonshire and Nottinghamshire projects sought, via additional material and professional resourcing, to provide the kind of basis upon which schools and teachers could identify their needs and, with appropriate support, act to meet them. Whilst none of the four has rejected formal in-service provision as a source to be tapped, all have taken the school and its practice as the point at which to begin.

This development, from 'taking' in-service education to 'making' in-service education, Betty would argue had its roots in 'the action, research and development work [which] has been undertaken in the small rural school'. Yet Hopkins (1986) asserts that change of this kind is recognizable in a number of OECD countries as a consequence of the increased recognition of weaknesses in the 'top-down' or 'centre-periphery' models of teacher and curriculum development. The extent to which a link exists between loss of confidence in 'top-down' approaches at national levels and the style of local initiatives such as we have cited is arguable. Rural schooling has been largely ignored by national agencies of curriculum renewal and teacher development, and it is much more likely that the innovative approaches to be found in rural areas are, and have been, constructed more to overcome problems of accessibility and to meet the particular and peculiar needs of the small rural school context, than to conform to a change in national fashions of in-service development.

Yet what characterizes the schemes of small school support and professional development which have emerged more prominently over the last decade? A term frequently and, in our view, incorrectly, used to describe them is 'school based'. Here, it is necessary to avoid a confusion in terminology between *school-based* and *school-focused* development. School based development we regard as defining action which is limited to the teachers of a school working strictly within the confines of that *school* to effect improvement in its curriculum. Whilst such a constraint does not deny the possibility of tapping outside expertise, it does imply a parochialism which acts as a confinement of the possibilities of that wider exchange which is the hallmark of an extended professional. In other words, school-based development, because it is first and foremost concerned with the school itself, may overlook the individual professional needs of its teachers. Particularly, whilst a large comprehensive school may have both the material and professional resources to operate in a school-based fashion, a small rural primary school does not. Any tendency therefore to create a school-based model of development for small rural schools is likely to run the risk of generating restrictions upon thinking and action.

School focused in-service, on the other hand, implies that while the developmental action will occur within the school and its classrooms, the thinking, planning, analysis and reflection which surround and inform the action will draw upon very much wider professional resources than the school itself can provide. It implies too, that a balance must be struck between the priorities of the school overall and the professional needs of the individual teachers whose activities deliver the curriculum which the pupils receive. In this respect, Howey (1986) in warning of the dangers of simply responding to the needs of the school *per se* cautions that:

'... an emphasis in dealing with problems at the school level or with significant clusters of people within a school should not result in a restricted view of continuing education. Multiple needs and interests among the practising professionals must be addressed, many of which are idiosyncratic in nature. While there are many forms of in-service which speak to individual needs and interests, school focused in-service should also be able to address individual interest and concerns as well as those cross-cutting curricular and organizational concerns which eventually define the scope and nature of a school'. (p45)

Howey, of course, in defining the concerns which school-focused development must embrace, assumes 'school' to be a typically large urban unit. Rural educators, working towards the generation of a school-focused style, cannot make that assumption, for the school units they have in mind are too small, individually, to provide the necessary professional foundations for wide cooperative action which can take account both of school and of individual professional needs. School-focused development in rural areas necessarily involves the 'federating' or 'clustering' of several schools to achieve an adequately sized teacher group as the basis for developmental action. That necessary bringing together of several small schools automatically makes school-focused development in rural areas distinctively different from that which a large urban school might generate. Particularly where a federation of small schools has been externally created by a local authority, fears at the school level may centre both upon the extent to which the local authority intends to use the federation to re-shape curriculum to its own preferred design and upon the degree to which the autonomy of each headteacher and his staff may be eroded. As we saw in the account of the Litcham Federation, the secondary headteacher was mindful of offending small schools' sensibilities, whilst in the Northamptonshire scheme, headteachers were exercised about the effect which a coordinator might have upon their traditional rights of decision. With respect to the nature of school-focused styles of development, it is also important to note that, while such an endeavour in a large urban school necessarily includes its headteacher, a federation of small schools may contain anything from five to ten headteachers, all possessing the rights, responsibilities and traditions of the British headteacher. The strains which such complexity creates are ones which it is necessary to identify so that they may be reconciled to provide a mutually profitable way of federated working.

The first strain, with regard to school-focused development, Henderson (1979) sees embedded in the dual nature of teaching:

> 'At one pole is the concept of the teacher as a professional, implying that he should have exclusive control over his professional development. At the other pole is the concept of the teacher as an employee, implying that training should be controlled by the employer'.[6]

The resolution of that strain is crucially dependent upon the view which a local authority takes of the level of professionalism of its teachers. Where an authority defines the professionalism of its teachers as deficient, the advisory staff may feel unable to trust the teachers' capacity to work in autonomous professional groups to improve both their capacities and those of the school. On the other hand, if an authority regards its teachers as professionally responsible, it may be prepared to accord them considerable freedom to exercise their judgments over the direction of developments.

A second major strain within federated systems of school-focused development lies in the need for all its members to re-inspect and, where necessary, to reinterpret their roles. The headteachers of small schools are, as we pointed out in chapter 5, ideally placed to cooperate with their school colleagues, because their role, unlike that of their urban confreres contains a substantial practitioner element. Yet if, in a federated system, headteachers choose to emphasize their role as that of sovereign head in a context which recognizably demands a measure of professional practitioner equality as the basis of cooperation, then strain is likely between them and their assistant teachers. Ohlson, as we may recall indicated the ease with which the development of cooperation was possible between himself and his headteacher colleagues, but admitted the failure to engage the assistant teachers in cooperative activity across the same three schools.

Interpretations of the nature of hierarchy and the nature of profession which at both school and authority level are crucial shapers of the school-focused activity which small school federations generate. The influence which such interpretations can have upon the cooperation of small schools in rural areas can be seen in the accounts of inter-school cooperation to be found in *Schools in Concert*, the 1983 Report of the Schools Council (Wales). The work which it reports was carried out within the remit of the Council's Programme One which was aimed at supporting local school initiatives in the search for 'practical solutions to the difficulties of curriculum development in rural schools, in the context of their relative isolation and limited resources'.

Groups of small schools in the counties of Clwyd, Gwent, Gwynedd and Powys participated. The project was funded in 1980 and concluded with a conference in March 1983, so that the time for planning, implementation and evaluation was necessarily brief. There was no formal expectation that the groups of schools involved would interrelate or receive funded support after the end of the project. The types of search for 'practical solutions' across the four counties were very diverse, each one revealing particular perspectives on how school-focused initiatives might be organized. Brief accounts of two of the local projects are given below to illustrate differences in perspective.

Small Schools in Concert: Powys

Eight small schools were invited to participate and the local project was initiated by a meeting between the eight headteachers, the Project Director (an LEA Adviser), the Principal Coordinator (the Assistant Director of Education for Schools) and the Schools Council Field Officer. This meeting was followed by a series of meetings held in the participating schools for all the teachers to discuss current work and 'to decide what practical steps could be taken as a result of this cross-fertilization of ideas and by sharing human and physical resources'. These meetings and a questionnaire yielded fifty ideas which could be pursued. By dint of grouping some of the individual items, a shorter list of potential activities was achieved.

Some of the activities drew in all the schools, whilst others brought together small groups of teachers. So, for example, a project 'Our School' was undertaken in the first term by all schools and culminated in a joint exhibition. The idea of an inter-school magazine 'for the children and by the children' was introduced and schools took it in turn to collate, edit and publish it. Sub-groups of teachers worked upon specialist areas. One group planned and implemented one day workshops to introduce teachers and pupils to new techniques and materials in art and craft. Another group worked upon developmental plans for local studies, whilst a third group cooperated in the preparation and publication of a list of local resources including individuals and organizations willing to assist teachers with teaching materials and visits. The Physical Education Adviser and the Science Adviser were able to provide consecutive sessions and workshops for junior children and their teachers. The music organizer coordinated school music activity which provided a musical end to the project itself.

Small Schools in Concert: Gwent

Gwent is a county which is committed by its own policy statement to closing small schools and replacing them with area schools. Nonetheless, the Schools Council's invitation to participate in the project was accepted and the Authority's advisory team selected a group of five small schools 'in the knowledge that they already demonstrated "good practice" in the utilization of local resources'. It would seem that the LEA had no view of informal cooperation developing between the chosen schools, for two were in the north of the county, two were in the south, and one was in the centre.

The Report describes the inception of the local project as follows:

'Early discussions between headteachers and advisers were centred on the existing curriculum in those schools which had agreed to take part in the project. These were frank and open analyses of the schools' situation in which weaknesses in the curriculum were identified. Headteachers were then asked to consult with their staffs about any particular activity which might be improved'. (p17)

The requested consultation highlighted three deficiencies:

1 A weakness in the area of science teaching in the schools.
2 A lack of staff expertise in science.
3 A sense of isolation from teachers working in similar environments.

The advisers and the headteachers, on the basis of the consultations, determined the aims of the group. These were:

'To implement, and then to evaluate, a range of strategies designed to stimulate the teaching and the learning of science. Particular emphasis was to be placed on the use of personnel such as advisers, college lecturers, parents, other teachers, etc.' (p17)

Of the project's developmental style, the Report observes:

'Within the framework of these aims the participating staffs were allowed to choose their own strategies for introducing science into their curriculum. Guidance in this matter was available from a senior adviser who agreed to act as science consultant to the group'. (p17)

And

'The developmental work was mainly school based. Schools worked separately in organizing their own strategies for the introduction of science teaching and then reported on their progress at group meetings which were held half-termly in the participating schools'. (p18)

The form of the inter-group meetings is described as follows:

'All staff were invited to attend, as well as advisers and the Schools Council Field Officer; the interest generated by this project was illustrated by the additional attendance of ancillary staff, parents and governors at their respective schools. At each school the work produced by the pupils was displayed and the headteachers described the strategies they were pursuing and the resources being used'. (p20)

Much interesting activity developed across the course of this project, notably in the ways in which the schools tapped outside expertise, ranging from engineers and scientists provided by the British Association for the Advancement of Science to local people including farmers, clergyman, the school piano tuner and school dinner supervisors. Professional assistance too was drawn from the local college and the Manpower Services Commission. The use of visits and television programmes was assessed and work cards and science kits evaluated.

One of the advisory staff acted as internal evaluator and, 'Headteachers also presented their own evaluation of the success of their strategies ...'. Two quite different perspectives are apparent in the reports of the Powys and Gwent experiences. Whilst the structure of their beginnings was similar in that each was inaugurated with a meeting between LEA officials and headteachers, the purposes were different. In Powys, the first meeting selected a strategy whereby all the teachers in all the schools could be brought together to articulate ideas and to identify cooperative ventures. In Gwent, the first meeting concerned itself with recognizing weaknesses in curriculum. The strategy born of that meeting was for headteachers to consult the individual staffs on the matter of curriculum deficiency and to identify the priority deficits. Extraordinarily, all five schools appear to have identified the same deficits. In Powys, the practical activity which emerged from the teacher consultations was both common and diverse. An initiating project and a thread of music teaching across the schools formed a unifying link, whilst groups of teachers from the participating schools worked on different curricular aspects. Pupil exchange and combined environmental studies outings also fostered group identity. In Gwent, the distance between schools prevented exchange and cooperation of that kind and each school worked as a single unit, reporting progress at half-termly intervals.

Operating at the face value of the reports from each county, one can suggest that, whilst the projects in both counties encouraged the teachers to be proactive towards their teaching and curriculum, what that meant in each of the counties was very different. In Gwent an area of curriculum was identified as inadequate and each school was required to set about its remediation. The leadership of headteachers is evident in both projects, yet the Powys report whilst it fulsomely acknowledges the contributions of the headteachers, uses the term 'teacher' throughout its account of the project. By contrast, the role of the headteachers is dominant in the Gwent report as identifier of deficit and as describer and evaluator of 'their' strategies.[7] In Gwent, setting aside the half-termly meetings, the schools worked independently in a *school-based way*. In Powys, the concern was not about the improvement of a pre-specified area of curriculum, but about encouraging teachers to identify areas in which they could deploy their talents, cooperate across schools and work in a *school-focused way*.

The impression one is left with, after reading the two reports, is of one endeavour seeking to create a style of inter-school working which, so far as it is possible, diminishes the effect of hierarchy and aims towards a horizontal form of professional cooperation across schools to achieve *school-focused* development. The other endeavour is one characterized by a pronounced hierarchy which emphasizes both a more vertical form of professional cooperation and the individual schools as separate loci of activity. One extends the professional orbit, while the other restricts it.

As we pointed out in chapter 5, a small rural school, in which staff relationships are harmonious, provides a sound basis for internal cooperation, because teachers are aware of one another's work and because the unit of operation is small enough for the teachers to take a whole-school view of the curriculum. Thus, whilst its size makes it a quite inappropriate foundation for *school-based* in-service activity, it is ideal in size for developmental activity arising from wider *school-focused* in-service. Given that several schools can be provided with the resources to foster inter-school cooperation, the small school can, whilst retaining its own identity, become one of several crucibles of development. Yet, if a *school-focused* approach to development involving several schools is to be predicated on an assumption of professional cooperation, a radical reappraisal of the traditional roles of headteacher and class teacher becomes necessary, for professional cooperation implies a measure of equal participation. Ladley (1983), the then headteacher of a rural school, at the close of a Schools Council supported study of the essential criteria for small school cooperation, offered this description of the headteacher's role:

'It is from his assessment of the strengths and weaknesses of himself as a teacher, his assistant staff, and of his local school and community situation that he will be able to decide, first of all what sort of grouping, if any, is right for his school. From this he will decide what the in-service needs of he and his colleagues are and what they can give to any cooperative venture as well as what they may hope to gain from one ... The activities undertaken by a group of schools, whether for pupils or as part of their in-service work, must be clearly focused on a particular need which has already been recognized. This focusing is a fundamental duty of the headteacher. He must make it clear to all concerned what purpose is to be met through coming together and the aims he sets must be easily comprehended, be ones that the staff feel confident they can meet, and be assessed frequently. In other words the headteacher must take on the responsibility of not only being the stimulator for change but of being the regulator of it'. (p39)

We dissent not at all from Ladley's perfectly legitimate assertion that a headteacher's task is to lead and to have responsibility for the educational effectiveness of his school. However, what Ladley's prescription of the headteacher's role defines out of existence is the possibility that his teachers, as professionals, can share in that leadership, in the definition of curriculum needs, in the identification of their in-service requirements and in the construction of appropriate forms of cooperation. The teacher, within Ladley's prescription, becomes the familiar 'assistant teacher' of the elementary tradition. He emphasizes hierarchy at the expense of professionality.

If one envisages a federation of small schools operating an active school focused approach, the opposition of the traditional roles of headteacher and assistant teacher must be abolished to avoid developmental stalemate. We were told recently by an adviser of two meetings which he had attended within the space of a week; one of the headteachers of a group of small schools searching for ways to co-operate and one of assistant teachers in the same schools. In the headteachers' meeting, objections were raised to one of the assistant teachers, an expert in her field, leading a group course. Also a barrier to development was noted as a consequence of what they saw as a tendency for the assistant teachers to 'leave it all to us'. In the teachers' meeting, the expressed sentiment was that the headteachers 'took it all to themselves'. Given the relative lack of power which class teachers possess, the logic of the affair is that until headteachers reconceptualize their roles to take account of wider cooperative working, it is impossible for teachers to reconceptualize how they might respond to a context of greater professional equality. Moreover, such a reshaping of roles would undoubtedly bring benefit to rural headteachers, for in our view their professional task is very demanding. It is not only that they have a full-time teaching commitment in addition to their responsibilities as head, but also, whether they live in the village or not, there are expectations that they will participate in community affairs to a much greater extent than their urban equivalents.

There is also a crucial need for local authorities to appraise the posture they are prepared to adopt in relation to the school-focused nature of small school cooperation. Inescapably, local authorities have a right and a duty to ensure that the curricula which their schools offer are appropriately developed. One way to achieve this end is by a tight control of in-service provision and development which takes little account of the professional needs of teachers and their capacity to be proactive. Another is to repose trust in the professional integrity and judgment of teachers and to provide them with a framework for action which, whilst it grants them freedom of action, also contains an element of accountability.

Signs of that necessary reconceptualization of local authority, headteacher, and teacher roles are evident in a number of developments directed to inter-school cooperation and here, the initiative of the Cornwall LEA provides an example. School clusters, beginning in a grassroots way, have, since 1984, received the recognition of the LEA in terms of financial and other support. To achieve financial support, school clusters must satisfy the LEA that what they propose to undertake is likely to strengthen the work of the schools. Moreover to gain further financial support school clusters must demonstrate that they are effective. In that way they are accountable. Two brief accounts of the early life of two clusters provide examples of their approach.

The Inception of the Border Cluster

Wilson *et al* (1985), the headteachers of the four small schools forming the cluster, report that the aim formulated was:

'To promote contact between the four schools and to establish a partnership which will be of benefit to children and staff in academic, social and recreational areas'. (p31)

The targets they envisaged were the upgrading of the curriculum, the development of professional cooperation and enlarging peer group contact. First priority was assigned to staff development and developing a cluster identity. Arts was chosen as an area of the curriculum which all four schools identified as an area to improve.

In the first term the cluster used its financial resources to organize an in-service music course, employed a part-time specialist music teacher to teach across the schools and to provide in-service input and drew in the music adviser to run a series of workshops designed to develop practical professional skills and to explore ways of integrating music with other areas of curriculum. Wilson *et al* observe of these sessions:

'This dual function of the course — improving staff expertise and breaking down staff isolation — ensured that at the end of the course (which had almost 100 per cent attendance) we had learned something and we all knew each other well'. (p31)

The practical outcome of course activity and the help of their 'resident music expert' yielded an integrated approach to music, demonstrated in the coming together of the children from the four schools to present their work and to participate in music, drama, dance and art activities. Planning for the spring term focused on a project 'The Sea and Shipwrecks'. Cluster meetings identified resources and ideas and each member of staff undertook responsibility for organizing aspects of the planned activity. The Exeter and Devon Arts Centre was tapped and a residential project organized for the older children. Children from the four schools were brought together in various combinations for visits and shared work. During the term, a music firm was harnessed to provide a course on basic keyboard skills required for the Yamaha Keyboard. With a further year of funding guaranteed the cluster planned to broaden their view of the arts with attention to writing and art and to begin their work with in-service courses within the cluster. Also included in the plan was the one-term employment of a dance specialist (akin to that of the music specialist) and exchange and discussion of curriculum documents in an attempt to define a cluster arts policy.

Wilson *et al* observe of the early progess of the cluster:

'By concentrating on staff development we feel a great empathy now with teachers from the other cluster schools and the advice of these teachers is easily and readily sought.

We have adopted a pattern of staff development based on in-service work, then practical classroom demonstrations, and then a purposeful getting together of children'. (p33)

The Inception of the Devichoys Cluster

Rowan *et al* (1985), the headteachers of the five small schools, point out that a basis for professional cooperation already existed across four of the five schools prior to the official development of the cluster. Previously, four of the schools had set up an in-service course centred upon the Open University's course *The Curriculum in Action* which was led by one of the teachers. It was during the course that the idea of working as a cluster emerged and the principle established that 'each member of our staffs should have an equal say in cluster activities'.

The first two terms of the cluster's life were very much a time in which cluster identity was emphasized and shaped. A Cluster Carol Concert brought the schools together as participants and from the musical activity which preceded it emerged the Early Music Group in which the specialism present in one of the schools was placed at the disposal of the others. Inadequate games facilities prompted an approach to the local comprehensive school and secured the use of its sports hall. Its pottery teacher, an enthusiastic supporter of the cluster was drawn into its work. With the extra financial support from the LEA, it was possible to hire a professional theatre company for a joint drama workshop for teachers and children. As can be seen, the first two terms of the Cluster's existence had been characterized by immediately possible activities which celebrate cooperation. Rowan *et al* observe that their *Curriculum in Action* course which ended during this time left them with the question: 'What do you intend to do now?'. That question the group faced and produced short and long term plans: the short term plans included:

1   Consideration of computer use and an evaluation of software.
2   The examination of science materials and the development of resource packs.
3   Consultation with an adviser on the HMI *English from 5–16* document.
4   The planning of an outdoor education curriculum for all age groups and involving the development and implementation of a maritime project based upon group in-service activity.

An LEA view of the cluster scheme is provided by Fryer (1985), first Deputy Secretary of Education for Cornwall:

'I am pleased that clusters are developing in an individual way which was always part of the scheme of things. It was never the intention that there would be a particular pattern for cluster development — more a framework provided by the LEA within which clusters could develop their own personality. This is happening with varying amounts of funding and does give, more richness to the overall scheme. Just as clusters should be individual, then schools within the clusters should retain their individuality and integrity. Schools need not always take part in joint activities and, indeed, in many of the clusters one sees particular schools opting out of some activities whilst joining in others — this, I believe, is healthy'. (p2)

A view from the clusters is provided by Bone *et al* (1985), members of the South Launceston Cluster:

'The strength of the Cornish initiative has been in the origin of the motivation. It has been the Clusters that have been able to decide on the direction that we should take. By providing resources without 'strings' each pilot has been able to realize its own ideas. We have been able to opt in and choose our own paths of development rather than have preconceived ideas fed from the centre'. (p38)

It is in those combined views that we get indicators of what is required as the foundation for professional *school-focused* development involving small schools. A first essential is that an LEA is prepared to create a framework, which, whilst it offers support, grants a considerable measure of freedom to local professional judgment so that teachers can be proactive in determining lines of improvement.

As can be seen from the brief accounts of the early months of the Border and Devichoys clusters, the teachers are identifying priorities and working towards them. Certainly, in one of them, a principle of professional equality has been enunciated, and across both, is an awareness of the need for in-service development provided from within and from outside the professional group. In this latter respect, the group, because it has control over the conduct of its own affairs can tailor the time, nature and quantity of in-service input to its recognized professional need. The granting of an additional financial resource, neither generous nor parsimonious, whilst it may allow the purchase of needed equipment and mobility, also gives the opportunity to buy the most precious developmental commodity of all — time — for if teachers cannot have time to visit, meet and plan, then their potential for achievement is made that much the poorer.

A Reflection

There is increasing evidence, at the national level, of a growing interest in the provision of in-service education with a *school-focused* perspective. Here, as at the time of Hadow and Plowden, it may be that the grass roots activity of small rural schools will be cited as pioneering endeavours to be emulated. That, however, does not provide grounds for complacency. Just as the largely unquestioned role relationships of headteachers, postholders and classteachers in larger schools so readily create barriers to effective school and curriculum development, so may the traditional roles of headteacher and classteacher frustrate a full realization of the potential inherent in the interrelation of small schools. An underlying theme in this chapter has been that cooperation should engage teachers professionally rather than hierarchically, for in our view that is the way in which the motivation of all the participants stands most chance of being engaged.

At the present time, it is possible to witness a unique event in rural education, for, as we have already noted, in 1985, the central government, by ways of its educational support grants began a programme of financial support to pilot schemes which are sufficiently long-term to allow an extended exploration of ways in which small schools can be helped to enrich the education they provide. In respect of such grants, no expectation can be held of them becoming a permanent feature of the rural scene. The financial aid which they provide allows experimentation in terms of how additional resources such as transport and extra educational equipment, and human resources such as cluster and federation coordinators and teacher consultants may be deployed to enrich teacher expertise and, thereby, the curriculum. In our view, the question which all of the schemes should address is: What are the major strategies and the essential conditions required to realize a culture of professional equality as the foundation of small school cooperation? That, for us, is the major question, because if we can approach an answer to it, we will be on the way to realizing a form of proactive *school-focused* development which harnesses the professional advantages resident in the small school — even in a cold educational climate.

Notes

1 The title is suggested by Johnston's (1981) paper in which he argues that 'the really important debate about the future of the smaller schools in rural and sparsely populated areas should be about the conditions of its effective life' rather than what he refers to as 'mere stagnant survival'.

2 Professor M. Galton, personal communication.

3 Discrepancy between rural school needs and course provision is not necessarily confined to the teachers. Parson-Jones (1983) records the perceptions of the secretary/ancillary members of small rural schools with regard to their in-service provision. She observes: 'Like rural teachers they are handicapped by their in-service courses being geared to the [needs of] secretaries in larger schools. They gain more information from the informal discussions than from official sources' (p19).

4 The terms 'federation' and 'cluster' have been used in previous rural initiatives where two or three schools have been formally amalagamated under one headteacher as a single school employing the existing sites and buildings. In this chapter we use the two terms as they are currently employed to signify schools which, although they retain their separate identities, cooperate as a group of schools.

5 In personal communication with the authors.

6 Cited in Hopkins, D. (1986) p19.

7 That assistant teachers were not conspicuously present at the concluding conference held in 1983 is evident from one of the five recommendations which it made:

> 'To convene a conference on the theme of cooperation in small rural primary schools within a period of not more than two years and to include a significant proportion of assistant teachers in its membership'. (p44)

Chapter 10

Education and Community Development: What Can the School Do?

This book began with an account of two struggles, each one concerned with a local authority's proposal to close a small rural school and with the organized opposition that was aroused to defeat that plan. The imminent prospect of hanging, it is said, concentrates a man's mind wonderfully. Something similar might also be said about the impending closure of a school; it compels protagonists and antagonists alike to articulate, more lucidly than previously, their beliefs about education.[1] In the cases we considered, despite their differing outcomes, it was possible to discern two quite distinct sets of beliefs about primary education and how best it might be provided in rural areas. We referred to them as the 'official' and the 'grass-roots' perspectives.

According to the official view, small rural schools were an educational liability and an expensive one at that. The educational problems focused on their inability to provide an adequately broad curriculum because of their small and isolated staffs. Furthermore, the limited peer groups invariably found in these schools offered little competition and little social or academic stimulus to pupils. A dispersed pattern of provision was presented therefore as being inherently likely to offer an inferior educational experience to the pupils it was supposed to serve as well as being economically inefficient; the solution, ideally, was rationalization, or as the Americans more bluntly put it, consolidation.

The grass-roots perspective saw matters differently in every respect. The individualized attention to pupils that small rural schools were able to provide and the personal qualities of the teachers were valued more highly than whatever superior facilities larger schools might enjoy and the range of subject expertise that could be found in a larger staff. An atmosphere which fostered cooperative rather than competitive behaviour was seen, and welcomed, as a distinguishing feature of these schools. Far from giving pupils an inferior education, they were depicted as offering an education which dovetailed with the small-scale characteristics of rural communities. And if they entailed higher unit costs, they were the one tangible asset that rural inhabitants received for the rates they paid.

We went on to argue that from the time of Hadow, the small rural school had been officially defined as a cause for educational concern. The exact nature of the deficiency had varied according to the educational issues, priorities or fashions that were prevalent at any one time, but always the particular characteristics of these schools had been depicted as rendering them educationally pathological. Judged by criteria that were derived from the experience of providing primary education in concentrated urban areas, they were deficient, but stemming from the many cases of individual closure, a nationally organized counter-ideology developed which rejected the urbanized assumptions built into the official ideology. It asserted that the scale and organization of primary education found in urban areas was not a universal ideal that should be transposed into the very different social context of sparsely populated areas.

In the middle sections of this book we have examined the assertions and counter-assertions which are embraced by these two ideological positions and which we summarized at the end of chapter 1. It is a task that has been made difficult by the comparative paucity of empirical data which surround these issues; in a predominantly urban society, education in rural areas has been a marginal activity for educational researchers too! On the basis of the material which does exist, we have endeavoured to develop the argument that small rural schools do have distinctive characteristics which can reasonably be thought of as potential advantages if we can escape from the assumption that the typically urban model represents the 'one best system'. If rural teachers can be encouraged to develop those potential strengths of their schools, and are supported when they do so, we have the best chance of enhancing the quality of the primary education provided in rural areas. That may not be an easy task, but so long as small schools serving rural populations are thought of as simply smaller versions of large urban schools, and are expected to function in the same way, they will continue to appear educationally deficient. In the previous chapter we saw signs of a recognition of this in some of the pilot projects that have been initiated in a number of rural authorities.

In this final chapter, we intend to give rein to our imaginations and to become frankly speculative. The issue we will address is one that has been implicit in much of what we have previously considered — the relationship between the school and its wider community. It is here that the official and the grass-roots perspectives diverge most radically. According to the official view, the relationship is essentially a contractual one, in which schools are bound by their formal responsibilities to parents, local authority and government to provide a satisfactory education for the children in their care. Necessarily, that contractual relationship is the foundation upon which education in any school rests. The question is whether, in circumstances where people know and have confidence in each other, it need be a restraint upon the educative relationships between the school and the community it serves.

A Contractual Relationship

In any assertion of the value of establishing cooperative links across the boundary between the school and its environment there is a recognition that education is not confined to what takes place inside schools. Children's learning and development is affected by their experiences both within and outside school. A contractual arrangement between teachers and parents acknowledges this in relation to pupils' home life, but it resists the idea that the character of community life outside the home might be significantly associated with children's development, or at least that the school can assume any responsibility for it.

An appropriate starting point for examining a contractual relationship is the Plowden Report. It firmly established in all subsequent educational planning the virtue of good relationships between a pupil's school and his home community and initiated in its train a welter of research and policy making designed to strengthen the home-school connection. The Report boldly asserted that:

> '. . . educational policy should explicitly recognize the power of
> the environment upon the school and the school upon the
> environment'. (para 80)

Its conception of 'environment' was, however, somewhat narrower than is implied in this statement of an organic, mutual connection; for it was restricted to parents. Thus, in its section 'The Home, School and Neighbourhood', it did not explore what the relationship might be between the school and the neighbourhood *as neighbourhood,* but perceived the latter as constituting parents (or, more accurately, occupational categories of parents). It championed the need for schools to possess close links with their communities, but its emphasis throughout was on parents. The significance of parents was that through their attitudes and child rearing practices, which may or may not have supported the work of the school, they affected children's responses to, and capacity to benefit from, schooling. The purpose of close links with the community was to enable the school more effectively to influence the parents and bring them into closer agreement with the practices of the primary classroom so that they could reinforce the work of the teachers.

The view that neighbourhood or community is essentially comprised of parents as *parents* leads to the view that other adults in the local environment outside the school cannot be thought of as being significantly related to the primary school. Even when the Report proposed a 'community school' it virtually excluded the community:

> 'Our third general purpose is about the 'community school'. By this we mean a school which is open beyond the ordinary school hours for the use of children, parents and, exceptionally, other members of the community'. (para 12)

Its view of the community school in the rural area was, in fact, no different from that which it prescribed for inner cities — a colonizing strategy whereby the influence of the school could be extended beyond its normal boundary and outside its normal hours in an attempt to buttress its educational programmes with its pupils.[2]

The Plowden Report, more than any other educational publication, made the value of school and community links an indispensable element in educational policy. It would now be difficult to envisage anybody responsible for planning primary school provision being insensitive to it, and as we have seen earlier, the creation and maintenance of these links have been identified as constituting one of the essential managerial functions of all primary schools. It also legitimated a particular view of those links which has been incorporated into the official perspective. Except where LEAs designate schools as 'community schools' (and there is much ambiguity in the way that is interpreted) the link is a contractual relationship with parents.

According to this, the responsibility of the local education authority is limited to ensuring that all children receive their educational entitlement, a curriculum which is broad, balanced, differentiated in line with their individual abilities, but relevant to their needs and to national priorities. To this end, it is considered essential to harness the cooperation of parents in support of the school's enterprise, but any more extensive concern, say for example, with the social development of the wider community, is beyond the scope of that contractual obligation. The school is not a resource for the local neighbourhood, except in so far as it provides its children with their primary education;

similarly, the local environment cannot be called upon as a resource for the school except in so far as certain elements of it (the parents) can be enlisted to lend their encouragement to the work of the professional teachers. It may be that the presence of a school does contribute to the formation of a sense of local identity, just as it is possible that other adults may contribute to the school, for instance through fund-raising, but they are incidental bonuses. They are outside the contractual relationship between the LEA and its professional representatives in each school, and the parents of the school's pupils.

It is perhaps useful to look at this in the light of contemporary efforts to improve the quality of schooling because what underpins recent government inspired moves is the view that education is a generic endeavour. The aims for education are considered to be common to all pupils; their needs are uniformly prescribed and seen as being independent of the social context in which they are growing up. It follows from this that the curriculum which pupils encounter should be the same, regardless of where they live. It will, for sure, have to be differentiated according to differences in their abilities, but there is no suggestion that it might need to be differentiated according to locality, because no matter what the nature of the social background, they enjoy the same curriculum entitlement which can be indicated through a national curriculum framework. Similarly, schools can also be perceived as institutions which are independent of their social or regional location; they exist to meet the common needs of pupils, and national priorities. Any one school is, by this reckoning, an outpost of a national system of educational provision; its quality is determined by the quality of its teaching staff, assisted by whatever parental support can be engendered for their efforts. Into this model of state education, a contractual relationship between teachers and parents fits perfectly well.

Equal Opportunity and a Relevant Curriculum

There is, throughout this official perspective, a self-evident and genuine concern not only with enhancing the quality of education, but also with improving educational equality. Notwithstanding the considerable variations that prevail between one LEA and another in the resources they provide for education, it seems eminently fair to insist that all children, whether they live in affluent suburbs, remote hill farms or in decaying inner cities, should receive the same curricular opportunities. Bolton (1985) explains why these two concerns have led to the current Governmental drive to establish a common curriculum:

'It is also understandable that when a nation is concerned about its standing in the world; and about the maintenance of its standards of living and the preservation of its social and cultural institutions; it should, among other things take a critical look at the education of its young people. But perhaps not so well understood is why that parallel debate about equal opportunity, egalitarianism and social mobility should move from school organization and issues such as selective and non-selective education to an emphasis upon internal school factors such as the curriculum and the ways in which teaching and learning are organized'. (p209)

The desire to achieve equal opportunities for all pupils has been a recurrent theme of educational reform in most developed countries, usually with similar results for rural schools. In Norway, for instance, there were two separate school laws (one for schools in towns and one for schools in rural areas) until 1959. Successive legislation has brought about a standardization of the state educational system so that rural schools have increasingly come to resemble town schools: multi-aged classes have been discouraged; the rural school year has been made comparable to the urban school calendar; the curriculum has become approximately equivalent and, so far as physical (and social) barriers have permitted, groups of small schools have been consolidated. Solstad (1981) points out:

'The impetus for these legislative reforms was the struggle for equality of educational opportunity'. (p303)

But whatever the motive, the cost of a common curriculum is that it renders the curricular principle of 'relevance' somewhat problematic. Part of the reason why the particular social environment that children inhabit is not considered material to a consideration of the education that they should receive is because the personal development of individual pupils and the social development of the communities in which they happen to live are viewed as separate things. In as much as they intersect at all, it is through the prescription that *their* curriculum should be relevant to enable them to deal more competently with their life outside school and eventually beyond compulsory schooling. The exemplars that are given of relevance are, however, invariably in terms of *national* priorities rather than *local* needs.

Dearden (1981) offers one criticism of this, from the point of view of the individual pupil:

'What perhaps needs to be said . . . is that it is a fallacy, and also an educationally disastrous mistake to infer from the premise that society needs x the conclusion that therefore everyone must learn x, whether 'x' is engineering, science, electronics or French . . . it looks very much like a species of overkill to impose a compulsory 'national need' version of balance on everyone, regardless of ability and inclination, or more likely inability or disinclination'. (p116)

And similarly, when we survey the immense variations that exist in standards of living between one locality and another, and the significant social and cultural differences that exist, the confidence in some communities and the deprivation in others, it starts to become clear that relevance in the curriculum is attainable only to the extent that LEAs are able to respond to their own social contexts. A relevant curriculum, suggests the Inspectorate:

'. . . increases [childrens] understanding of themselves and the world in which they are growing up; raises their confidence and competence in controlling events and coping with widening expectations and demands; and progressively equips them with the knowledge and skills needed in adult working life'. (HMI, 1985a, para 116)

The world in which they are growing up is not only the cosmopolitan world of national priorities, but the more immediate community of local needs. For primary age children especially, it is in the *local* context that they can have the opportunities to develop the competence to shape their lives and to respond to the demands and expectations that are placed upon them. But that is not an individualistic enterprise, for we are all of us social beings — the unique product of the interplay between our individual personality and a particular set of cultural circumstances which have influenceed us and which we, in turn, can influence. At the earliest age, a child brings to school the stamp of the community upon his or her upbringing, in thoughts, feelings and attitudes, and is also, in however small a way, capable of contributing to the development of that community. In fact, we would argue, being able to contribute to the social development of the community from which children substantially draw their identity is as fine a way as any of encouraging their individual development.

Any set of aims for schooling is an answer to the question: What sort of people do we want our children to be? That question entails another: What sort of society do we want ours to be? It is possible, therefore, to view the matter of curriculum relevance from the other end, that is to say, community needs. As Sockett (1986) puts it:

'Yet what is crucial is for the communities themselves to be helped to articulate a perspective on their future. Young people, and the schools in particular must be close to the heart of those debates. We need strategies which will allow the inventiveness of teachers full rein within such communities, accepting the risks that will entail. You can define it as a strategy of self help, or if you have different politics, community action'. (p10)

In short, national priorities are local needs, and a relevant curriculum requires schools to be responsive to their communities.

Local Needs, Personal Identity and Schools

Hargreaves (1982) in his examination of the adolescent youngster in an urban setting depicts, unsentimentally, the decline of community. Particularly, he focuses upon the former workaday urban neighbourhood and demonstrates how similarities of occupation, the interlocking of kin and friendship networks and the intermingling of old and young have substantially disappeared. In the face of change and diversification in industry and occupation, the rational planning of new housing developments and the attendant dispersal of established relationships, bonding community interests have dissolved. Hargreaves harbours no nostalgia for the dirt and the disease of the pre-war working class 'real community'. The point he seeks to emphasize is that the organic social connections which are the cement of community have decayed.

The dissolution of these communities has yielded for many people the relative privatization of their lives and relief from the social density of a crowded neighbourhood. However, the price to be paid has been the cost of personal anonymity. The consequences for the child growing up in the relatively depersonalized environments which have come to replace the older community settings, Hargreaves sees as serious. The fragmentation or loss of traditional cultural and social structure results in the absence of a set of community relationships wherein a child can find a clear cut identity. Put another way, the child has difficulty in finding a range of voices which provides a degree of harmony in responding to the question 'Who am I?' Within such a social vacuum, the problem for the child becomes that of finding a community within which he can root an identity. For Hargreaves, and indeed for many other commentators, the youth culture found in many urban schools represents 'an attempt to recover a sense of solidarity and community which is now lacking in the home environment'.

It might be argued that this thesis pertains to the secondary school adolescent, whereas our concern is with younger, primary children. To that we can reply that if, in urban areas, cohorts of youngsters do face problems of identity, such problems do not wait upon secondary transfer for their manifestation. Among teachers in primary schools there is concern over the signs of rootlessness and the disconnection between family, neighbourhood and school. A frequently voiced anxiety for such teachers is that to do with the difficulty of developing adequate parent-teacher contact and particularly the problem summed up in the statement, 'You never see the parents you really wish to see'. That very common remark betokens the degree of anonymity which many urban primary teachers would wish to see defeated.

It might also be objected that this thesis applies only to working class inner-city areas or redevelopment estates. Hargreaves doubts that, arguing that 'the middle classes have not remained entirely unaffected by many of the same social forces that have transformed working class life'.

> 'Behind the oak doors of detached houses on fashionable housing estates are hidden many personal and social problems which require solution: loneliness and distress and neglect do not belong uniquely to the working class "deprived"'. (p129)

Nor, we would want to add, do they belong uniquely to urban areas of the country because rural communities too have changed dramatically over the same period. While it is rare to find large parts of villages that have been demolished and reconstructed elsewhere according to a planner's blueprint, it is certainly the case that many who formerly worked on the land have moved into agricultural services and processing plants, whilst others continue to live in the village yet work in the town. In many rural settlements, familiar institutions, the pub and the shops have gone and the parish church no longer possesses individual rights to the vicar; rail links have been severed and bus timetables curtailed. Private housing developments have brought their quota of incomers, committed in some ways to rural living, yet urban in their bread winning. That said, it remains the case that, relative to urban contexts, present day rural communities are more likely to be characterized by face-to-face relationships. Networks of relationships are more likely to be overlapping because in small communities, a variety of groups and activities can only be sustained through community members filling more than one role. It is the absence of such relationships and networks that is the essence of Hargreaves' concern for the decline of community in urban areas. Even so, it is clear that the often romantic depictions of village life which appear in many Case for Retention documents owe as much to imagination as they do to experienced reality. In fact, if the real experience did not often contain an element of malaise, a sense of rural decline and of rural areas being neglected by central decision makers, the school campaign groups may have been less urgently stimulated into action.

Faced with these social trends which are to be found in quite diverse localities, and the implications they carry for the child's development of identity, many schools have become responsive to their communities. In secondary and in primary schools, and in urban and rural areas alike, there are teachers who work to the principles of strengthening the connections between school and neighbourhood, or of making extensive use of their cultural surroundings to give shape and relevant purpose to the curricular activities that they present to their pupils. Hargreaves offers a useful four-fold typology of these moves which, although set in the context of urban comprehensive schools, have general applicability.

First, there is the attempt to recreate a feeling of community within the schools, a strategy which usually takes the form of reducing the hierarchical social distance between teachers and pupils and between the head and the rest of the staff. A second strategy is to invite greater participation in the school's activities by those in the outside community; at the very least this implies elected representatives on parent-teacher associations and it can involve parents in certain kinds of classroom activities. A third development, although largely an option for secondary schools, turns the school into a community centre, sharing its facilities (and occasionally its educational resources) with other community groups. Finally, there is the attempt to develop a community-centred curriculum, to move beyond changes in the structure of the school and to alter the content of what is taught. The chief thrust of Hargreaves' work is in this last direction, the advocacy of a locally relevant curriculum for all of a school's pupils.

There is nothing in any of these strategies, designed as they are to alter the relationship between school and community, which is intrinsic to any particular locality; they appear as feasible (or as difficult) in a large primary school in an urban conurbation as in a remote village. Yet, when we look carefully at how they might be accomplished, certain differences can be detected which relate to the size of the school and the nature of its catchment community.

Consider the first development that Hargreaves mentions, the attempt to establish a sense of community within the schools itself. We have seen from our earlier discussion how the size and the formal structure of the school shapes peer group relationships. The extended peer group in the small school is an embryonic community of pupils, reinforced particularly, in those cases where the school serves a single village, by out-of-school relationships. In the larger school, with several forms in each year group, the organization of single age classes inhibits the formation of communal relationships which cut across those categories. A different strategy is required, which is why some headteachers of large schools, which could be organized conventionally, prefer multi-age, or as it is familiarly known, 'family' grouping. Similarly, the close, personalized relationships between teachers and pupils, the 'family atmosphere' that is acknowledged to be one of the major characteristics of many small rural schools is conducive to creating among pupils a sense of communal belonging. And among the teachers, the small size of the staff and above all, the fact that the head is a full-time teacher, makes it easier for him, if he so wishes, to build an element of professional equality into their relationships. Larger schools have to work within the constraints that a more formal structure imposes.

The same is true when schools endeavour to involve members of the outside community in the school's activities. The greater scale of the school's operations and the more probable anonymity of urban neighbourhoods in which a lesser proportion of parents will know each other, mean that urban schools invariably rely on the formal mechanisms of parent-teacher association meetings and written communications. A rural school, whether it wishes it or not, it caught up in a web of informal relationships (which are likely to include non-parents as well as parents of the current pupils); all of the school's ancillary workers are liable to live locally and to know, and be known by, many others. The school is accessible to the outside community in a way that urban schools rarely can be, because its connections are more organic.

In making these comments, we are not intending to draw any

invidious comparisons, but simply to reiterate what we have been arguing throughout this book — that schools are different by virtue of their size, their location and the structure of the communities they serve. Teachers must work with the opportunities and within the constraints that their situation provides, wherever they are found. The following little incident that we were told about is a perfect illustration. A chief education officer, in his monthly schools newsletter, suggested that it would be a worthwhile idea for small groups of parents to be invited to take lunch at the school; through informal conversation over the table they might gain a better understanding of the teachers' work with their children and the teachers could get to know them better. The head of a two-teacher school, perhaps seeing the suggestion as more mandatory than the CEO intended, said, as she was chatting to a group of parents in the playground at the end of the school day, 'I wonder if you would like to come, a few at a time, and have lunch in the school?'.

'Why ever would we want to do that?', asked one parent.

'Well', said the headteacher, 'It would give us a chance to talk about what we do in school and you could tell me about the children'.

'We do that already', said another parent, 'Like we are now and at Harvest and the Christmas Fair'.

'Why should we want to do that?', repeated the first parent, suspiciously, 'Is there something up?'

Attempts to arrange informal lunch-time meetings or efforts to creat a healthy parent-teacher association are thoroughly appropriate in urban schools as means of extending the school-community link beyond a purely contractual relationship. In small scale rural contexts, where school-community relationships are more organic, there is a different set of energies that might be released.

Can we then envisage a small rural school responding to its community in the way Hargeaves finally records, by aiming to build a more locally relevant curriculum? Even to ask the question in a predominantly urban society, committed to the principle of equal educational opportunity for all, is to invite incredulity. It summons forth images of Morris dancing and rustic crafts, or the whimsy of the pre-war *Handbook of Suggestions* that we referred to in chapter 2. There have been some vigorous examples of that approach to primary curriculum development in urban areas, notably the Educational Priority Area projects, but these were indelibly linked in the public eye (if not in the project teams' view) with 'compensatory education' and making up for the cultural deficiencies of 'deprived areas' in inner cities. Would the purpose be the same in rural schools?

An example might help, and to expedite matters we will take a rather dramatic one.

A Locally Relevant Rural Curriculum

The Western Isles (otherwise known as the Outer Hebrides) off the north-west coast of Scotland, have a combined population of about 30,000 living mostly in small villages. Farming, fishing, textile manufacturing and an increasing service sector are the main economic activities. Primary education is provided by a very dispersed pattern of small schools which is characteristic of rural Scotland. Of the fifty-nine schools, forty-three have three teachers or less.[3]

Following local government reorganization, the Western Isles Island Council was formed in 1975 and became the spur to a series of interrelated developments aimed at invigorating the cultural, educational and economic life of the islands. The primary school Bilingual Education Project (BEP) was one component of this innovation, which connected with a community venture involving adult education and the establishment of pre-school play groups. As one of the principal project team members, MacLeod (1977) remarked:

> 'As with many other areas in the country it was felt that the conception of education tended to be rather restricted to the work going on inside the school. To a large degree this work bore little relationship to the issues and problems in the community. Even the language used in the schools was not that of the community and it is only now through structures such as the Bilingual Education Project that the language and the curriculum of the school are being closely linked with the community'. (p43)

Gaelic was the normal spoken language of 80 per cent of the islands' population; it had figured in the schools' curriculum but as a subject that was to be taught rather in the way that French might have been taught. Only in recent years had it been thought worthy for use as a teaching medium and local authorities in Gaelic speaking areas had begun to assist schools to develop curricular materials and teaching approaches for bilingual children. This was the aim of the Bilingual Education Project, to establish a curriculum that would enable children to learn through Gaelic as well as through English.

Murray and MacLeod (1981) saw the project's activities being underpinned by:

'. . . the attempt to discover and to fulfil the special needs of the bilingual child in terms of the local and national communities to which that child naturally belongs'. (p245)

In the initial year, 1975–76, the project concentrated on the first three age groups; the work was then rapidly extended to cover the full seven years of primary schooling. From its inception, the principle was made explicit that teaching through Gaelic could only constitute an enriching contribution to the entire curriculum if it was closely tied to the children's out of school experiences and that substantial use would, therefore, need to be made of the resources which the local physical and social environment provided. Teachers who were enthusiastic about the project agreed that 'direct investigations outside the school would be an integral part of the work on any theme'.

Murray and MacLeod interpret this as a link between the bilingual aims of the project and the aspirations for a locally-based rural curriculum:

'The adoption of a direct, 'hands-on' involvement with the local environment was crucially important. Excursions outside the school provided the teacher with a new ambience which made it easier for those who had not done so previously to use Gaelic as a teaching medium. Similarly, for the children this field-based approach provided a learning milieu in which they were naturally more confident in seeking and exploiting fresh experiences than had been the case in formal classroom work. Teachers and their classes also came into contact — as part of school's work — with local people, so the community's activities began to impinge upon the curriculum. In the long term this will profoundly affect the interaction of school, home and community in the Western Isles'. (p47)

One discovery, especially as the joint thrust on bilingualism and on locally relevant curricula moved to more structured work with the older children, was the absence of adequate and appropriate reference materials in Gaelic. Teachers began to develop their own, based upon the language use and current activities of their classes. Books, sometimes partly written by children and often illustrated by them, were published, and non-book materials were duplicated and distributed through a variety of individually negotiated arrangements with local development agencies. Murray and MacLeod observe:

'The pace and scale of these ad hoc publishing ventures were new in Gaelic. They attracted considerable publicity as well as affecting people's attitudes significantly'. (p250)

They were not, however, adequate to meet the needs of the schools that were being generated by the work of the Bilingual Education Project. So, by combining with other projects within the development innovation (for example, the Community Education Project) BEP was instrumental in establishing a Gaelic and English translation commercial publishing company (the first and only one). It was based in the Western Isles. Murray and MacLeod comment:

'It fills a serious gap which would inhibit the development of a relevant education. It provides a resource to which the community has access, and its own activity should stimulate and enable the community to make greater use of that access'. (p251)

The news was not all good. There were difficulties and disappointments, some of which we will refer to shortly. The immediate question is whether this particular effort at creating a locally relevant curriculum for rural primary children which links the work of the school closely with its neighbouring community carries any significance for other rural areas. It is tempting to suggest not; the Western Isles are remote, cut off from the mainstream of urban and industrial society in so many ways, yet internally united, culturally and linguistically. Murray and MacLeod indicate the opposite conclusion:

'Although people in minority cultures may tend to have more need for new structures to compensate for the lack of adequate provision in the past, it is likely that the approach being adopted here will be of relevance to rural communities generally. In the Western Isles, the essential first step was making a firm commitment to the value and importance of the local community as the foundation upon which all development work in education, or elsewhere, must be built'. (p253)

That is the foundation principle. Reformulating rural education so that it demonstrates that firm commitment to the local community may sound innocent enough; it is actually radical. We can get an insight into that by considering the second case study in the first chapter. There, a member of Ings Downton School action group asked:

'Would all those parents go to all that trouble to defend a school that they did not think was providing a good education for their own children?'

The question was, of course, rhetorical. It not only conveyed its own judgment about the school, it also indicated that the parents felt they knew the school well enough to make that judgment and to form the commitment to defend it. That is something that education officers occasionally find hard to take seriously. 'How', we have heard them assert, 'can parents without any professional knowledge make an informed judgment about the quality of a school?'. If parents are satisfied, it is assumed to be because they lack the knowledge of anything better; they have only the memories of their own schooling, a generation earlier, as a basis for comparison. Thus, the argument runs, their opinions are tied to the limits of their own experience.

Here, from an official perspective, we can see a different principle at work. There is a firm commitment to the local children, to their educational opportunities and curriculum entitlement, but an equally firm rejection of the belief that local parents (or any other element of the community) can be the foundation for this. The notion of 'curriculum entitlement' seems to impute to education authorities the prerogative of guardian of the child's interests which might need to be protected against the ignorance or self-interest of their parents. Development work in education rests on the judgment of professionals. But this ignores two things.

Firstly, it overlooks the fact that each parent's knowledge of the school includes something that is not available to a local education officer (or councillor) or a member of the Inspectorate who is making a professional assessment. That is the intimate knowledge that is gained from seeing one's own children, not any children, but one's own children, going to and from school every day. Only parents have that experience. They know the daily triumphs and disappointments, the moments of excitement and the occasions of boredom. Through their children and their friends, through the casual conversation with neighbours, through the everyday incidents they observe and take part in, and their sense of the routines and rituals of the school, parents have a particular (but of course partial) knowledge of the school which is denied to any outsider. As Gibson (1985) expresses it, 'they know it feelingly'. Or, to put it quite differently, the professional is likewise tied to the limits of his experience.

Secondly, it ignores the fact that parents have hopes and aspirations for their children's education, which may well derive from local values, but which must carry legitimate weight, even when they differ from the views of professionals. When we looked at the broad aims that are held out for schooling, we noted that they were a set of ideals for what we wanted our children to become, and no group has a monopoly, in a liberal democracy, on the right to make judgments about that. Sockett (1986) puts it well:

'Being asked to comment on the Cockcroft foundations list, say, as an item to be agreed within the schools' objectives, may not elicit too many enthusiastic responses from parents; yet on inter-personal relationships and matters within the ethos of the school *any* adult can comment with value'. (p9)

So the principle which Murray and MacLeod enunciate, if it is taken seriously, is not so innocuous. It implies that the adult community is capable of making a significant contribution to the education its children receive in schools; it suggests that a primary education can be based upon local knowledge; it rejects the distinction between individual development and the regeneration of community life. We need to consider each of these in turn.

Enlisting Other Adults

Adults in the community can, and in many cases do, contribute to the quality of their school's curriculum through their efforts as volunteer helpers. We saw this in the school we described in chapter 6. They made needlework and cookery possible; by their presence they made it possible for the whole school to be divided into small groups for one afternoon; using their time and their private cars they enabled the two teachers to take their pupils outside the school, to the museum, for instance, and to meet other adults (the potter) who had skills to contribute to their curriculum. But also their very presence in the school, the naturalness in the way the headteacher gave them responsibility, spoke of a commitment to the value of local people. We can only speculate, but it seems likely to us that the children heard those messages of partnership.

Ringby is not a unique school in this respect. The Rural Schools Project in Gwent which we spoke of in the previous chapter, enlisted local community support:

'Local personnel such as parents, farmers, craftsmen, clergymen and dinner supervisors were used in varying degrees by all the schools. Some were used to provide a stimulus for the learning of science whilst others taught small groups on a regular basis ... Even the school piano tuner was used to introduce a study of sounds in one school'. (p19)

Similarly, we know of a school in which the caretaker stays on, after her contractual caretaking duties are completed, for half-an-hour to listen to children read, and another, in which a native French speaker who lives in the village delivers a ten-minute lesson every morning of the week. In another school known to us, the secretary, a local person, was hired not only because of her designated typing skills, but also because she has grade 5 level on the piano. Examples are numerous. What is significant about a number of them is that the volunteer is not simply given mundane tasks to perform, such as repairing books (useful though that is) but is asked to sustain a contribution to an important area of the curriculum.

In all of these cases, local adults have been persuaded that they have a positive contribution to make to the child's education. That may not always be easy to accomplish, as Murray and MacLeod illustrate:

'For example, one teacher took her pupils aged between five and seven, across the moor to watch a group of local men cutting peat. On the way, the teacher and her pupils spoke easily about their surroundings in Gaelic (as the project intended). And the men, as they worked, conversed in Galeic as usual. When the teacher and her pupils arrived, however, the men greeted them in English, and continued to talk in English until the teacher intervened to ask them to speak in Gaelic, as they would normally have done outside the school context to the local children and the local teacher'. (p247)

Nor may it be easy to convince teachers' professional associations of the appropriateness of using voluntary help with the curriculum inside the school. Enlisting other adults may offend professional proprieties but is a practice of self-help which may become increasingly significant in rural areas and not only in regard to their schools. We will discuss that further before the end of the chapter.

A Locally-relevant Curriculum

Can a worthwhile curriculum be based upon the locality and avoid the charge of parochialism? Gibson (1985) expresses that uncertainty, arguing that for all that the curriculum should arise from 'community needs, ideals and richnesses', nonetheless, 'there is a world elsewhere':

'While the justification of the curriculum must be rooted in existing, familiar cultures, and must strengthen those roots, it must also offer to students the potential to transform those roots, even to opt out of the culture, the community into which he or she has been born'. (p31)

Forsythe (1983) directs the uncertainty specifically towards rural schools. Not only parochialism, but a form of covert social control is a possibility:

'We stub our toe on a controversy which remains vital today: are rural schools to train children to stay or to leave rural life?' (p207)

But children, it has to be remembered, do not come empty-headed to school. They come with a wealth of experience and common-sense knowledge derived from living their lives within their various communities outside schools which, on the whole serves them well. A locally relevant curriculum in their formal schooling is not simply a confirming experience for all that they already know, but an initiation into ways of reflecting and acting intelligently and imaginatively upon what they currently know and do. If it is not that, it is not likely to be any sort of education, only a selection ritual by which the more talented are encouraged and enabled to depart their community. The purpose of basing the curriculum substantially in the things and the people that pupils are familiar with, is not to persuade them to remain, when their schooling is over, within their community or origin, any more than it is to persuade them that the good life will be found elsewhere. It is to allow them to look critically and caringly at the particular world they inhabit and to develop the skills and the will to contribute to its development. Whether, in the end, they choose to stay or to leave that world is another matter which will in any case be dependent upon a great many other factors, but such an approach to their curriculum should not debar them from leaving. What it should do is to enable them to recognize that they have a choice, and thereby, to make an *informed* decision about whether to stay or to go. What it should provide them with is an understanding of the nature of community, an understanding which they can put to use wherever they choose to spend the rest of their lives.

If the concern is that the academic curriculum may be distorted, it can only be said that there is no reason to suppose that the major concepts and ways of thinking that the formal curriculum demands cannot be derived from familiar surroundings. A great advantage in doing so, as many teachers acknowledge, is that it more readily engages the pupil's interest; the curriculum becomes relevant in precisely the sense that the Inspectorate describe, 'that it is seen by pupils to meet their present and prospective needs'. Moreover it has the potential to alter the relationship between pupil and teacher by making the child less dependent on the teacher. They already know something about the local environment and its culture (possibly more than the teacher at one level), and if that is the basis for the curriculum, pupils have some access to it independently of the teacher. Solstad (1981) makes this point in relation to an innovation designed to implement a locally relevant curriculum in the Lofoten Islands of Norway:

> 'It should be noted that within this project the teachers came to realise that the teaching situation with a locally relevant curriculum had to be based on new 'rules' for defining knowledge and for performing the roles of teacher and student. The teachers indicated that local knowledge had to be taught through methods different from those applied to the traditional school programme. The students should have the opportunity to benefit from their local status by discovering or creating knowledge about the local community'. (p317)

To the extent that teachers were able to work within this new frame, pupils became more as partners in their own education, with the confidence that breeds. That, we suggest, should stand them in good stead, whether they leave their community or stay. Either way, they can take it with them.

The Lofoten Project was, however, far from being an unqualified success. Reflecting on it at the time, one teacher commented, 'We have the ghost of a compulsory curriculum hanging over us'. Solstad remarks:

> 'Despite the fact that the new national curriculum plan (the Monsterplanen) has no compulsory teaching plans in the traditional sense, many teachers felt bound by that concept. Consequently, they found themselves facing the dilemma of deciding whether to direct their efforts towards local knowledge or to give the students a 'safe' education through the school's ordinary curriculum'. (p318)

Hargreaves makes much the same point in relation to English comprehensive schools. So long as they need to prove themselves by their academic examination results, 'there can be no full development of a community-centred curriculum in the secondary school'.

In the primary sector, perhaps the options are more open, but if rural schools are to be responsive to their communities and if their teachers are to develop curricula that can be said to be relevant to their pupils, they will need the encouragement to innovate. The ghost of a national curriculum framework may need to be exorcised.

Education and Community Development

We have seen that the Western Isles project to reform the curriculum of the primary schools was but one of a series of inter-related innovations aimed at bringing about the development of those communities. In this respect it reflected a conviction that has gained momentum in various parts of the developed world during the last decade that educational improvement is closely connected with rural development.[4] It is a growing trend in Norway says Solstad (1981); McLean (1981) implies the same in Australia, and in America, McLaughlin (1982) concluded from an evaluation of a range of rural education projects:

> 'A careful examination of the case studies suggests that the success of rural school improvement programmes depends on how well they fit local community needs as well as local educational needs'. (p283)

The reason McLaughlin offers is that the natural linkages between school and community in rural areas means that what affects one affects the other. What is good for the pupil is good for the community! It is an assumption that not everybody shares.

Forsythe (1983), for example, suggests that it is at least possible that 'the interests of rural children and the interests of the surrounding community may conflict'. The reason for that, she argues, is because the community stands to benefit simply by the presence of a local school, while the interests of the pupils relate to what takes place within the classroom. If we view a pupil's primary school education as being largely independent of the community in which he or she is growing up and see its direction as being an academic matter for professionals to decide upon, and if we view the benefits that can accrue to the community as passively as Forsythe appears to do there is a real possibility of a conflict of interests. If, on the other hand, we ask of schools that they should be responsive to their communities, the simple divergence of interests which she describes, starts to look less plausible. But we do need then to ask how it is that schools, in harness with their communities, might best foster the all-round development of the child, and contribute to community life.

Consider the following familiar situations; they are ones that we happen to know something of, but they are typical of the sort that can be found at various times in rural schools up and down the country:

'A junior class has been doing a project about the local area at the turn of the century. Much of the material they had to research for themselves and now, at the end of it, they are performing a play, devised by their teacher, to illustrate elements of their theme. They are in costume — some of which their parents made and some of which is genuine and borrowed from some older local inhabitants. The class is on stage at the front of the room; a group of adults (mainly parents) form the audience at the back of the room.

Some older girls are playing netball in the playground. A mother is among them, coach, referee and organizer of the team. She once played netball for the county.

The whole school is gathered in the canteen together with some forty or fifty old people who are being served with tea and cakes. They have all just returned from the local church where the pupils have performed a Christmas concert; they will repeat their performance in two days time for the parents.

Three pupils are in the front room of a house down the road from the school. They are interviewing the lady who lives there about the evacuation that took place into the village during the early part of the war.

A group of pupils is gathered round a pea harvester. The farmer has demonstrated how it works and they are asking him about the economics of it. He tells them and he goes on to talk about the harvesting in his grandfather's time when he farmed the same land.

A widower has come into the school to see the headteacher. He has received a letter from the DHSS which he cannot understand; she will explain it and help him to fill in the form.

On a Saturday afternoon there are a dozen or more adults in the school, mainly parents and a few whose children have long since left the school. They are painting, plastering and generally labouring. The old school house is being converted into additional space for the school. The local authority has provided the paint.

Three mornings a week there is a playgroup which is run by some of the mothers; it uses a room at the back of the school and a stretch of grass outside. Two fathers and a few junior boys dug the sand-pit'.

What can we see in these sketches? Most visibly there are some repeated instances of cooperation between people who, by virtue of their various connections with the school and the locality share something in common. There are examples of relationships being established within and across generations. In every case there are people of very different ages assuming some form of responsibility for what goes on within the community.

These are adults who are making a contribution to the work of the school. The most tangible example of this is with the paint brushes, and for a headteacher who wishes to enlist the active support of parents that is a good place to begin. That is where Robin, whose school we visited for an afternoon in chapter 6, started. When he became head at Ringby, he inherited a run-down dilapidated building and he set to work, with the local authority and the parents, to improve it. It was the quickest and most effective way to demonstrate his commitment to the importance of the local community because the results are so visible and immediate. It was some time before he spoke to parents about the curriculum. But the farmer, demonstrating modern agricultural technology and reflecting on the social changes on farms, the lady who once housed evacuee children, the mother who not only teaches netballing skills, but also shows what it is to have pride in the skill that one has, are also contributing to the quality of the school. And for all of them, the traffic is two-way. The sense of community pride is enhanced by a community asset which members of the community have helped to improve, and, quite apart from the enjoyment of the social intercourse, those who contribute to the school's curriculum benefit themselves. To teach somebody something is also to teach yourself something.

There are also in those cameos, children contributing to the life of their community; they are organizing and producing events which are valued by an older generation, and in doing so, they are experiencing what social responsibility is and what it is to have a voice in local affairs. They are also teaching the adults; the play for instance is their interpretation to the parents of their histories;[5] the Christmas concert is a confirmation to an older generation of the continuity of the village's identity. At times such as those, young people become 'significant others' to older people.

It could be said that incidents such as we have briefly outlined could occur, and do occur in urban schools. That is quite true, but there is a difference. Where there is a close-knit network of relationships from the school out into the community, where, in other words, people know each other well, events sponsored by the school affirm a sense of community, not just a connection between parents and the school. Pupils can stage a play for their own parents as easily in an urban school as in a rural school, but staging it for the community is a more improbable undertaking.

It goes without saying that schools exist to enable young people to be more competent in their personal lives, less reliant on others and conscious of their obligations to others. To the degree that a school can successfully respond to its local environment, it can set in motion a further set of resources and help to foster what we might call an 'educative community' — people of different ages, in a context which is familiar to them, cooperating in a variety of ways so that they become more capable of meeting individual and social needs. Commenting on education and community development programmes in Australia, Randell (1981) asserts:

'A high community morale affects children's attitudes to learning'. (p71)

It sounds a plausible hypothesis, and so does the converse; the way in which children undertake their learning affects a community's morale.

Another way of putting that might be to refer to the idea of 'self-help', an idea which is gaining currency as a partial solution to the numerous problems of service provision in rural districts.[6] The direction was signalled several years ago by the National Association of Local Councils (1978):

'Clearly with the present economic climate and the general attitude of government to public expenditure, rural self-help will become even more important. Without it, even more rural facilities are likely to be at risk. If self-help is to provide acceptable substitute services or facilities, public and government alike must accept that it may take unorthodox forms and therefore be administratively untidy'. (para 28)

The test is whether the schools, and government, can recognize the potential in unorthodoxy.

There is one further feature of those briefly sketched moments which may only be guessed. Behind each of them was a teacher who did have a 'firm commitment to the value and importance of the local community'. In any educational programme the commitment of the teacher is a fundamental requirement.

The more that any proposed curriculum change calls for alterations in teaching method or underlying principle, the more important become the teachers as determinants of success. The Bilingual Education Project found this, as Murray and MacLeod realized:

> 'It became evident to the team at an early stage that a school's acceptance of the original invitation to participate did not necessarily mean that the school would welcome change, nor that individual teachers were prepared or even willing to become agents of change. The project works in an area involving complex and emotionally charged attitudes — toward language, toward schooling, toward cultural traditions and toward the local community'. (p245)

Some schools, it is reported, accepted selected aspects of the programme; in others there was a dramatic change to the curriculum. Teachers clearly differed in the view they took of the local cultural traditions as a basis for the curriculum and of teaching through the indigenous language. We are taken back to that underlying principle: '... the essential first step was making a firm commitment to the value and importance of the local community as the foundation upon which all development work in education, or elsewhere, must be built'.

In somewhat more ordinary circumstances, Forsythe (1983) makes a very similar point. Noting that 'relations between the teacher in a small rural school and members of the local community can vary over a very wide range', she reports:

> 'The evidence suggests that success is most likely to be achieved if the teacher has had previous experience of living ... in a small community, and if the teacher has a personal link with the local area'. (p160)

It helped if the teacher had previously acquired, through residence, an understanding of life in rural communities characterized by face-to-face contact, and also if they had kinship links with the area which 'provided them with a firm anchor in the community'. It is easy to imagine why that should be, but as a matter of policy, what it suggests is that there are good grounds for including in the training of teachers an element which focuses on the nature of rural communities and their relationships with the schools which serve them. It would be of benefit to those who wish to teach in such schools. The identical argument for incorporating courses on teaching in inner cities has, after all, been accepted without question.

With one or two exceptions[7], such courses do not exist at initial training level and furthermore, the rationalization of teacher education which took place in the 1970s has resulted in its consolidation in urban areas so that now, far fewer students ever encounter a small rural school even as an incidental part of their pre-service training. At in-service level, the situation can be not very different. Newly appointed headteachers are often required to undertake a short management course. Crossman (1985) gives his experience of that, and it is probably not untypical:

'I was appointed headteacher in a four-teacher village school, a seemingly natural career progression, after teaching exclusively in urban primary schools. Superficially the task appeared similar to my previous teaching experience, the headship role like the one I had observed. The reality was different ... The immediacy of the situation required me to revise my assumptions and practice without adequately considering the causes underlying the problem. A short LEA course for heads of small rural schools reinforced my concern. The visiting practising experts were from large urban schools, implying a view that their scaled-down practice would suit the needs of small rural schools'. (p1)

The schools are different; the role of teacher and (especially) of headteacher is different. To recognize that would indicate forms of training which sought a curriculum and management more in harmony with the nature of small schools and rural communities rather than one which suggested that they should adapt large urban school practice to their circumstance and cope as best they can.

Crossman puts his finger on another characteristic of the way our thinking about education affects rural schools. Moving from urban class teaching to a small rural school headship, and then to headship of a large urban school is a common career progression. The danger is that because the urban model of what headship entails is so much to the fore, as well as being rewarded with higher salary and status, ambitious heads of small rural schools may merely rehearse the management style appropriate to large urban schools. But rather as Hadow recommended the practice of young teachers serving an apprenticeship in small rural schools because of what they might learn there and later carry with them, about individual and group methods of teaching,[8] something similar might be said for novitiate head-teachers. In a small school in an rural community, they might learn how to make a school responsive to its social context, and that would serve them well if and when they came to be promoted to larger headships in different social locations.

The Future For Small Schools

So long as successive governments continue to reach for standardized answers to the questions of how to improve educational quality and how to ensure greater equality of opportunity, the future for small rural schools will look bleak. They will continue to be viewed as an aberration and the educational debate in rural areas will remain locked into the issue of closure, or mere survival. The moves towards greater centralization which we have been forced to remark upon frequently in this book, suggest that that is the most likely prediction. And yet, we retain a certain optimism.

Earlier in this book, we quoted Taylor's view, in 1978, that 'there must be a limit in a democracy to the extent to which educational policy can be pursued in the teeth of public opposition'. Nearly a decade later, and several hundred school closures later, we might be seeing just where that limit lies. That is not to say there will be no more school closures, but we do sense a growing disillusion with the belief that centralized solutions can answer local problems. In this country and in other parts of the developed world, there are signs of a growing conviction that local resources and local talent are required to deal with the issues which confront local communities. And paradoxically, there are signs that central governments recognize it also. In the previous chapter, we outlined some of the ways in which this has begun to take place with regard to education in rural areas. In this chapter we have been speculating on ways in which it might develop.

But however eager schools are to combine their strengths, and however rich are the local resources which schools might draw upon, some external support is necessary. As we saw in chapter 9, it brings in additional talents which the teachers have defined as being neces-sary; it also buys for them that most essential of components — time. In a predominantly urban nation, facing an unpredictable future, the education of rural children is not likely to be headline news. There will be no massive handouts for rural schooling, but the scale of support may not be the crucial matter. In fact, if McLaughlin (1982) is correct, the American experience suggests that:

'... heavily funded efforts [are] not necessarily more successful than those operating on small local budgets'. (p282)

What is crucial is that the support is used to make clear and then to amplify the potential advantages that stem from the size of small rural schools and the more intimate relationship they are capable of establishing with their local communities.

Equality of educational opportunity is best served by recognizing differences that inevitably exist and seeking ways of responding to them rather than by endeavouring to impose a common educational experience on all children. To identify and bring together the potentials which the small rural primary school and its community together possess is to address the matter of quality in relation to the social foundations on which, in the end, any worthwhile education rests.

Notes

1 Assuming the school to be held in reasonably high esteem by parents. If it is not, it is likely to be closed with scarcely a word being spoken.
2 The Educational Priority Area projects that were set up, under the general direction of A.H. HALSEY, as a result of the Plowden Report, took a very much more positive stance towards their communities.
3 Data from MURRAY and MACLEOD (1981)
4 See DARNELL and SIMPSON (1981), a report of the conference *New Directions in Rural Education* organized by Western Australia Education Department and OECD/CERI.
5 An interesting feature of the Lofoten project is that, like that in the Western Isles, there was a shortage of books about the local area, its economics, industry and cultural history. These, when they were produced for school use, were bought and read avidly by local adults.
6 The National Council for Voluntary Organisations has, for example, published a manual to encourage rural self-help initiatives (see WOOLLETT 1981).
7 For example, Aberdeen College of Education.
8 See chapter 2.

Appendix: The Illustrative Study: Calculation of Costs

Capital Costs to the LEA

Option A (1 School)   £(000)

Costs to remodel and extend school 1 to accommodate 350 pupils	564
Cost of equipment and furnishing (10 per cent of building cost)	56
Revenue from sale of four county primary schools (assuming average net sale price of £25,000)	100
Net capital cost to LEA	£520

Option B (7 Schools)

	£(000)
Costs to remodel schools to accommodate anticipated pupil numbers will be:	
School 1	9
School 2	40
School 4	55
School 5	60
School 6	50
School 7	42
Total remodelling costs	256
Total remodelling costs to LEA (excluding voluntary-aided school 5)	196
Cost of equipment and furnishings (10 per cent of building costs)	25
Cost of new school 3 (including equipment and furnishings)	120

Total costs to LEA	341
Revenue from sale of existing school 3	25
Net capital cost to LEA	£316

Option C (5 Schools)

Costs to remodel schools to accommodate anticipated pupil numbers will be:	£(000)
School 1	9
School 2	123
School 4	55
School 5	60
School 6	50
Total remodelling costs	297
Total remodelling costs to LEA (excluding voluntary-aided school 5)	237
Cost of equipment and furnishings (10 per cent of building costs)	30
Total costs to LEA	267
Revenue from sale of school 3 and school 7	50
Net capital cost to LEA	£217

Recurrent Costs to the LEA

Recurrent costs are calculated (at 1985 prices) for the five major items of expenditure: teachers' salaries; transport costs; premises related costs; welfare assistants' and clerical staff salaries; capitation and supplies.

Teachers' Salaries

At present, seventeen full-time teachers are employed in the area and the total salary costs are £177,400, giving an average salary cost of £10,400 per teacher. Estimates for all three options are made on the basis of this figure. It is assumed that the extra costs of any additional scale posts in a large school will be cancelled out by there being fewer headteachers' allowances.

On present staffing policies, the one area school in option A will qualify for 13.5 teachers, making for salary costs of £140,400. Option

B requires seventeen teachers with an annual salary expenditure of £177,400. Option C will result in one four-teacher school, three schools with three teachers and a two-teacher school — in total fifteen teachers at a cost of £156,000.

Transport Costs

With option A it is assumed that transport will be required for all pupils except those who are currently attending school 1 who do not qualify for transport provided by the authority. In other words, approximately 290 pupils will need to be bussed. This is a considerable increase over the present total of eighty-nine pupils for whom transport is provided and it is assumed that some economy of scale will be possible, unit costs being £130 rather than the current £141 per pupil. The total transport costs for option A, on this assumption, will be £37,700. For option B, transport costs will remain at £12,500.

With option C, transport will be required for the eighty-nine pupils who currently require it. In addition, thirty-four pupils transferring from school 3 to school 2, and fifty-three pupils transferring from school 7 to schools 5 and 6 will require transport. This makes for a total of 176 pupils, and again it is assumed some economy of scale will be possible, the cost being calculated on the basis of unit transport costs of £135. The total expenditure on transport in option C will therefore be £23,800.

Premises Related Costs

In calculating an estimate for these costs, the assumption is made that the costs per school will be proportional to the floor area of the school. The size required to bring all schools to the standards set by the 1981 Schools Premises Regulations is calculated (on the further assumption that only 60 per cent of the floor area is used for teaching purposes) and costs estimated accordingly. On this basis, premises related costs for the three options are:

Option A   £29,600
Option B   £48,400
Option C   £38,900

Welfare and Clerical Assistants

The current scheme for the provision of non-teaching support allocates a set number of hours according to the size of the school. The area school of 349 pupils would qualify for forty-five hours per week; the total number of hours of support in the seven schools of option B would be eighty-five, and in five schools (option C) would be seventy-five. This would result in annual costs of:

Option A	£ 5,400
Option B	£10,200
Option C	£ 9,000

Capitation and Supplies

Capitation allowance for primary pupils is calculated on a per capita basis, except that there is a small schools supplement which comes into effect in schools with less than fifty pupils on roll, resulting in the capitation being increased by approximately 20 per cent. At present, half the pupils in the schools benefit from this and it would remain the case under option B. The area school proposal would remove it altogether, and option C would remove it in all except the two-teacher school. On this basis, annual costs would be:

Option A	£11,300
Option B	£12,600
Option C	£11,600

The costs of the three opinions are summarized below. All figures are in £ thousands.

	Option A (1 school)	Option B (7 schools)	Option C (5 Schools)
Capital Costs	520,000	316,000	217,000
Recurrent Costs:			
Teacher's Salaries	140,400	177,400	156,000
Transport Costs	37,700	12,500	23,800
Premises Related Costs	29,600	48,400	38,900
Welfare/clerical Salaries	5,400	10,200	9,000
Capitation and Supplies	11,300	12,600	11,600
Total Recurrent Costs	224,400	261,100	239,300

Bibliography

ADDISON, S. (1982) *Small Rural Schools Project: 1974–1982,* Northamptonshire Education Authority

ADDISON, S. (1985) 'Small schools — A local authority's approach', *Primary Education Review*, 24, pp8–9

ALEXANDER, R. (1984) *Primary Teaching.* Holt Rinehart and Winston.

ARCHBOLD, A. and Nisbet, J. (1977) 'Parents attitudes to the closure of small rural primary schools', *Scottish Educational Studies*, 9, 2, pp122–7

ASSOCIATION OF DISTRICT COUNCILS (1986) *The Rural Economy at the Crossroads.*

ASTON UNIVERSITY. (1980) *The Social Effects of Rural Primary School Reorganization, Second Interim Report*, University of Aston.

ASTON UNIVERSITY (1981) *The Social Effects of Rural Primary School Reorganization, Final Report.* University of Aston.

BARKER, R.G. and GUMP, P.V. (1964) (Eds) *Big School, Small School*, Stanford University Press.

BARON, G. (1977) Open University broadcast, 'School and community', Unit 13, *Decision Making in British Education Systems.*

BARR, F. (1959) 'Urban and rural differences: — Ability and attainment'. *Educational Research*, 1, 2, pp49–60

BENNETT, S.N. *et al* (1984) *The Quality of Pupil Learning Experiences*, Laurence Erlbaum Associates.

BENNETT, S.N. *et al* (1986).

BENNETT, S.N. (1987) 'Task processes in mixed and single age classes', *Education 3–13*, March.

BENNETT, S.N., O'HARE, E. and LEE, J. (1983) 'Mixed age classes in primary schools: A survey of practice.' *British Educational Research Journal*, 9, 1, pp41–56

BETTY, C (1985) *The Nottinghamshire Small Schools Project*, Nottinghamshire LEA.

BLYTH, W.A.L. (1960) 'The sociometric study of children's groups in English schools', *British Journal of Educational Studies*, 8, pp127–47.

BLYTH, W.A.L. (1965) *English Primary Education, Vol. 1*, Routledge and Kegan Paul.

BLYTH, W.A.L. and DERRICOTT, R. (1977) *The Social Significance of Middle Schools*, Batsford.

BOARD OF EDUCATION, (1937) *Handbook of Suggestions for the consideration of teachers and others concerned in the work of public elementary schools,* HMSO.

BOLTON, E.P. (1985) 'Curriculum 5–16', *Educational Review,* 37, 3, pp199–215.

BONE, B., CRISPIN, P. and WILSON, C. (1985) 'The South Launceston Cluster', in *Second Small Schools Conference,* Cornwall Education Committee.

BURSTALL, C. (1974) *Primary French in the Balance,* NFER.

CAMPBELL, R.J. (1985) *Developing the Primary Curriculum,* Holt, Rinehart and Winston.

CAMPBELL, W.J. (1980) 'School size: Its influence on pupils'. in FINCH, A. and SCRIMSHAW, P. (Eds) *Standards, Schooling and Education,* Hodder and Stoughton.

COATESWORTH, D. (1976) 'Is small still beautiful in rural Norfolk?' *Education,* 10 October 1956, pp275–6.

COMMISSION FOR LOCAL AUTHORITY ACCOUNTS IN SCOTLAND (1984) *Value for Money Study on School Occupancy Costs.*

COMMUNITY COUNCIL OF NORTHUMBERLAND (1985) *Jobs for School Leavers in Rural Northumberland.*

CONNOR, (1977) *The Parish Primary School and The Rural Community,* Norfolk County Planning Department.

COOLEY, C.H. (1902) *Human Nature and the Social Order,* Scribner.

CROSS, G.R. and REVELL, (1975) 'Note on grammar school selection in a rural area', Bulletin 7, NFER, March.

CROSSMAN, D.R. (1985) *An Exploration of Rural Teachers' Perception of their Task and its Relation to In-Service Provision,* unpublished MA dissertation, University of East Anglia.

CUMBRIAN ASSOCIATION FOR RURAL EDUCATION, (1978) *The Case for the Small Rural School.* Cumbrian Association for Rural Education.

CUMBRIAN ASSOCIATION FOR RURAL EDUCATION (1986) *Primary Children and School Transport in Cumbria,* Cumbrian Association for Rural Education.

CUMMINGS, C.E. (1971) *Studies in Educational Costs.* Scottish Academic Press.

CURRY, N. and WEST, C. (1981) 'Internal economics of scale in rural primary education', in CURRY, N. (Ed) *Rural Settlement Policy and Economics,* Gloucestershire Papers in Local and Rural Planning, 12.

DAHLOFF, U. and ANDRAE, A. (1973) *Process Analysis of Non-Graded Rural Schools,* Institute of Education Report, University of Goteborg, 1.

DARNELL, F. (1981) 'Equality and opportunity in rural education'. in DARNELL, F and SIMPSON P.M. (Eds) *Rural Education: In Pursuit of Excellence,* National Centre for Research on Rural Education, University of Western Australia.

DARNELL, F. and SIMPSON, P.M. (1981) (Eds) *Rural Education: In Pursuit of Excellence,* National Centre for Research on Rural Education, University of Western Australia.

DEARDEN, R.F. (1968) *The Philosophy of Primary Education: An Introduction,* Routledge and Kegan Paul.

DEARDEN, R.F. (1981) 'Balance and coherence: Some curricular principles in recent reports.' *Cambridge Journal of Education,* 11, 2, pp107–18.

DES (1965) Circular 10/65, HMSO.

DES (1966) Circular 10/66, HMSO.

DES (1977a) *Education in Schools: A Consultative Document*, (Green Paper), HMSO.

DES (1977b) *Local Authority Arrangments for the School Curriculum*, Circular 14/77, HMSO.

DES (1977c) *Falling Numbers and School Closures*, Circular 5/77, HMSO.

DES (1978) *Special Educational Needs* (The Warnock Report), HMSO.

DES (1979) *Local Authority Arrangements for the School Curriculum: Report on the Circular 14/77*, HMSO.

DES (1980) *A Framework for the School Curriculum*, HMSO.

DUNNE, E. (1977) 'Choosing smallness: An examination of the small school experience in rural America', in SHER, J. (Ed) *Education in Rural America*, Westview Press.

EDMUNDS, E.L. and BESSAI, F. (1977). 'Small schools', *Headteachers' Review*, 68, 3, November, pp54–6. See also *Headteachers' Review*, 69, 1, pp2–5, March 1978.

EDWARDS, M. (1985) *Norfolk's Policy Towards Rural Primary Schools*, address to an Education Workshop Examining Primary Education in Rural Areas, Norwich 9 March, unpublished.

FINCH D. (1986) *A Study of the Social Environment of Small Rural Schools, with Particular Reference to the Nature of Inter-personal Relationships*, unpublished study, School of Education, University of East Anglia.

FINDLAY, I.R. (1973) *Inequality in Education in the Sparsely Populated Area*, paper presented to the Comparative Education Society of Europe Conference, September.

FORSYTHE, D. (1983) (Ed) *The Rural Community and the Small School*, Aberdeen University Press.

FRANKENBERG, R. (1966) *Communities in Britain*, Penguin Books.

FRYER, D. (1985) 'A summary of the main points raised at the conference'. *The Second Small Schools Conference*, Cornwall Education Committee.

FTHENAKIS, W.E. and BAUER, H.E. (1977) *Compensatory Education of Children Living in Socio-Cultural Isolated Areas (of Upper Bavaria)*, Council of Europe Symposium on Pre-School Education in Sparsely Populated Areas, September.

GAY, J.D. (1985) *The Size of Anglican Primary Schools*, Culham College Institute Occasional Paper No. 7, Culham College Institute.

GALTON, M and SIMON B. (1980) *Inside the Primary Classroom*, Routledge and Kegan Paul.

GIBSON, R. (1985) 'How do we justify the curriculum?', in CASSIVI, D. and MACNEIL, K. (Eds) *Dialogue on Curriculum*, University of Cape Breton Press.

GILDER, I.M. (1979) 'Rural planning policies: An economic appraisal', *Progress in Planning*, II, 3, pp213–271

GITTINS REPORT, CACE (Wales) (1967) *Primary Education in Wales*, HMSO.

GREGORY, R. (1975) 'The educational advantages of the small primary school', *Forum*, Summer, 17, 3, pp79–82.

HADOW REPORT (1926) *The Education of the Adolescent,* Report of the Consultative Committee of the Board of Education, HMSO.

HADOW REPORT (1931) *Report of the Consultative Committee on the Primary School,* HMSO.

HARGREAVES, D.H. (1967) *Social Relations in a Secondary School,* Routledge and Kegan Paul.

HARGREAVES, D.H. (1972) *Interpersonal Relations and Education,* Routledge and Kegan Paul.

HARGREAVES, D.H. (1982) *The Challenge for The Comprehensive School: Culture, Curriculum and Community,* Routledge and Kegan Paul.

HARTLEY, D. (1985) *Understanding the Primary School,* Croom Helm.

HIND, I.W. (1977) 'Estimates of cost functions for primary schools in rural areas', *Australian Journal of Agricultural Economics,* 21, 1, pp13–25.

HIND, I.W. (1981) 'Some aspects of the provision of educational services in rural areas', in DARNELL, F. and SIMPSON, P.M. (Eds) *Rural Education: In Pursuit of Excellence,* National Centre for Research on Rural Education, University of Western Australian.

HIRST, P. (1965) 'Liberal education and the nature of knowledge', in ARCHAMBAULT, R.D. (Ed) *Philosophical Analysis and Education,* Routledge and Kegan Paul.

HMI (1974) *Education in Invernesshire,* Scottish Education Department.

HMI (1978) *Primary Education in England (A Survey by HMI),* HMSO.

HMI (1982) *Education 5–9: An Illustrative Study by HMI,* HMSO.

HMI (1983) *9–13 Middle Schools: An Illustrative Study by HMI,* HMSO.

HMI (1984a) *Education Observed (A Review of the First Six Months of Published Reports by HM Inspectors),* HMSO.

HMI (1984b) *Education Observed II: (A Review of Published Reports by HM Inspectors on Primary Schools and 11–16 and 12–16 Comprehensive Schools),* HMSO.

HMI (1984c) *Educational Provision and Response in Some Norfolk Schools: Report by HM Inspectors,* HMSO.

HMI (1985a) *The Curriculum from 5 to 16: Curriculum Matters 2,* HMSO.

HMI (1985b) *Education Observed III: Good Teachers,* HMSO.

HMSO (1972) *A Framework for Expansion,*HMSO.

HMSO (1981) *Education (Schools Premises Regulations) 1981,* HMSO.

HMSO (1985) *Better Schools,* HMSO.

HOEGMO, A. and SOLSTAD, K.J. 'The Lofoten Project: Towards a relevant education', in *10th Interskola International Conference, Innovation and Rural Education,* ERIC/CRESS.

HOPKINS, D. (1986) *Inservice Training and Educational Development: An International Survey,* Croom Helm.

HOWEY, K. (1986) 'School Focused Inservice: Synthesis Report', in HOPKINS, D. (Ed) *Inservice Training and Educational Development: An International Survey,* Croom Helm.

HOYLE, E. (1974) 'Professionality, professionalism and control in teaching, *London Educational Review,* 3, 2, summer, pp15–17.

HOYLE, E. and BELL, R. (1972) *Problems of Curriculum Innovation I. Units 13–15, The Curriculum Context and Design,* Open University Press.

JAMES REPORT (1972) *Teacher Education and Training*, HMSO.

JOHNSTON, R. (1981) 'The survival of the small school', in Scottish Education Department, *Off the Beaten Track*, HMSO.

KING, R. (1978) *All Things Bright and Beautiful? A Sociological Study of Infants' Classrooms*, John Wiley and Sons.

KOGAN, M. (1978) *The Politics of Educational Change*, Fontana.

LACEY, C. (1970) *Hightown Grammar: the school as a social system*, Manchester University Press.

LADLEY, G. (1983) 'Professional development for headteachers in the Clun Forest, Shropshire', in *Small Schools in Concert*, Schools Council for Wales.

LAWTON, D. (1984) *The Tightening Grip*, Bedford Way Papers No. 21 Institute of Education, Heinemann Educational Books Ltd.

LEE (1961) 'A test of the hypothesis that school reorganisation is a cause of rural depopulation', *Durham Research Reivew*, 3, pp64–73.

LEESE, O. (1978) 'Politics and power in curriculum reform', in RICHARDS, C. (Ed.) *Power and the Curriculum*, Nafferton Books.

LEWES, G. (1980) 'The disadvantages and advantages of small rural schools' in WATKINS, R. (Ed) *Educational Disadvantage in Rural Areas*, Centre for Information and Advice on Educational Disadvantage.

LORTIE, D.C. (1975) *School Teacher: A Sociological Study*, University of Chicago Press.

MACKAY, G.A. (1983) 'The economic context', in FORSYTHE, D. (Ed) (1983) *The Rural Community and the Small School*, Aberdeen University Press.

MCLEAN, D. (1981) 'Community involved education: A rural experiment', in DARNELL, F. and SIMPSON, P.M. (Eds) *Rural Education: In Pursuit of Excellence*, National Centre for Research on Rural Education, University of Western Australia.

MCLAUGHLIN, M. (1982) 'What worked and why', in NACHTIGAL, P.M. (Ed) *Rural Education: In Search of a Better Way*, Westview Press.

MACLENNAN, S. (1985) *Principles and Practicalities in the Early Teaching of a Foreign Language*. University of East Anglia/British Council.

MACLEOD, F. (1977) 'The Western Isles community education project', in 10th Interskola International Conference Report, *Innovation and Rural Education*, ERIC/CRESS.

MCPHERSON, G.H. (1972) *Small Town Teacher*, Harvard University Press.

MCWILLIAM, E. (1978) *100 Years of a Village School: Bransombe School 1878–1978*, Private publication.

MARSHALL, D.G. (1985) 'Closing small schools or when is small too small?', *Education Canada*, Fall pp10–16.

MASSEY, G.D. (1978) *School Transport: A Comparative and Quantitative Study*, unpublished MEd. thesis, University of Bath.

MEAD, G.H. (1934) *Mind, Self and Society*, University of Chicago Press.

MEYENN, R.J. (1980) 'Peer networks among middle schools pupils', in HARGREAVES, A. and TICKLE, L. (Eds) *Middle Schools: Origins, Ideology and Practice*. Harper and Row.

MILBURN, D. (1981) 'A study of multi-age or family grouped classrooms', *Phi Delta Kappa*, March, pp513–4.

MINISTRY OF EDUCATION (1959) *Primary Education*, HMSO.

MORDEY, R. and JUDGE, E. (1984) 'Rural service provisions and rural settlement policy', *Brunswick Environmental Papers No. 47*, School of Planning and Environmental Studies, Leeds Polytechnic.

MOORHOUSE, E. (1985) *A Personal Story of Oxfordshire Primary Schools*, private publication.

MURRAY, J. and MacLeod, F. (1981) 'Sea change in the Western Isles of Scotland: The rise of locally relevant bilingual education', in SHER, J.P. (Ed) *Rural Education in Urbanized Nations*, OECD/CERI Report, Western Press.

NASH, R. (1977) *Conditions of Learning in Rural Primary Schools*, Report to the Social Science Research Committee.

NATIONAL ASSOCIATION OF LOCAL COUNCILS (1979) *'Rural Life, Change or Decay'*.

NEWBY, H. *et al* (1978) *Property, Paternalism and Power*, Hutchinson.

NEWBY., H. (1980) *Green and Pleasant Land?*, Penguin Books.

NEWSOM REPORT (1963) *Half Our Future*, Report of the Central Advisory Council for Education, HMSO.

NIAS, J. (1984) 'The definition and maintenance of self in primary teaching', *British Journal of Sociology of Education*, 5, 3, pp268–80.

NORDIC COUNCIL OF MINISTERS (1977) *Pre-Schools in Sparsely Populated Areas: A Report of Recent and Current Experiments in Finland, Norway and Sweden*. Secretariat for Nordic Cultural Cooperation.

NORFOLK COUNTY COUNCIL (1985) *Development Plan Guidelines for Primary Schools*, Norfolk County Council.

NORFOLK COUNTY PLANNING DEPARTMENT (1976) *The Walsham Area Study*, Norfolk County Planning Department.

NORTHAMPTONSHIRE COUNTY COUNCIL (1984) *The School Curriculum: A Framework of Principles*, Northamptonshire County Council.

OHLSON, P. (1983) 'A co-operative teaching venture in Cornwall', in *Small Schools in Concert*. Schools Council for Wales.

PAHL, P.E. (1965) *Urbs in Rure*, Weidenfeld and Nicolson.

PARSONS-JONES, E. (1983) *Northamptonshire Rural Schools Enrichment Project*, unpublished DipEd dissertation, University of Leicester.

PLOWDEN REPORT, CACE (1967) *Children and their Primary Schools*, HMSO.

POLLARD, A. (1985) *The Social World of the Primary School*, Holt, Rinehart and Winston.

PRIMARY SCHOOLS RESEARCH AND DEVELOPMENT GROUP/SCHOOLS COUNCIL (1983) *Curriculum Responsibility and the use of Teacher Expertise in the Primary School*, University of Birmingham Department of Curriculum Studies.

RANDELL, S. (1981) 'The responsibilities of schools in local development', in DARNELL, F. and SIMPSON, P.M. (1981) (Eds) *Rural Education: In Pursuit of Excellence*. National Centre for Research on Rural Education, University of Western Australia.

'MISS READ' (1960) *Village School*, Penguin Books.

RICHARDS, C. (1982) 'Primary education 1974–80', in RICHARDS, C. (Ed) *New Directions in Primary Education*, Falmer Press.

ROGERS, R. (1977) 'Closing village schools: What the LEAs are up to', *Where*, 133, November.

ROGERS, R. (1979) *Schools Under Threat: A Handbook on Closures*, Advisory Centre for Education.

ROSS, J.A. (1980) 'The influence of the Principal upon the curriculum decisions of teachers', *Journal of Curriculum Studies*, 12, pp219–30.

ROWAN, P., COLLINSON, P., DAVEY, P., HAIGHTON, P. and CORWOOD, A. (1985) 'The Devichoys Cluster', in *Second Small Schools Conference*, Cornwall Education Committee.

RYDERG, H. (1971) 'Vart Behov av Region Politik Halmstad Uben og Sjogren' cited in DAHLOFF, V. and ANDRAE, A. (1973) *Process Analysis of Non-Graded Rural Schools*, Institute of Education Report, University of Goteborg.

SAVILLE, C. (1977) 'Perceptions of teachers' in-service education needs in rural areas', in 10th Interskola Internation Conference, *Innovation and Rural Education*, ERIC/CRESS.

SCHOOLS COUNCIL (1975) *Small Schools Study*, unpublished field officers' team report.

SCHOOLS COUNCIL (1983) *Primary Practice,* working paper 75, Methuen.

SCHOOLS COUNCIL (WALES) (1983) *Small Schools in Concert*, Schools Council Committee for Wales.

SCOLEY F.T. (1983) 'Rural primary education: Current issues', in *Small Schools in Concert*, Schools Council for Wales.

SCOTTISH EDUCATION DEPARTMENT (1974) *Education in Invernesshire*, HMSO.

SCRUPSKI, A. (1970) 'Administrative support for teacher and teachers legitimation of administrative authority', Ed.D dissertation, Rutgers University, cited in WEBB, R.B. (1981) *Schooling and Society*. Collier Macmillan.

SHANKS, D and WELSH, J (1983) 'Transition to secondary school', in FORSYTHE, D. (Ed) *The Rural Community and the Small School*, Aberdeen University Press.

SHAW, M. (1976) 'Can we afford villages?', *Built Environment Quarterly*, 17 June, pp135–7.

SHER, J.P. (1977) (Ed) *Education in Rural America: A Reassessment of Conventional Wisdom*. Westview Press.

SHER, J.P. (1978) *Revitalizing Rural Education: A Legislator's Handbook*, National Conference of State Legislatures.

SHER, J.P. (1981) *Rural Education in Urbanized Nations*, OECD/CERI Report, Westview Press.

SHER, J.P. and TOMKINS, R.V. (1977) 'Economy, efficiency and equality: The myths of rural school and district consolidation', in SHER, J.P. (Ed) *Education in Rural America: A Reassessment of Conventional Wisdom*, Westview Press.

SIGSWORTH, A. (1984) *Rural Teachers' Perceptions of Their Task*, paper presented at the British Association for the Advancement of Science, University of East Anglia.

SIMPKIN, T. (1980) 'The economics of smallness: The case of small primary schools', *Educational Studies*, 6, 1, pp79–91.

SKINNER, J. (1980) 'Combatting the professional isolation of teachers in rural schools', in WATKINS, R. (Ed) *Educational Disdvantage in Rural Areas*, Centre for Information and Advice on Education Disadvantage.

SMITH, C.A. (1948) *The Mental Testing of Hebridean Children*, Scottish Council for Research in Education.

SOCKETT, H. (1976) *Designing the Curriculum*, Open Books.

SOCKETT, H. (1986) *The School Curriculum: A Basis for Partnership*, Address to an Invitation Conference of Education Officers and Advisers, Llandudno, 15 January.

SOLSTAD, K.J. (1981) 'Locally relevant curricula in rural Norway: The Lofoten Islands examples', in SHER, J.P. (Ed) *Rural Education in Urbanized Nations*, OECD/CERI Report, Westview Press.

STANDING CONFERENCE OF RURAL COMMUNITY COUNCILS, (1978) *The Decline of Rural Services*.

TAYLOR, B. (1978) 'Week by week', *Education*, 6 October, p299.

TAYLOR, P.H., Reid, W., HOLLEY, B. and EXON G. (1974) *Purpose, Power and Constraint in the Primary School Curriculum*, Macmillan.

THOMAS (1972) 'When small schools die, they die alone', *Education*, September, pp168–9.

THOMAS, R.S. (1983) 'Children's Song', in THOMAS R.S. *Selected Poems 1946–68*, Granada Publishing.

THOMPSON, E.P. (1967) 'Time, work discipline and industrial capitalism', *Past and Present*, 38, pp60–1.

TWINE, D. (1975) 'Some effects of the urbanization process on rural children', *Educational Studies*, 1, 3, pp209–16.

TYACK, D.B. (1974) *The One Best System*, Harvard University Press.

WARNER, P.W. (1973) 'Aspects of school transport in a rural scene', in *Aspects of Education*, Journal of Hull Institute of Education, 17, pp19–37.

WARNOCK REPORT (1978) *Special Educational Needs: report of the Committee on Enquiry into the education of handicapped children and young people*, HMSO.

WEBB, R.J. (1981) *Schooling and Society*, Collier Macmillan.

WILLIS, P. (1977) *Learning to Labour*, Saxon House.

WILSON, A., DREW, J. DAVY, J. and ALEXANDER, I. (1985) 'The Border Cluster', in *Second Small Schools Conference*, Cornwall Education Comittee.

WOODS, P. (1980) *Teacher Strategies*, Croom Helm.

WOOLLETT, S. (1981) *Alternative Rural Services: A Community Initiatives Manual*, National Council for Voluntary Organizations.

Index